SYSTEMS ANALYSIS AND DESIGN

Dr. Bechoo Lal

Toronto Academic Press

Systems Analysis and Design

Dr. Bechoo Lal

Toronto Academic Press
224 Shoreacres Road
Burlington, ON L7L 2H2
Canada
www.tap-books.com
Email: orders@arclereducation.com

ISBN: 978-1-77469-749-8

ABOUT THE AUTHOR

Bechoo Lal, PhD. became a Member (M) of IAENG: International Association of Engineers, USA with membership (108820) in 2010, a Senior Member (SM) in 2019. I am doctorate PhD in Computer Science, PhD- Information System from University of Mumbai, Master from Banaras Hindu University (BHU), PGP- Data Science from Purdue University, USA. Currently working as a Associate Professor in Department of Computer Science & Engineering, KLEF- KL University Vijayawada Campus Andhra Pradesh, India. His research areas are data science, big data analytics and Machine Learning.

Contents

3 Requirements Modeling 47

4 Data and Process Modeling 93

List of Figures

List of Tables

List of Abbreviations

BPM	Business Process Management
BPM	Business Process Model
BPMN	Business Process Modeling Notation
CMM	Capability Maturity Model
CMMI	Capability Maturity Model Integration
DBMS	Database Management System
DFD	Data Flow Diagram
DPS	Data Processing Systems
DSS	Decision Support Systems
FAQs	Frequently Asked Queries
FDD	Functional Decomposition Diagram
GLB	Graham-Leach-Bliley
GUIs	Graphical User Interfaces
HCI	Human-Computer Interaction
HIPAA	Health Insurance Portability and Accountability Act
ISD	Interface Structure Diagram
ISO	International Organization for Standardization
IT	Information Technology
JAD	Joint App Development
MIS	Management Information Systems
O-O	Object-Oriented

OS	Operating System
PCIDSS	Payment Card Industry Data Security Standards
PIM	Personal Information Manager
POS	Point-of-Sale
RAD	Rapid Application Development
SAD	Systems Analysis and Design
SAN	Storage Area Network
SDLC	Software Development Life Cycle
SQL	Structured Query Language
TCO	Total Cost of Ownership
UI	User Interface
UML	Unified Modeling Language
UX	User Experience
XP	Extreme Programming

PREFACE

Systems analysis and design (SAD) is a dynamic and engaging subject in which analysts always learn new methods and strategies to design more effective and efficient systems. Nevertheless, regardless of the strategy or methodology utilized, every analyst should be familiar with a fundamental set of abilities. Every information systems project has four stages: planning, analysis, design, and implementation. Every project requires analysts to gather requirements, model the business needs, and create blueprints for how the system should be built. Every project also requires understanding organizational behavior concepts such as change management and team building.

This book reflects the dynamic characteristics of the industry by keeping students focused on practicing SAD while offering the basic set of skills that we feel every systems analyst needs to know today and in the future. The authors of this book came to this conclusion after researching the topic. This book is based on our practical expertise as systems analysts and our experience teaching SAD to students in various settings.

This book comprises eight chapters. The first chapter, "Introduction to System Analysis and Design," provides an overview of the field and covers the basic concepts and terminology used in the book.

The second chapter, "System Development Life Cycle," covers the different phases of the system development process, including planning, analysis, design, implementation, and maintenance. The third chapter, "Requirements Modeling," covers identifying and documenting a system's requirements. The fourth chapter, "Data and Process Modeling," covers designing the data and processes used in the system.

The fifth chapter, "Architecture Design," covers the process of designing the overall structure of a system, including the hardware and software components that will be used. The sixth chapter, "User Interface Design," covers designing the interface with which users will interact. The seventh chapter, "Managing Systems Implementation," covers the process of implementing and managing the transition from the old system to the new one.

Finally, the eighth chapter, "Managing Systems Support and Security," covers the ongoing process of maintaining and securing a system. This includes monitoring the system for potential issues and ensuring that it meets the organization's needs. This book is intended for students, IT professionals, and anyone interested in understanding the process of designing and implementing systems.

—Author

CHAPTER 1

INTRODUCTION TO SYSTEM ANALYSIS AND DESIGN

UNIT INTRODUCTION

System analysis and design is a term used in business to describe analyzing a business issue to make enhancements to it by advanced methodologies and practices. Designing organizations, improving performance, and obtaining objectives for expansion and profitability are all linked to system analysis and design. The emphasis seems to be on systems in action, the link among subsystems, and their role in attaining a common goal (Hawryszkiewycz, 1988).

System analysis is the process of analyzing a system to ascertain its efficiency, the areas in which it may need improvement, and the quality of its output. Companies are complex systems that consist of a wide variety of interrelated subsystems. Any change to one part of the system will affect other parts, some of which may be predictable and others not. Systems certification is a way of thinking that has been used to examine and improve computer-based applications. It provides a model for illustrating a given system's internal and external influences. When a computer is integrated into a business setting, it affects the company and the employee. Access to reliable data can boost performance and give you a sense of accomplishment. An employee's career might be threatened, employee morale might fall because of disengagement, and customers might feel threatened because of the company's perceived technological incompetence. Systems, methods, and technology are the core objectives of system design and analysis (Glover et al., 2012).

Systems design and Systems analysis are the two primary categories of the larger field of systems development. Designing a new system, whether to replace an existing one or to supplement it, is what we call the "system design process." But first, we need a thorough understanding of the current system and a strategy for optimizing its usage of computers. To put it another way, system analysis is the process of gathering information, analyzing it to find problems, and then using that information to provide solutions. It is the responsibility of the systems analyst (Whitten & Bentley, 2008).

Consider the stocking area of a clothing store and how it's managed. The retailer needs a system analyst to "computerize" its stock area activities to improve inventory management and get more up-to-date information for reordering. Insight into the store's workflow is necessary before developing a data collection, file maintenance, and report generation system. It is important to know what kinds of reports are generated, how they are used, and what kinds of forms are used for manual data storage (including purchase orders, requisitions, and invoices) (Kindred, 1985).

Furthermore, to move on, look for details regarding lists of rearranged notifications, stock-on-hand data, open purchase orders, and other reports. Discover wherein the data comes from, whether in the stockroom, the accounting department, or the purchasing department. On either hand, you should comprehend the current system's operation and, more particularly, how data flow through the system (Mandal, 2006).

Everyone should know the retailer's motivations for changing its current business practices. Does the company have issues keeping track of orders, merchandise, or money? Does it appear to be handling inventory records s? Is a more effective system required before it can increase operations?

Once you have gathered these facts, you may only start figuring out where and how a computer-based information system may help all its users. Before engaging in any additional analysis tasks, a systems study and information collection must be completed (Shlaer & Mellor, 1988). Systems analysts help with more than just the latest problems. They have been called upon frequently to aid in administrating a company's planned growth. Considering that the apparel industry now lacks any standardized framework, this investigation looks ahead to the possibilities. Analysts examine the company's projected needs and any alterations that should be made to fulfill those needs. In this example, as in the vast majority of others, analysts may advise on improving things. It's common to have more than one option (Fridman, 2014).

Managers and employees within the company are advised by systems analysts on which alternative to select based on factors such as the solution's suitability for the particular organization and setting, as well as the likelihood of employee support. The time required to establish one alternative relative to others can occasionally be crucial. Important considerations can include costs and advantages. The administration, which would invest in and utilize the result, finally decides which option to adopt.

After making a decision, the recommendation is put into effect. New information-gathering needs, file specifications, operating processes, equipment requirements, and human resource requirements are all accounted for in the plan's comprehensive scope. The system's design, like a plan for a structure, specifies all the parts that would make up the whole (Izadi et al., 2009).

The designs for the warehouse's storage areas would detail the processes for taking sales and order information from customers and keeping it safe, whether that data is stored on paper forms or in a computerized format like a magnetic tape or disk. The designs would also define the roles that computers and humans would play. Different layouts call for different ratios of human to computational labor. The stockroom staff will also require knowledge about the company. Every design outlines the system's intended output, like sales analyzes, invoices, purchase summaries, and inventory reports. It will be up to the systems analysts to choose which outputs to utilize and how to generate them.

The analysis specifies the system's proper course of action. Design explains how to achieve the goal. Take note that individuals are involved in all of the processes above. Both employees and managers have solid insights into what functions well and what does not, what creates difficulties, and where changes are required. Notably wherein changes would be accepted and wherein changes would not. People continue to be the main components of organizations, despite technology. As a result, interacting with people and communicating effectively are crucial aspects of the systems analyst's job (Satzinger et al., 2011).

Learning Objective

At the end of this chapter, students will be able to:

- Learn the different phases and methodologies of the system development life cycle;
- Learn how to identify and analyze system requirements;
- Learn how to design and implement effective solutions to business problems;
- Understand the importance of testing and maintenance in the system development process;
- Learn how to document and communicate the system design effectively to stakeholders;
- Learn how to work effectively as a team in the system development process;
- Understand the impact of technology on system analysis and design;
- Learn how to use tools and techniques to support system analysis and design;
- Understand the ethical and legal considerations in system analysis and design.

Key Terms

- System analysis
- System design

- Systems models
- Interface
- Abstract models
- Processor
- Schematic models
- Flow system models
- Dynamic system models
- Management information systems

1.1. BUSINESS SYSTEM CONCEPTS

The system is a commonly used word. The word system is widely used. It has become fashionable to attach the word system to add a contemporary flair when referring to things or processes. People speak of exercise system, investment system, delivery system, information system, education system, computer system etc. System may be referred to any set of components, which function in interrelated manner for a common cause or objective (Karagiannis et al., 1996).

1.1.1. Definition

The word "system" comes from the Greek word "*systema,*" which means a structured relationship between operational parts or elements. Because a system is intended to accomplish one or more goals, it already exists. The system of telephone, the system of manufacturing, the system of accounting, the system of transportation, and, for more than 20 years, the computer system are all systems that we use daily (Hammer et al., 1974). Similar to this, we refer to the organizational and business systems as interconnected divisions (subsystems) like sales, personnel, production, and a data system. As a single, autonomous system, none of such subsystems is handy. However, when they are correctly coordinated, the business may run efficiently and successfully (Opdahl & Henderson, 2005).

There are more than 100 interpretations of the word "system." Still, they all seem to center on the idea that a system is a well-planned network of interrelated components working together to achieve an objective. An element can be a system in a multi-level structure, a physical part (such as the engines, wings, or automobile), or a managerial action (such as planning, organizing, and controlling). The element could be basic or sophisticated, simple or complicated. A single computer having a memory, keyboard, and printer can be one of them, as well as a group of intelligent terminals connected to a mainframe. In either scenario, every element is a part of the overall system and is required to contribute to the system's success. For the development of a good system under this approach, the elements must be grouped in an organized manner (Chapple & Moon, 2005).

Therefore, there are three main implications of studying systems concepts:

- A system should be created to accomplish a specific goal;
- The elements should be interconnected and dependent on one another; and
- Priority is given to the mission of the company as a whole rather than the goals of its subsystems. For instance, the organization's privacy,

secrecy, and security policy should be followed while computerizing personnel applications. Selected data (such as payroll) should also be accessible to the accounting division upon request (Negash & Gray, 2008).

1.2. CHARACTERISTICS OF A SYSTEM

Our definition of a system implies that all systems share specific properties, including structure (order), interaction, dependency, integration, and a primary goal (Grover & Saeed, 2007).

1.2.1. Organization

Organizational structure and order are indicated. The structure helps in reaching objectives. Such a system's organizational structure can be seen in the chain of command that extends from the CEO down to the lowest-paid employees (Bittner, 1965). Such an arrangement can depict the authority structure, establish the flow of formal communication, and outline the chain of command between a system and its subsystems. The essential parts of a computer are the input device, the output device, the central processing unit, and the storage unit. They are a cohesive system for generating information whenever connected (Grunig et al., 2013).

1.2.2. Interaction

The way that every element interacts with the other elements is known as interaction. For instance, in a company, employees, and payroll must work together in purchasing, manufacturing, advertising, and sales (Pike et al., 2009). A computer system's CPU and input device must communicate to solve an issue. The arithmetic unit uses the main memory's data and programs to calculate (Vander & Knol, 2014).

1.2.3. Interdependence

The term "interdependence" explains the interconnected nature of various parts of a whole, such as a business or a computer network. They have been partnered and synchronized under a plan. One subsystem's output is the input required by another, resulting in the former's inability to operate effectively without the latter (Wageman, 1995). When systems function, this dependency is essential. An all-encompassing information system is developed to accommodate the needs of authorized individuals (department heads, managers, etc.) who want easy access via remote terminals. Organizational members and the human resources infrastructure are interdependent (Rusbult & Van Lange, 2003). In conclusion, no subsystem may operate independently because it depends on the information (inputs) it obtains from other subsystems to carry out its necessary functions. More examples of interdependence include the work of systems analysts, programmers, and the operations staff at a data center (Keohane & Nye, 1987). The user initiates the process of computerizing an application, followed by analysis, design, coding, testing, and finally, operation by the computer operator. Without the necessary input from other members of the computer center subsystem, none of these people may do the necessary tasks(Figure 1.1) (McMillan, 1997).

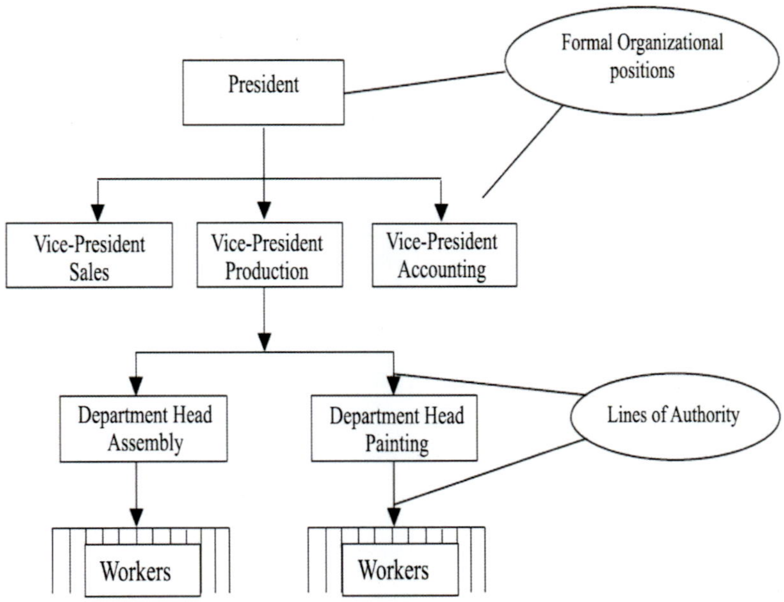

Figure 1.1. Illustrations of organization structure.

Source: Creately, Creative Commons License.

1.2.4. Integration

Integration is the whole view of a system. Synthesis has been utilized after analysis to achieve the organization's primary objective. Integration is all about how systems are connected. Sharing a physical feature or location is only the beginning (Davies, 1998). As such, it demonstrates that, even though each system element performs a unique function, the components work together to form the whole. Generally speaking, successful integration results in a synergistic impact and a bigger overall influence than if every element operates alone (Bartle, 2001).

1.2.5. Central Objective

A system's primary goal is its final characteristic. Real or declared goals are both acceptable. Although a goal that is announced may be that goal, it is normal for a company to declare one goal and work toward another (Gaskell, 1988). The key idea here is that for system implementation and conversion, consumers must understand the main goal of a computer application earlier in the analysis. Organizational and political factors frequently obscure the true goal. To determine the true goal of the suggested change, the analyst should work around these barriers (Canitrot, 1980).

Did you Know?

System analysis and design deal with planning the development of information systems through understanding and specifying in detail what a system should do and how the components of the system should be implemented and work together.

1.3. ELEMENTS OF A SYSTEM

The typical work environment for a systems analyst is fast-paced and ever-evolving. We might be part of a business, a commercial program, or a virtual network (Randers, 1997). When reassembling a system, it is essential to keep in mind the following details:

- Inputs and outputs;
- Environment;
- Boundaries and interface;
- Processor(s);
- Control;
- Feedback.

1.3.1. Outputs and Inputs

One of a system's primary objectives is to generate an output that is useful to the user. Goods, services, and content should all be designed with the end user in mind (Kunz & Rittel, 1970). Inputs are people, materials, and information put into the system to be processed. Output is the final product of any processing (Watson, 2002). A system, like a business, requires input to produce output. Inputs include human labor, financial resources, and physical materials. It is critical to note that determining the output is the first step in characterizing the input type, quantity, and consistency needed to operate a system. The user needs of a proposed computer system, or the output that the computer is anticipated to provide to satisfy the requirements of the user, are, for instance, the first thing to be determined in systems analysis (Sharp et al., 2007).

1.3.2. Processor(s)

A processor is the element of a system that turns input into output. It is the portion of a system that has been operating properly. Depending on the needs of the output, processors may modify the input totally or partially. This indicates that processing would adapt to changing output needs. Sometimes, input is modified to aid the processor in handling the transformation (Farhat et al., 1987).

1.3.3. Control

In a system, the control element acts as the director. The decision-making system controls the order of operations for input, output, and processing. To ensure the organization's continued success, management acts as a decision-making body to control the flow of resources into, within, and out of business. The operating system (OS) and supplementary applications matter regarding how a computer operates. The output specifications establish the nature and amount of input needed to keep the system balanced (Noor & Babuška, 1987).

Understanding the attitudes of the individual in control of the area in which a computer has been considered might be crucial to the success or failure of the installation in systems analysis. Management support is necessary to secure control and support the change's goal (Mackie, 2000).

1.3.4. Feedback

In a dynamic system, control is accomplished by feedback. In a cybernetic process of a certain kind that incorporates control and communication, feedback evaluates the results of the process by comparing them to a benchmark. The information gathered from the output is communicated back to the input and/or the management (Controller) so that it can be considered. After comparing the output to the performance requirements, changes to the input or processing may affect the outcome (Guo, 1997).

Feedback can be informative or directive, favorable or negative. Positive feedback improves how well the system functions. It is typical in style. Generally, negative feedback gives the controller data for taking action. There are many ways in which feedback plays a vital role in the study of systems (Babuška & Rank, 1987). Analysis can relay to the consumer that their initial concerns about an app were well-founded and that the app in question requires some adjustment. After the system is implemented, there is yet another type of feedback. The user notifies the analyst of the new installation's efficiency. The user's needs are frequently considered when making improvements (Wagner et al., 2005).

1.3.5. Environment

The environment is the "supra system" in which an organization operates. It is the origin of outside factors that have an impact on the system. It is often used to determine the proper functioning of a system. For instance, the company's environment, which can include suppliers, competitors, and others, may impose restrictions and, as a result, affect the actual efficiency of the company (Kyritsi et al., 2002).

Remember

The most common system analysis techniques are blocking diagram (system analysis), fault tree analysis (system analysis) event tree analysis.

1.3.6. Boundaries and Interface

The restrictions that define a system's components, functionalities, and relationships with other systems at its interface should serve as its boundaries. For example, a commercial bank's teller system is solely responsible for the deposits, withdrawals, and activities related to customers' checking and savings accounts.Not included may be mortgage foreclosures, trust transactions, and similar occurrences (Tezduyar, 2003).

Lines limit the reach and effectiveness of any system. In an integrated banking-wide computer system design, a customer with a mortgage and a checking account at the same bank may utilize the teller system to pay the premium by writing a check, which is subsequently processed by the mortgage loan system (Bramble & King, 1996). Thanks to current advancements in system architecture, it is feasible to have money transferred directly from a bank account to creditors, regardless of location. This indicates that to design a system successfully; it is essential to understand the boundaries of a particular system to determine the nature of its interaction with other systems (Bieler et al., 2014).

1.4. KINDS OF SYSTEMS

The frame of reference through which a system is viewed has been associated with the system's approach to evaluation. Systems are categorized in various ways (Naikar et al., 2003). The most general classifications are:

i. Physical or abstract;
ii. Closed or open;
iii. "Man-made" information systems.

1.4.1. Physical or Abstract Systems

Physical systems are tangible objects that can operate either statically or dynamically. For instance, the desks, officers, and chairs are physical components of the computer center and make it easier for the computer to function (Liu et al., 2017). They are visible and countable; hence they exist. On the other hand, a computer with programming seems to be a dynamic system. In response to user demands or changes in the priority of the data requested, information, output, programs, and applications change (Gunes et al., 2014).

Conceptual or non-physical things are abstract systems. They could be as simple as formulas for the interactions between groups of factors or models for the conception of abstract physical phenomena. A model is a picture of an existing system or a future one. Using models makes it easier for the analyst to comprehend the connections present in the system that is the subject of the investigation. The goal is to identify the important components and crucial linkages in a complicated system (Leitao et al., 2016).

1.4.2. Open or Closed Systems

The degree of independence is an additional criterion for classifying systems. An open system has several connections to its surroundings. It allows contact over its border; it gets input from outside sources and gives products to the outside world.

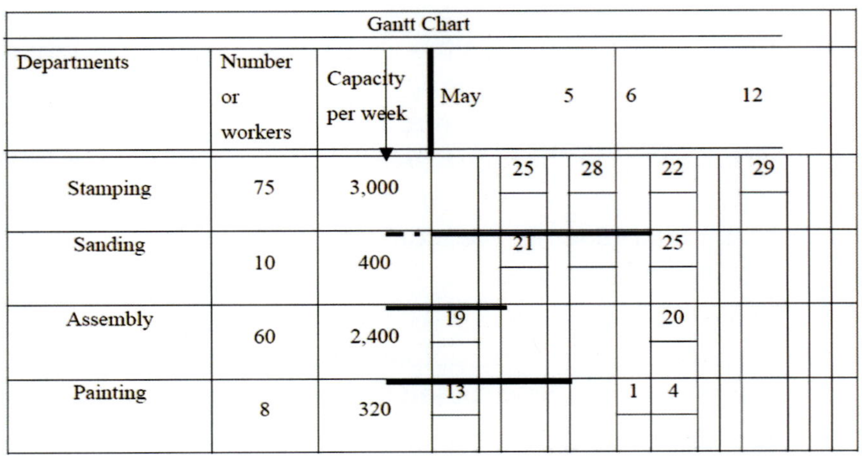

Figure 1.2. Depiction of Gantt chart.

Source: Smartsheet, Creative Commons License.

Information systems fall under this category since they must evolve along with the users' needs (Bigo, 2006). In contrast, a closed system is protected from the environment. An entirely closed system is uncommon in real life. In systems analysis, programs, computers, and organizations have long been considered open, dynamic systems influenced by their context (Figure 1.2) (Schiff, 2003).

An open system seems especially relevant in light of current business challenges, including computer fraud, invasions of privacy security measures, and computational ethics. Since a system is considered open if it may be associated with other users and the environment, systems analysis often includes these factors before approving a new system (Fleetwood, 2017). Methods performed locally within the user's application domain are the focus of the technical side of systems analysis. Being open to new suggestions also necessitates flexibility on the part of the analyst. It necessitates that the system under development is reactive to the evolving needs of users and the surrounding ecosystem (Landauer, 1987).

There are five essential properties of open systems:

1. **Input from Outside:** Open systems are responsible for autonomous regulation and adjustment. When everything works as it should, an open system eventually reaches a steady state, often known as equilibrium. When things are purchased and sold in a retail business without the business experiencing either an out-of-stock situation or an overstock situation, this is an instance of a steady state. When there is a rise in the price of items, there must either be an equal and opposite increase in the prices charged to customers or a reduction in the amount spent on operating expenses. This reply will determine whether the company will remain in a steady condition (Pondy & Mitroff, 1979).
2. **Entropy:** Every dynamic system has the inherent tendency to deteriorate with time, which can increase entropy or a loss of energy. Open systems can combat the effects of entropy by either actively searching for new inputs or modifying their processes to return to a stable state. In our hypothetical situation, if the company does not adjust its pricing in response to an increase in the cost of goods, it would become unprofitable, which could lead to the company's collapse and a state of disorder (Klimontovich, 1999).
3. **Process, Output, and Cycles:** The output of open systems is generated in cycles along a continuous flow route (Thompson & Goldstein, 2005).
4. **Differentiation:** Open systems have the propensity to have their components and functionalities become more and more differentiated. Humans and machines increasingly assume complementary but distinct roles in the modern workplace. This quality argues persuasively for

the expanding significance of the idea of the system in the minds of systems analysts (Reagan et al., 1987).

5. **Equifinality:** The phrase signifies that objectives are accomplished through a variety of pathways and various courses of action. Generally speaking, there is more consensus on the desired results than optimal approaches (Lyman, 2004).

Knowing system characteristics enables analysts to clarify their role and connect their actions to achieving the company's goals when undertaking a system project. Analysts are an integral element of the business. To prevent the system from "running down," they have the chance to adjust the organization to modifications through a digital application. Information feedback from top executives and the new system's primary user is essential to this procedure (Jennings et al., 2003).

A general understanding of systems theory is often referenced in the theme of how information systems are designed. The purpose of adjusting the system's goals or outputs is to increase efficiency (Kapsali, 2013).

1.4.3. Manmade Information Systems

Information should ideally lessen ambiguity surrounding a situation or event. For example, if you know that the wind is calm, it is less difficult to imagine that the time spent on the boat will be pleasant. The data system serves as the basis for communication between the client and the analyst (Li et al., 2014). This gives directions, orders, and feedback. It establishes the type of connections between decision-makers. Employees at all levels can view it as a central location for decision-making. This foundation describes an information system as a collection of tools, processes, and OS built around client-based criteria to generate data and deliver it to the consumer for planning, management, and execution. In systems analysis, it is crucial to remember that considering a different system entail enhancing one or many such standards (Marchuk et al., 2012).

Several professionals are unaware that a company has several information systems, every of which serves a specific function and supports the flow of data, decision-making, communications, control, and efficiency. The three main types of information systems are computer-based, informal, and formal (Buzina & Engovatov, 2020).

1.4.4. Formal Information System

The organization that the organization chart represents serves as the foundation for a formal information system. The chart uses boxes to represent positions and lines representing lines of authority to show their connections. It worries about how authority, communication, and workflow are organized (Guarino, 1998). Top management formally disseminates information to the target user inside the organization through orders, memoranda, or reports. Additionally, this structure enables input for follow-up up the chain of command. The environment in Figure 1.1 input form motivates top management to choose a policy. Policies are broad statements that outline what a company should do. For implementation by lower-level management, policies are converted into directives, rules, and regulations. The result is an indicator of worker performance (Hall, 1999).

1.5. SYSTEMS MODELS

Models are utilized more frequently and in more different ways than in any other subject other than systems analysis. Beginning with a model of the reality (facts, connections, procedures, etc.) that the system has been concerned with, the analyst next proceeds to analyze the model. Each computer system interacts with the outside world, an issue, or another reality. A telephone switching system, for instance, consists of subscribers, dialing, phone handsets, conference calls, and other components. The analyst starts by simulating this reality before thinking about the system's tasks (Klahr et al., 1987).

The advantages of abstracting complicated systems into model form are demonstrated using various business system models. The main models are schematic, static, flow, and dynamic system models (Ackoff & Gharajedaghi, 1996).

1.5.1. Schematic Models

A schematic model is a 2-D diagram showing a system's components and how they are connected. Information flow, material flow, and data feedback are all represented by various arrows. The system's many components are shown as boxes (Harari, 1979).

1.5.2. Flow System Models

A flow system model depicts the movement of the information, energy, and materials that keep the system in place. These models have a logical flow that is well-organized. PERT (Program Evaluation and Review Technique) is a well-known illustration (Chen & Zhang, 2009). To find the crucial path, it manipulates particular values. It then interprets the relationships and relays them back as a control. The likelihood of completion within a time frame is considered with time, resources, and performance requirements, as depicted in Figure 1.3 (Showalter et al., 1978).

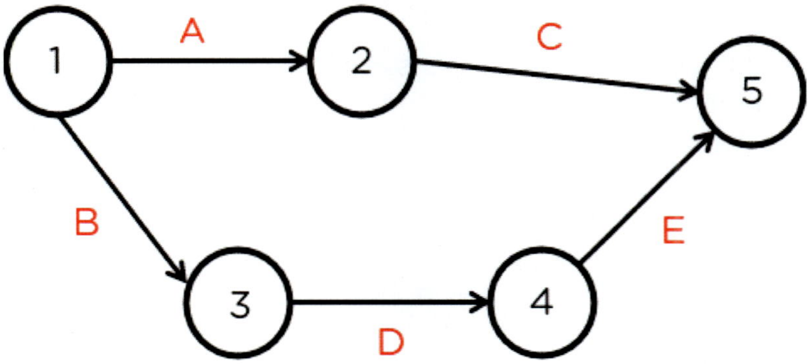

Figure 1.3. Diagram of PERT.

Source: Simplilearn, Creative Commons License.

1.5.3. Static System Models

This type of model exhibits one pair of relationships such as activity–time or cost – quantity. The Gantt chart, for example, gives a static picture of an activity- time relationship. Planned activities (stamping, sanding etc.) are plotted in relation to time are shown in figure 1.3. The date column has light lines that indicate the amount of time it takes to complete a given activity. The heavy line represents the cumulative time schedule for each activity (Adrot et al., 2000). For instance, the stamping division is expected to begin working on order number 25 on Wednesday and finish that same day. Orders number 28 and 22 each have one day scheduled, order number 28 has two days, order number 22 has four days, and order number 29 has two days (May 10–11). The line outside the stamping office had been there for six days. The broken line shows a two-day delay in the department's schedule. The arrow indicates the effective date of the chart (Xiang et al., 2011).

1.5.4. Dynamic System Models

Organizational structures are dynamic systems. A dynamic model imitates the organization or application type with which analysts are tasked. It shows a dynamic, ever-changing system. It comprises:

i. System inputs;
ii. The processor by which transformation occurs;
iii. The program(s) necessary for processing;
iv. System outputs.

1.6. CATEGORIES OF INFORMATION

Information on managerial levels and managerial decisions falls into three areas. Strategic information is the 1st level, which refers to long-term planning strategies that directly concern high management. Data on population growth, financial investment trends, and human resource shifts will interest top corporate executives who are in charge of developing policies and selecting long-term objectives(Berger, 2002). Such data is gathered using a DSS (decision support system; Hearst, 2006).

Managerial information makes up the 2nd level of information. Middle management and department leaders can use it immediately for control and implementation. Instances include cash flow forecasts, annual financial statements, and sales analyzes (Berger, 2002). Planning that has been done for months instead of years will benefit from this data. Utilizing management information systems (MIS) is maintained (Keil et al., 2005).

Operational information, which is short-term, everyday information used to run departments and execute the day-to-day laws and regulations of the organization, is the third type of information. Instances include daily absence reports from employees, past-due purchase orders, and current stock levels. Operational information is established through DPS (data processing systems). The same is seen in Figure 1.4 (Maddox et al., 2005).

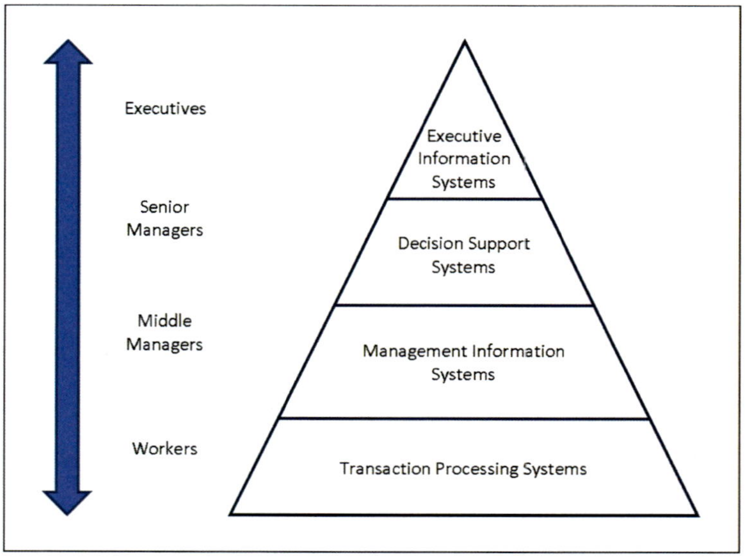

Figure 1.4. Levels of management and information in an ordinary organization.

Source: Chris Kimble, Creative Commons License.

The two main categories of decision-making, unstructured, and structured, are also linked to the nature of the data and managerial levels. Closed, steady, and mechanical organizational processes are typically more computational, structured, and dependent on routine decision-making for control and planning (Ma et al., 2016). A computer system can easily back up judgments at this level of management. Adaptive, open, and dynamic systems, in contrast, tend to lack structure in the decision-making procedure and increase the uncertainty linked with making decisions. It is challenging to obtain computer support due to a lack of structure and extra-organizational and missing data (Aust & Huber, 2001).

Thus, before choosing the system necessary to manufacture it, the analyst must decide on the data needed, the required information level, how it is arranged, and what format it is. Having a foundation in systems theory and companies is also important for this reason (Alba et al., 1980).

1.6.1. Informal Information Systems

The formal information system is a hierarchical framework created to further business objectives. The emphasis placed by a corporation on the control to assure performance often limits employee communication. An unofficial information system grows as a result (Clancy & Collins, 1979). It is an employee-based system created to address personnel and professional needs and resolve employment-related issues. Additionally, it directs data upward through oblique routes. This is a helpful mechanism in this regard as it operates within the confines of the company and its declared policies (Macdonald, 1996).

To understand how much support may be anticipated for a potential installation, the analyst must understand the power-authority-influence network, the command line, and how decisions are made. Additionally, understanding how the employee-based system functions from the inside out helps conduct exploratory analysis. Employee engagement and cooperation are essential to avoiding sabotage and educating users. A suitable interface with informal communication channels might represent the distinction between the failure and success of new technologies, as computers can't deliver trustworthy information without client-staff support (Ackerman & McDonald, 2000).

1.6.2. Computer-Based Information Systems

The third class of information systems relies on computing devices to control operational processes within a company. Today, a computer is a necessary information source. Computers are frequently utilized in systems analysis to solve issues. This implies that the analyst needs to be knowledgeable about computer technology and skilled at managing people at an organizational level (Leifer, 1988).

1.6.3. Management Information Systems (MIS)

Management techniques used to run a business are significantly altered by the advent of technology. The type of information required to resolve a problem also depends on the manager's position within the business. Low-level management needs comprehensive internal data to make daily, well-organized control choices. High-level management needs compiled data from various sources to accomplish goals since long-term objectives are their main priorities. Regardless of the situation, management decisions are based on timely, accurate, relevant, complete information and all of the above. The MIS has met these information criteria in a timely and responsive manner (Majchrzak & Markus, 2012).

MIS aims to give management a thorough understanding of particular operations through a person-machine system and a fully integrated collection of data processing tasks. Essentially, it's a composite of information systems. It must function in real-time, responding to inquiries as soon as they come in to be effective. Additionally, management data must be accessible early enough to influence a choice. Information management systems (MIS) should include file definition, file maintenance and update, transaction, and inquiry processing, and one or more databases linked to an organization's database to function effectively. Each relevant data file in the MIS might be updated simultaneously by a single transaction. Reduced data redundancy (duplicate) and replication time mean that data can be kept current at all times (Shah, 2014).

The database, a non-redundant group of connected data items that can be handled by application programs and made accessible to multiple users, is a crucial component of MIS. Every document should be connected in some way. The ability for several programs to utilize the same records or files is known as data sharing. Access to information is made possible through a database management system (DBMS). It is a software component that manages almost all operations affecting the database (Davis, 2003).

A database system has the following benefits:

- The number of programs created, and processing time are both significantly decreased;
- All of the programs utilize the same centralized file storage;
- The duplication of storage space has been removed;
- Information is stored only once in a database and may be retrieved quickly and efficiently (Ehie, 2002).

The need to hire specialist employees and the importance of data security are two main drawbacks of databases. Users of MIS often fall into the middle and upper levels of management, operational managers, and support workers. Predictions, specific analytical requests, long-range strategies, and monthly reports are all things that middle and upper management use MIS for (Ajayi & Omirin, 2007). Short-term planning, periodic reporting, and exception reports are the main uses of MIS for operational managers. The support team appreciates the MIS for its particular information and report analysis that aids management in controlling and planning. Most employees in an organization are responsible for giving information for utilization in MIS. Information stored in the system no longer belongs to the user who initiated it and is instead made accessible to all authenticated users (Mason & Mitroff, 1973).

The conventional MIS of today has several issues. Since most MIS reports are historical, they frequently date. Several installations have databases that don't meet user requirements, which is another issue. This indicates that several MIS environments just haven't been compatible with the user's actual environment. Ultimately, a poor or incomplete database update compromises the dependability of all clients (Asemi et al., 2011).

Getting the approval and support of those who would interface with the system is a significant issue in MIS design. Employees who feel their employees are at risk may oppose the deployment of MIS. The analyst must convince the correct people to modify their behavior for the installation to be effective while also knowing technology and human psychology (Nasir, 2005).

1.6.4. Decision Support Systems (DSS)

The minimal support top management receives from MIS for making decisions is one argument given in the literature for management's dissatisfaction with it. DSS expands MIS's capability. It supports management's decision-making. It's a constantly changing model and is significantly influenced by operations research (Mohemad et al., 2010).

Gorry and Morton are credited as being the first individuals to use the term "decision support system" (DSS). The phrase has a straightforward etymology:

- Decision-making in difficult circumstances is emphasized rather than processing, retrieving, or reporting information.
- Support demands for decision-making scenarios that can be computer-aided and have adequate "structure" to support computers.
- The word "system" emphasizes how integrated problem solving is by implying a combination of machine, man, and decision environment (Sprague, 1980).

The concept of interactive computer-based systems assisting unstructured decision-making was first introduced to management decision systems in the early 1970s and has since been broadened to encompass all systems except transaction processing systems. An interactive computer-based system was typically needed in the early definitions to assist users in using data and models to tackle unstructured problems. Many authors believe DSS is a subset of MIS, separate from MIS, or an extension of MIS. The literature generally agrees that DSS belongs to the second generation of computer systems (Arnott & Pervan, 2008). MIS. Production MIS and personnel MIS are examples of MIS that combine transaction processing, report preparation, and online inquiry capabilities with an integrated focus on certain functional areas and then add predefined reports for management. External sources of data, statistical and accounting models, and interactive query abilities are all added to DSS. The result is a framework created to assist senior management, in particular, in handling "what if" unstructured problem situations at all management levels. This system can assist in decision modeling and ad hoc data analysis tasks (Eom & Kim, 2006).

ACTIVITY 1.1

What are the categories of information?

The knowledge of an issue at a symptomatic level is part of the intelligence stage of decision-making; it necessitates a detailed examination of the issue and a thorough analysis of the factors and their interactions. The possibility of developing a wise decision increase with management's knowledge of the root of a problem. A DSS may offer intelligence through statistical software and information retrieval (Husain, 2019).

The evaluation of alternative options is the main emphasis of the design phase of decision-making. Decision design throughout this step can involve computer-based deterministic or stochastic models. In designing decisions under uncertainty, DSS is crucial. The model's outcome(s) is the foundation for the decision-making phase of choice (Liu et al., 2010).

1.7. SUMMARY

A system is an organized set of interconnected pieces linked by a plan to achieve a specific objective. It is characterized by interaction, organization, integration, dependency, and a primary objective. System analysts must consider a system's output and input, processors, controls, feedback, and the environment when building it. Systems can be categorized as closed or open, abstract or physical, or man-made information systems. A system could be dynamic, static, or schematic. An information system is an open system that accepts inputs and enables user involvement. An open system's primary characteristics include external input, processing, output, and cycle-based functioning with feedback and differentiation. Organizations need a specific kind of information system to handle three levels of information. A long-term planning and executive-level strategic information system. Managerial information systems are useful for top and middle-level management in ensuring that policies are carried out as intended. Operational information systems help with the day-to-day information necessary to manage a business. Future emphasis will be placed on decision support systems (DSS) rather than information processing; this will call for a computer-aided environment and emphasize a combined man-and-machine and decision environment.

REVIEW QUESTIONS

1. What is the goal of system analysis and design?
2. What are the various activities involved in system analysis and design?
3. How can system analysis and design be used to improve business operations?
4. What are the different types of systems involved in system analysis and design?
5. How can system analysis and design help to identify potential problems in a system?
6. What are the different stages of system analysis and design?
7. What are the benefits of using system analysis and design?
8. What techniques are used in system analysis and design?
9. What steps are involved in the system analysis and design process?
10. What are best practices for developing effective systems using system analysis and design?

MULTIPLE CHOICE QUESTIONS

1. What is the primary goal of system analysis and design?

a. To develop a working system
b. To create an efficient system
c. To improve an existing system

d. To analyze a system

2. What is a requirement analysis?

a. A type of system design

b. A process of assessing user needs

c. A type of system analysis

d. A process of analyzing data

3. What is the purpose of system design?

a. To create a working system

b. To analyze a system

c. To improve an existing system

d. To develop an efficient system

4. Which of the following is an example of a system design?

a. Algorithms

b. Software architecture

c. Database design

d. All of the above

5. What is the primary focus of system design?

a. Creating a working system

b. Analyzing user needs

c. Implementing a system

d. Developing an efficient system

Answers to Multiple Choice Questions

1. (c) 2. (b) 3. (d) 4. (d) 5. (d)

REFERENCES

1. Ackerman, M. S., & McDonald, D. W., (2000). Collaborative support for informal information in collective memory systems. *Information Systems Frontiers, 2*(3), 333–347.
2. Ackoff, R. L., & Gharajedaghi, J., (1996). Reflections on systems and their models. *Systems Research, 13*(1), 13–23.
3. Adrot, O., Maquin, D., & Ragot, J., (2000). Diagnosis of an uncertain static system. In: *Proceedings of the 39th IEEE Conference on Decision and Control (Cat. No. 00CH37187)* (Vol. 4, pp. 4150–4154). IEEE.
4. Ajayi, I. A., & Omirin, F. F., (2007). The use of management information systems

(MIS) in decision making in the South-West Nigerian Universities. *Educational Research and Reviews, 2*(5), 109.

5. Alba, J. W., Chromiak, W., Hasher, L., & Attig, M. S., (1980). Automatic encoding of category size information. *Journal of Experimental Psychology: Human Learning and Memory, 6*(4), 370.
6. Arnott, D., & Pervan, G., (2008). Eight key issues for the decision support systems discipline. *Decision Support Systems, 44*(3), 657–672.
7. Asemi, A., Safari, A., & Zavareh, A. A., (2011). The role of management information system (MIS) and decision support system (DSS) for manager's decision-making process. *International Journal of Business and Management, 6*(7), 164–173.
8. Aust, U., & Huber, L., (2001). The role of item-and category-specific information in the discrimination of people versus nonpeople images by pigeons. *Animal Learning & Behavior, 29*(2), 107–119.
9. Babuška, I., & Rank, E., (1987). An expert-system-like feedback approach in the hp-version of the finite element method. *Finite Elements in Analysis and Design, 3*(2), 127–147.
10. Bartle, R. G., (2001). *A Modern Theory of Integration* (Vol. 32). American Mathematical Soc.
11. Berger, E. J., (2002). Friction modeling for dynamic system simulation. *Appl. Mech. Rev., 55*(6), 535–577.
12. Bieler, T. R., Eisenlohr, P., Zhang, C., Phukan, H. J., & Crimp, M. A., (2014). Grain boundaries and interfaces in slip transfer. *Current Opinion in Solid State and Materials Science, 18*(4), 212–226.
13. Bigo, V., (2006). Open and closed systems and the Cambridge school. *Review of Social Economy, 64*(4), 493–514.
14. Bittner, E., (1965). The concept of organization. *Social Research*, 239–255.
15. Bramble, J. H., & King, J. T., (1996). A finite element method for interface problems in domains with smooth boundaries and interfaces. *Advances in Computational Mathematics, 6*(1), 109–138.
16. Buzina, D., & Engovatov, I., (2020). Information system for the content of natural and man-made radionuclides in building materials. In: *E3S Web of Conferences* (Vol. 175, p. 11022). EDP Sciences.
17. Canitrot, A., (1980). Discipline as the central objective of economic policy: An essay on the economic program of the Argentine government since 1976. *World Development, 8*(11), 923–928.
18. Chapple, W., & Moon, J., (2005). Corporate social responsibility (CSR) in Asia: A seven-country study of CSR web site reporting. *Business & Society, 44*(4), 415–441.
19. Chen, Z., & Zhang, Y., (2009). Well flow models for various numerical methods. *International Journal of Numerical Analysis & Modeling, 6*(3).
20. Clancy, D. K., & Collins, F., (1979). Informal accounting information systems: Some

tentative findings. *Accounting, Organizations and Society, 4*(1, 2), 21–30.

21. Davies, J., (1998). Mechanisms of endosseous integration. *International Journal of Prosthodontics, 11*(5).
22. Davis, G. B., (2003). Management information systems (MIS). *Encyclopedia of Computer Science,* 1070–1077.
23. Distelberg, B., & Sorenson, R. L., (2009). Updating systems concepts in family businesses: A focus on values, resource flows, and adaptability. *Family Business Review, 22*(1), 65–81.
24. Ehie, I. C., (2002). Developing a management information systems (MIS) curriculum: Perspectives from MIS practitioners. *Journal of Education for Business, 77*(3), 151–158.
25. Eliasoph, N., & Lichterman, P., (2003). Culture in interaction. *American Journal of Sociology, 108*(4), 735–794.
26. Eom, S., & Kim, E., (2006). A survey of decision support system applications (1995–2001). *Journal of the Operational Research Society, 57*(11), 1264–1278.
27. Farhat, C., Wilson, E., & Powell, G., (1987). Solution of finite element systems on concurrent processing computers. *Engineering with Computers, 2*(3), 157–165.
28. Fleetwood, S., (2017). The critical realist conception of open and closed systems. *Journal of Economic Methodology, 24*(1), 41–68.
29. Fridman, E., (2014). *Introduction to Time-Delay Systems: Analysis and Control* (Vol. 1, pp. 1–11). Springer.
30. Gaskell, C. M., (1988). Direct evidence for gravitational domination of the motion of gas within one light-week of the central object in NGC 4151 and the determination of the mass of the probable black hole. *The Astrophysical Journal, 325*, 114–118.
31. Glover, J. D., Sarma, M. S., & Overbye, T., (2012). *Power System Analysis & Design, SI Version* (Vol. 1, pp. 1–10). Cengage Learning.
32. Grover, V., & Saeed, K. A., (2007). The impact of product, market, and relationship characteristics on interorganizational system integration in manufacturer-supplier dyads. *Journal of Management Information Systems, 23*(4), 185–216.
33. Grunig, L. A., Grunig, J. E., & Ehling, W. P., (2013). What is an effective organization? In: *Excellence in Public Relations and Communication Management* (pp. 65–90). Routledge.
34. Guarino, N., (1998). *Formal Ontology in Information Systems: Proceedings of the First International Conference (FOIS'98)* (Vol. 46). Trento, Italy. IOS press.
35. Gunes, V., Peter, S., Givargis, T., & Vahid, F., (2014). A survey on concepts, applications, and challenges in cyber-physical systems. *KSII Transactions on Internet and Information Systems (TIIS),8*(12), 4242–4268.
36. Guo, R. M., (1997). Modeling and simulation of run-out table cooling control using feedforward-feedback and element tracking system. *IEEE transactions on Industry Applications, 33*(2), 304–311.

37. Hall, A., (1999). Using formal methods to develop an ATC information system. In: *Industrial-Strength Formal Methods in Practice* (pp. 207–229). Springer, London.
38. Hammer, M. M., Howe, W. G., & Wladawsky, I., (1974). An interactive business definition system. *ACM SIGPLAN Notices, 9*(4), 25–33.
39. Harari, H., (1979). A schematic model of quarks and leptons. *Physics Letters B, 86*(1), 83–86.
40. Hawryszkiewycz, I. T., (1988). *Introduction to Systems Analysis and Design* (Vol. 1, pp. 1–5). Prentice-Hall, Inc.
41. Hearst, M. A., (2006). Clustering versus faceted categories for information exploration. *Communications of the ACM, 49*(4), 59–61.
42. Husain, T., (2019). An analysis of modeling audit quality measurement based on decision support systems (DSS). *Measurement, 275*, 310–326.
43. Izadi, I., Shah, S. L., Shook, D. S., & Chen, T., (2009). An introduction to alarm analysis and design. *IFAC Proceedings Volumes, 42*(8), 645–650.
44. Jennings, D. F., Rajaratnam, D., & Lawrence, F. B., (2003). Strategy-performance relationships in service firms: A test for equifinality. *Journal of Managerial Issues,* 208–220.
45. Kapsali, M., (2013). Equifinality in project management exploring causal complexity in projects. *Systems Research and Behavioral Science, 30*(1), 2–14.
46. Karagiannis, D., Junginger, S., & Strobl, R., (1996). Introduction to business process management systems concepts. In: *Business Process Modeling* (pp. 81–106). Springer, Berlin, Heidelberg.
47. Keil, F., Kim, N. S., & Greif, M. L., (2005). Categories and levels of information. In: *Category Specificity in Brain and Mind* (pp. 397–407). Psychology Press.
48. Keohane, R. O., & Nye, J. S., (1987). Power and interdependence revisited. *International Organization, 41*(4), 725–753.
49. Kindred, A. R., (1985). *Data Systems and Management: An Introduction to Systems Analysis and Design* (Vol. 1, pp. 1–20). Prentice-Hall, Inc.
50. Klahr, D., Langley, P., Neches, R., & Neches, R. T., 1987). *Production System Models of Learning and Development* (Vol. 1, pp. 1–22). MIT press.
51. Klimontovich, Y. L., (1999). Entropy and information of open systems. *Physics-Uspekhi, 42*(4), 375.
52. Kunz, W., & Rittel, H. W., (1970). *Issues as Elements of Information Systems* (Vol. 131, p. 14). Berkeley, CA: Institute of Urban and Regional Development, University of California.
53. Kyritsi, P., Cox, D. C., Valenzuela, R. A., & Wolniansky, P. W., (2002). Effect of antenna polarization on the capacity of a multiple element system in an indoor environment. *IEEE Journal on Selected Areas in Communications, 20*(6), 1227–1239.
54. Landauer, R., (1987). Electrical transport in open and closed systems. *Zeitschrift für Physik B Condensed Matter, 68*(2), 217–228.

55. Leifer, R., (1988). Matching computer-based information systems with organizational structures. *MIS Quarterly*,63–73.
56. Leitao, P., Karnouskos, S., Ribeiro, L., Lee, J., Strasser, T., & Colombo, A. W., (2016). Smart agents in industrial cyber–physical systems. *Proceedings of the IEEE, 104*(5), 1086–1101.
57. Li, J., Li, Q., Liu, C., Khan, S. U., & Ghani, N., (2014). Community-based collaborative information system for emergency management. *Computers & Operations Research, 42*, 116–124.
58. Liu, S., Duffy, A. H., Whitfield, R. I., & Boyle, I. M., (2010). Integration of decision support systems to improve decision support performance. *Knowledge and Information Systems, 22*(3), 261–286.
59. Liu, Y., Peng, Y., Wang, B., Yao, S., & Liu, Z., (2017). Review on cyber-physical systems. *IEEE/CAA Journal of Automatica Sinica, 4*(1), 27–40.
60. Lyman, R. L., (2004). The concept of equifinality in taphonomy. *Journal of Taphonomy, 2*(1), 15–26.
61. Ma, S., Fildes, R., & Huang, T., (2016). Demand forecasting with high dimensional data: The case of SKU retail sales forecasting with intra-and inter-category promotional information. *European Journal of Operational Research, 249*(1), 245–257.
62. Macdonald, S., (1996). Informal information flow and strategy in the international firm. *International Journal of Technology Management, 11*(1), 219.
63. Mackie, R. I., (2000). An object-oriented approach to calculation control in finite element programs. *Computers & Structures, 77*(5), 461–474.
64. Maddox, W. T., Filoteo, J. V., Lauritzen, J. S., Connally, E., & Hejl, K. D., (2005). Discontinuous categories affect information-integration but not rule-based category learning. *Journal of Experimental Psychology: Learning, Memory, and Cognition, 31*(4), 654.
65. Majchrzak, A., & Markus, M. L., (2012). Technology affordances and constraints in management information systems (MIS). In: Kessler, E., (ed.), *Encyclopedia of Management Theory* (Vol. 1, pp. 1–17). *Sage Publications, Forthcoming.*
66. Mandal, A. K., (2006). *Introduction to Control Engineering: Modeling, Analysis and Design* (Vol. 1, pp. 1–25). New Age International.
67. Marchuk, A., Marinin, I., Krivorotko, O., Komarov, V., Karas, A., & Khidasheli, D., (2012). 3D GIS integrated natural and man-made hazards research and information system. In: *Proceedings of the 2012 Joint International Conference on Human-Centered Computer Environments* (pp. 225–229).
68. Mason, R. O., & Mitroff, I. I., (1973). A program for research on management information systems. *Management Science, 19*(5), 475–487.
69. McMillan, S. M., (1997). Interdependence and conflict. *Mershon International Studies Review, 41*(Supplement_1), 33–58.
70. Mohemad, R., Hamdan, A. R., Othman, Z. A., & Noor, N. M. M., (2010). *Decision Support*

*Systems (DSS) in Construction Tendering Processes.*arXiv preprint arXiv:1004.3260.

71. Naikar, N., Pearce, B., Drumm, D., & Sanderson, P. M., (2003). Designing teams for first-of-a-kind, complex systems using the initial phases of cognitive work analysis: Case study. *Human Factors, 45*(2), 202–217.
72. Nasir, S., (2005). The development, change, and transformation of management information systems (MIS): A content analysis of articles published in business and marketing journals. *International Journal of Information Management, 25*(5), 442–457.
73. Negash, S., & Gray, P., (2008). Business intelligence. In: *Handbook on Decision Support Systems 2* (pp. 175–193). Springer, Berlin, Heidelberg.
74. Noor, A. K., & Babuška, I., (1987). Quality assessment and control of finite element solutions. *Finite Elements in Analysis and Design, 3*(1), 1–26.
75. Opdahl, A., & Henderson-Sellers, B., (2005). Template-based definition of information systems and enterprise modelling constructs. In: *Business Systems Analysis with Ontologies* (pp. 105–129). IGI Global.
76. Pike, W. A., Stasko, J., Chang, R., & O'connell, T. A., (2009). The science of interaction. *Information Visualization, 8*(4), 263–274.
77. Pondy, L. R., & Mitroff, I. I., (1979). Beyond open system models of organization. *Research in Organizational Behavior, 1*(1), 3–39.
78. Randers, J., (1997). Elements of the system dynamics method. *Journal of the Operational Research Society, 48*(11), 1144–1145.
79. Reagan, M. K., Gill, J. B., Malavassi, E., & Garcia, M. O., (1987). Changes in magma composition at Arenal volcano, Costa Rica, 1968–1985: Real-time monitoring of open-system differentiation. *Bulletin of Volcanology, 49*(1), 415–434.
80. Rusbult, C. E., & Van, L. P. A., (2003). Interdependence, interaction, and relationships. *Annual Review of Psychology, 54*(1), 351–375.
81. Satzinger, J., Jackson, R., & Burd, S., (2011). *Introduction to Systems Analysis and Design* (Vol. 1, pp. 1–16). Книга.
82. Schiff, A., (2003). Open and closed systems of two-sided networks. *Information Economics and Policy, 15*(4), 425–442.
83. Shah, M., (2014). Impact of management information systems (MIS) on school administration: What the literature says. *Procedia-Social and Behavioral Sciences, 116*, 2799–2804.
84. Sharp, J. A., Meng, W., & Liu, W., (2007). A modified slacks-based measure model for data envelopment analysis with 'natural' negative outputs and inputs. *Journal of the Operational Research Society, 58*(12), 1672–1677.
85. Shlaer, S., & Mellor, S. J., (1988). *Object-Oriented Systems Analysis: Modeling the World in Data* (Vol. 1, pp. 1–6). Yourdon press.
86. Showalter, K., Noyes, R. M., & Bar-Eli, K., (1978). A modified oregonator model exhibiting complicated limit cycle behavior in a flow system. *The Journal of Chemical Physics, 69*(6), 2514–2524.

87. Sprague, Jr. R. H., (1980). A framework for the development of decision support systems. *MIS Quarterly,* 1–26.

88. Tezduyar, T. E., (2003). Computation of moving boundaries and interfaces and stabilization parameters. *International Journal for Numerical Methods in Fluids, 43*(5), 555–575.

89. Thompson, W. G., & Goldstein, S. L., (2005). Open-system coral ages reveal persistent suborbital sea-level cycles. *Science, 308*(5720), 401–404.

90. VanderWeele, T. J., & Knol, M. J., (2014). A tutorial on interaction. *Epidemiologic Methods, 3*(1), 33–72.

91. Wageman, R., (1995). Interdependence and group effectiveness. *Administrative Science Quarterly,* 145.

92. Wagner, C. R., Perrin, D. P., Feller, R. L., Howe, R. D., Clatz, O., Delingette, H., & Ayache, N., (2005). Integrating tactile and force feedback with finite element models. In: *Proceedings of the 2005 IEEE international Conference on Robotics and Automation* (pp. 3942–3947). IEEE.

93. Watson, J., (2002). Comparing the performance of male-and female-controlled businesses: Relating outputs to inputs. *Entrepreneurship Theory and Practice, 26*(3), 91–100.

94. Whitten, J. L., & Bentley, L. D., (2008). *Introduction to Systems Analysis and Design* (Vol. 1, pp. 1–15). McGraw-Hill Higher Education.

95. Xiang, J., Yanoo, K., Maeno, Y., & Tadano, K., (2011). Automatic synthesis of static fault trees from system models. In: *2011 Fifth International Conference on Secure Software Integration and Reliability Improvement* (pp. 127–136). IEEE.

CHAPTER 2

SYSTEM DEVELOPMENT LIFE CYCLE

UNIT INTRODUCTION

The system of analysis is responsible for providing meaning and direction to a system's development project. After obtaining a comprehensive grasp of user demands and difficulties, the analyst will approach a candidate system. It is determined that there is a workable solution, which is subsequently communicated (Weitzel & Kerschberg, 1989). Candidate systems frequently cross the borders of different types of users within an organization. For instance, users from the consumer orders department, consumer banking, the warehouse, as well as the accounting department could all be required to participate in the use of a billing system. Together with the research, the program representing every user works to carry out all the systems development programs. This helps to guarantee that all the users' requirements are satisfied (Isaias & Issa, 2015).

Learning Objective

After studying this unit, you will be able to:

- Identify and describe the stages of system development;
- Identify and explain the considerations for a candidate system;
- Develop a plan and demonstrate the ability to control for success in system development.

Key Terms

- System development
- Project selection
- Political consideration
- Working capital
- Candidate system

2.1. STAGES OF SYSTEM DEVELOPMENT LIFE CYCLE

The process by which analysts, developers, and consumers, develop, and operate an information system is known as a development life cycle technique. Even the sequence of the processes in such activities is unclear because of how tightly related the multiple business phases are to one another (Snee & Rodenbaugh, 2002).

2.1.1. Project Selection

Before resolving, an issue, one should understand the situation of the issue. An applicant system's foundation is the realization that it requires a process of needs and a management system to be improved. For instance, a supervisor might wish to investigate the purchasing system flow, or even a banking president might be receiving complaints about just the lengthy drive-in wait (Meade & Presley, 2002). Due to this need, an initial survey or study is being conducted to see if the different system may address the issue. It comprises investigating areas of duplication of work, bottlenecks, current ineffective practices, or whether some elements of the current system could benefit from a computerized system (Henriksen & Traynor, 1999).

The management wishes to provide an expert look at the issue if it is significant enough. Such a task takes dedication, especially if the analyst could be another contractor. The analyst's initial responsibility in better environments with established processes, even as standard, is to create a statement outlining the issue's nature, extent, and goal. After that, they check that for correctness with both the user. Only an approximate *"ballpark"* calculation of the project might achieve its developmental cost. However, a precise cost estimate for the following phase—the viability study—can be generated (Souder & Mandakovic, 1986).

2.1.1.1. The Impetus for System Change

The concept of transformation comes from the surroundings or the company itself. Ideas depending on the environment come from clients, suppliers, the government, and others. For instance, new rules governing unemployed compensation might necessitate changing the restructurings. Examining the distribution schedule, the qualifications of its truck drivers, and the volume of goods that must be delivered could result in customer complaints regarding order delivery. Upon investigation, every one of those concepts may result in an issue definition as the initial stage of the system's life cycle process (McHugh et al., 2019). Top management, users, and analysts inside the organization could also have changes in mind. Someone from the business may sense the desire to upgrade current programs or improve processes even as the organization alters its activities or deals with advancements in computer technology. Here seem to be a few instances (Wong et al., 2008):

- An organization purchases another one;
- A neighborhood bank opens a branch there;
- In one month, a department uses up 80% of its budget (MacLean et al., 2011);
- Each department head maintains that other departments must be eliminated even though two divisions perform virtually the same tasks;
- The usage of counterfeit (illegal) forms is revealed by a demand for a new form (Lukas et al., 2007).
- Top management also started investigations because of severe operational issues, high employee turnover, and labor-intensive tasks, including increased costs of finished product rejection. Other instances include:
- A senior executive vice president receives a report and questions the numbers;
- After reading an IRS independent audit, the firm comptroller begins to reflect (Kovoor-Misra, 2020);
- An executive gets an idea after reading regarding decision support with forecasting demand.

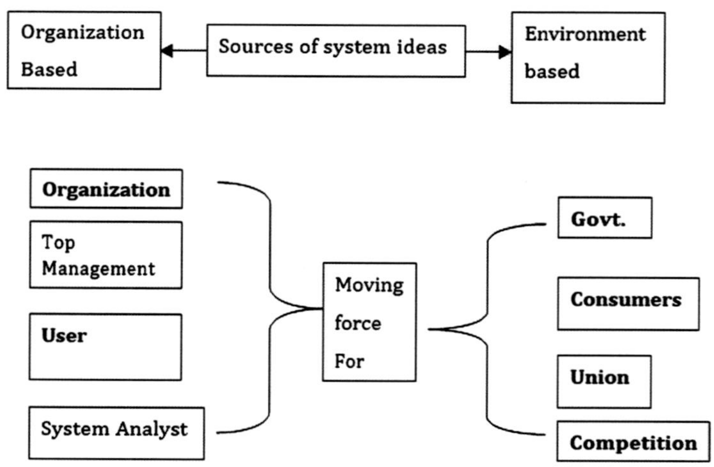

Figure 2.1. Major change agents.

Source: Business Jargon, Creative Commons License.

Each element is essential for an appropriate solution to a user's requested changes. A systems analyst is in a distinct position to notice patterns, and their specific areas of expertise make them valuable sources of inspiration. The analyst's position and professional standing lend credence to the recommendations (Figure 2.1) (Ferlie & Shortell, 2001).

2.1.2. Feasibility Study

The study is extended into a more in-depth feasibility assessment based on the preliminary research findings. A viability study evaluates the viability of a system idea. Effects on organization, customer needs' capability to be met, and efficient utilization of resources. It centers on three key issues (Bowen et al., 2009):

- How does a potential system address the user's demonstrated needs?
- What resources are being offered for a particular group of candidate processes? Is the issue worth addressing? and
- What effect will the candidate's system likely have on the organization? How does it integrate with the overall MIS strategy of the company?

Careful consideration must be given to every one of these issues. They center on the examination and assessment of the issue, the identification, and description of potential systems, the performing requirements and costs of each system, as well as the ultimate choice of the optimal system (Arain et al., 2010).

The goal of a feasibility report is to get a sense of an original problem size rather than to solve it. The study helps to clarify the problem formulation and decides which components of a problem should be incorporated into the system. As a result, estimates of benefits and costs are more precise at this point.

A formal request is about the feasibility of the study's findings. This is merely a report—a formalized document that outlines the character and reaches of the suggested remedy. The proposal outlines what is currently known or what will be done. The following are its components:

1. **A Phrased Explanation:** These of the issue that sparked analysis was the problem's statement.
2. **A Listing of the Study's Key:** Conclusions and suggestions are provided in the overview of the results and suggestions. It is perfect for a user who needs it (McLaughlin et al., 1998).
3. **Rapid Access to the Findings:** of the systems under

Did you Know?

Systems development life cycle phases include planning, system analysis, system design, development, implementation, integration and testing, and operations and maintenance.

study investigation. A summary of the findings is given, followed by suggestions and a reason for each.

4. **Details of Findings:** A description of the current system's practices and techniques, followed by a discussion of the goals and practices of the prospective system Details on outputs reports, data structures, and the costs and advantages of the product or system are included.
5. **Recommendations and Conclusions:** The proposed system's personnel assignments, prices, detailed projects, and deadlines are all specifically recommended (Orsmond & Cohn, 2015).

The plan has become a formal agreement when management examines it, opening the route for actual planning and execution. In the life cycle, it is a critical decision phase. The less promising projects fail here, while the more successful ones are implemented. Proposal modifications are usually made in writing based on the program's complexity, size, and cost. Verifying modifications before deploying the proposed project is just simple sense (Mills, 1978).

2.1.3. Analysis

An analysis is a thorough examination of the many tasks performed by a system and the connections between those tasks inside and outside the system. What should be done to address the issue is a crucial question. Establishing the system's limits and determining whether a candidate system must consider other connected systems are both aspects of analysis. Data on accessible files, decision-making processes, and activities processed by the current system are gathered during analysis (Choquet-Bruhat et al., 1982). Examples of analytical tools include data flow diagrams (DFDs), surveys, interviews, and on-site observation. A frequently used analytical tool, interviews demand specialized knowledge and consideration for the examined subjects. Preference for the gathering and analysis of data could be problematic. To gather the data necessary to perform the analysis, education, experience, and common sense are all prerequisites (Freud, 1937).

The researcher clearly understands what must be performed once the study is complete. Choosing a potential solution to the issue is the next stage. We shift from the conceptual to the physical parts of an entire lifecycle because of the design process (Freud, 1964).

2.1.4. Design

System design has been the most innovative and challenging stage of the life cycle of a system. The word "*design*" refers to both the end system and the development process. It refers to the technical requirements (similar to an engineer's blueprints) to put the prospective system into practice. The development and testing of programs are also included. Here, the main concern is: How must the issue be resolved? Figure 2.2 depicts the main design steps (Gemperle et al., 1998).

The first stage is deciding what format and how the output will be produced. There are additional samples of input and output available. Second, the master files (database) and input data must be created to meet the specifications of the planned output. Program development and testing, along with a list of the programs required to achieve the system's goals, take care of the operating (processing) stages. As both a final stage before implementation, mandatory document and evaluates the system's rationale in-depth as well as an assessment of the prospective system's influence on the customer and the organization (Stonebraker & Rowe, 1986).

Procedure flowcharts, records designs, reporting layouts, and a realistic implementation strategy are all included in the full report before the implementation stage. It is also necessary to have access to information about staff, finances, hardware, and facilities, including their expected costs. Projected expenses must now be somewhat close to operational costs (Kelly, 2003).

Programs are written by separate teams of developers in some businesses, whereas other businesses employ programmers who are also analyst programmers. For this discussion, we will suppose that analysis, as well as programming, are done by two different people. However, there are several tasks that the analyst should complete as programs are being written. Additionally, standard procedures should be created (Caulder & Raymond, 1999).

2.1.4.1. Implementation

System design is more innovative than execution. It is mainly involved with file converting and setting up user training sites. The telecommunications network, including testing of the networks, is covered under installation whenever the candidate network is integrated into endpoints or remote control (Maskin & Sjöström, 2002). User acceptance and user training are also tested during the final inspection. It may be necessary to provide substantial user training, depending on the system's design. Conversion typically occurs later or around the moment the customer is now being trained.

Extreme views of the developer as an individual who needs to be kept separate from other developing the system processes are standard. However, programming is a form of design. Because of the coding effort, the candidate state's estimated values should be changed. Programming offers a *"reality test"* for such analysts' *presumptions.* Thus, leaving developers out of the early system design is unwise (Frigo & Johnson, 2005).

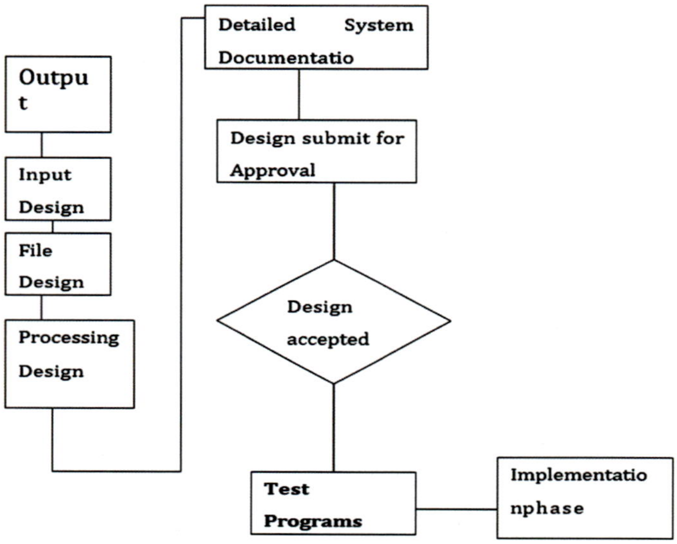

Figure 2.2. Procedures for system design.

Source: Business Jargon, Creative Commons License.

The system's capacity to access, modify, and return data via the file system is tested during the testing phase. *Test data* is fed into the computers and evaluated against the file(s) submitted for testing after the programs are made available. If acceptable, "*live*" data is used to execute the program(s). Instead, a diagnostic process is utilized to identify and fix program faults. Most conversions include parallel runs, in which the *"new"* and the "old" systems operate side by side. Although expensive, this strategy offers additional protection versus candidate fault conditions and allows the user team to build knowledge through use. Parallel processing, unfortunately, is not always an option. Running two online point-of-sale (POS) systems simultaneously is not conceivable for a retail chain. In either case, every old system is removed once the candidate system has shown itself (Love, 2004).

2.1.5. Post-Implementation and Maintenance

Evaluation and maintenance start once the deployment phase is finished and the user's staff has had time to adapt to a candidate system's changes. As with any system, software and hardware must be periodically maintained due to aging processes. Changes must be made if the new knowledge conflicts with the design requirements. To stay in line with design criteria, the hardware must also be maintained regularly. Maintenance is crucial to keep the new system up to standard (Fryling, 2010).

System improvements are also necessary because of user preferences, adjustments in organizational needs, or environmental conditions. When a bank raises its service fees on checking and savings accounts from Rs 3.00 to Rs 4.50 for required reserves of Rs 300, it is preservation as opposed to expansion. However, it would be an improvement if the same bank opted to offer personal loans on negative balances whenever customers overdraw their accounts. Additional testing and improvements to the evaluation program are required for this update (Wong, 2014).

2.1.5.1. Project Termination

A system project could be abandoned at any point before its implementation; however, doing so after it has passed the design stage is more challenging (and expensive). Projects are typically abandoned if it transpires during an assessment process that:

- The current design cannot satisfy the user's evolving goals or needs;
- Advantages first from the candidate system that has been observed do not warrant commitments to implementation;
- The user's funding unexpectedly changes, or design expenses are more expensive than initially projected during the feasibility analysis;
- The project's cost and time estimates have been substantially exceeded (Boehm, 2000).
- A system project could be ended at the customer's query in every scenario. Project cancelation contrasts with a new system crash. Numerous factors are at play when a new system fails to satisfy user needs:
- Not all user criteria were specified or understood.
- In the vital stages of developing the system, the customer was not involved directly.
- The developer, the researcher, or both lacked experiences.
- Under strict time limitations, the systems analyst (or planning committee) had to complete the assignment. Therefore, the feasibility assessment, as well as the system design, were not given adequate consideration.
- Poor implementation of training (Balachandra et al., 1996).
- The new application proved too much for the current hardware to manage.
- Customers in those other departments could not obtain data that such an old system had supplied because of the new system.
- The new system was not intuitive.
- Users' needs varied throughout time.

- The support personnel were rude (Unger et al., 2012).

There are a lot more reasons that might be added to the list. The critical thing is that even though improvements in software and hardware make the analyst's job more straightforward, the performance of such a system project relies here on the analyst's expertise, originality, and knowledge, in addition to the support of customer staff. This implies that now the analyst should be knowledgeable about cutting-edge software and technology in addition to interpersonal skills (De, 2001).

Remember

The systems development life cycle (SDLC) is a conceptual model used in project management that describes the stages involved in an information system development project, from an initial feasibility study through maintenance of the completed application.

2.2. CONSIDERATIONS FOR THE CANDIDATE SYSTEM

There is a greater need for software services in business today than the capabilities to fill that need. The components of demand are as follows:

- Functioning of the current system;
- Maintenance frequently accounts for over 50% of maintenance and concentrates on "patching" systems;
- Improvements involve significant changes to the program's architecture or tools;
- Solicitations for potential systems (Anthony et al., 2014).
- All these requirements call for human, economic, and technological resources. The technology department must provide the following on that human side:
- Equipment operators who operate computers;
- Data entry workers;
- Systems analysts should specify and create designs;
- To create computer programs from specified requirements, use applications programmers;
- Programmers for error correction (Moon et al., 2011);
- Managers, project directors, and supervisors will coordinate the jobs with the users.

Thus, the fundamental issue is balancing the customer's needs with the available resources. Technical, behavioral, and economic considerations influence how much any project is preferred over another (Lucas et al., 2021).

The system agency's capacity to manage a project is a technical factor. The accessibility of capable analysts, architects, and software experts to complete the assignment will determine many things. This is particularly true when developing complicated systems for giant organizations and constructing databases. Free-lance it to an external consulting business as an alternative to giving up on a project due to a lack of internal talent. The project's development costs must be compared against the anticipated overall benefits (Wilk et al., 2001).

The analyst's record of success, the user's previous experience with just a present structure, and the user's ability to persuade senior management to fund a potential system are all behavioral factors. Additional elements that affect financing a candidate system include political influences, which can favor one program over another, the standing of the institution, and its track record of effectiveness.

Economic consideration is possibly the most crucial one when choosing a project. It emphasizes the possible return on the investment in the system. Various calculations, selected variables, and other factors influence an acceptable rate. A yearly return on investment of well over 20% is recommended by system consultants (Tan et al., 2015).

2.3. POLITICAL CONSIDERATIONS

Along with the factors mentioned above, there is also the political aspect, which is partially behavioral. Suppose that executives of a production company are considering two automation control solutions: Teleconferencing network proposal A and a sales support structure proposal B, both intended to cut down on trip expenses. The committee backed Proposal B, which was supported by a powerful executive and had weak justifications. The appropriate individuals believed it should pass, so it did (Oakes, 1992).

When conventional methods fail to achieve the desired objectives, politics is the science of utilizing influence and forming alliances. A working relationship with both the final user is beneficial while developing system initiatives. Rarely does a user who was involved in creating a system criticize it. Politics could become involved if such a participatory relationship is introduced too late and encounters resistance. The key is to foresee opposition and change this into support as early as possible (Hung, 2012).

2.4. PLANNING AND CONTROL FOR SYSTEM SUCCESS

What could an analyst do now to guarantee a system's achievement? It is necessary first to create a strategy that outlines the process, some techniques, actions, resources, expenses, and a timeline for finishing the system. Secondly, a project team of researchers, developers, a systems advisor, and user representatives are required for more extensive initiatives. Compared to solo analysts performing the same tasks, teamwork's sharing of knowledge, communication, and cooperation can be incredibly productive. Lastly, to mirror the stages of system development—analysis, development, and implementation—the project must be broken down into more manageable modules (Venkatraman & Ramanujam, 1987).

Most of such work is managed and controlled as a project. The development life cycle's primary objective is to codify a project control method organized at three key levels. Required tasks are initially divided into smaller, more doable jobs. A task is often a well-defined, organized work unit one person can complete. The task's budget, time, and quality can all be easily managed. It is simple to finish without the assistance of other projects or project team members. If rework is required, it will only negatively affect other jobs unless time is of the essence (Guide, 2000).

Tasks with a broader scope and thus are intended to yield significant outcomes are included in the second level of the work unit. An action is a collection of activities that fulfill one step of the software development life cycle (SDLC) and are conceptually related.

A phase, or third degree of control, is a series of tasks that help a project reach an essential goal. The project's overall structure comprises milestones (Tsai et al., 2012).

The following steps were followed when planning a project:

- List the phases and the tasks that are contained inside every activity;
- Establish a budget for every phase and receive approval to move on;
- Periodically evaluate, document, and summarize activity progress;
- After a reporting month, create a project progress update (Fitriati & Mulyani, 2015).

In conclusion, the development of the system cannot be reduced to a process that only involves software and hardware. It is essential to verify and reevaluate the initial premises on which the specifications were built with the user's needs in mind. Making sure that all potential system features—technological, logical, and behavioral—are considered before installation and maintenance are crucial to managing the structural model (Migdadi & Abu Zaid, 2016).

2.5. SUMMARY

The system's life cycle is linked to system analysis and design (SDLC). Project plan, viability, assessment, designing, implementation, and post-implementation are the phases. The project concept arose from the surroundings or within the company. One problem has been identified; a first inquiry is carried out to establish whether or not a modification is viable. A feasibility study is done if the response is affirmative. The analysis is a careful examination of the numerous operations carried out by a system. The technical requirements used in constructing the candidate system are referred to as system design. Implementation is focused on the candidate system's specifics. Following the introduction, maintenance starts, which includes any upgrades, revisions, or deviations from the established requirements. Careful and frequently prolonged preparation is essential to ensure the system's success. The whole management procedure is critical to the system's practical completion.

REVIEW QUESTIONS

1. Why is a system proposal so crucial for system design?
2. What is system development life cycle?
3. What is the difference between analysis and design? Explain.
4. How would an analysis determine the users' needs for a system? Explain.
5. Distinguish between the initial investigation and feasibility study. In what way are they related?
6. How does system design simplify implementation?
7. What is testing?
8. How is testing different from evaluation?
9. There are several considerations in deciding on a candidate system. What are they? Why are they important?

MULTIPLE CHOICE QUESTIONS

1. Which of the following is the first step in the system development life cycle?

a. Planning
b. Analysis
c. Design
d. Implementation

2. What is the primary purpose of the SDLC?

a. To create a system
b. To analyze user requirements

c. To develop and maintain software
d. To provide feedback to the customer

3. **Which of the following is a phase in the SDLC?**
   a. Testing
   b. Deployment
   c. Construction
   d. Documentation

4. **What is the last step in the SDLC process?**
   a. Maintenance
   b. Implementation
   c. Testing
   d. Evaluation

5. **.......... is / are the most important and fundamental phases of SDLC.**
   a. Preliminary investigation
   b. Requirement Analysis
   c. Design, Testing and Implementation
   d. All of the mentioned above

Answers to Multiple Choice Questions

1. (a) 2. (b) 3. (a) 4. (b) 5. (d)

REFERENCES

1. Anthony, S. J., Annunziato, R. A., Fairey, E., Kelly, V. L., So, S., & Wray, J., (2014). Waiting for transplant: Physical, psychosocial, and nutritional status considerations for pediatric candidates and implications for care. *Pediatric Transplantation, 18*(5), 423–434.
2. Arain, M., Campbell, M. J., Cooper, C. L., & Lancaster, G. A., (2010). What is a pilot or feasibility study? A review of current practice and editorial policy. *BMC Medical Research Methodology, 10*(1), 1–7.
3. Balachandra, R., Brockhoff, K. K., & Pearson, A. W., (1996). R&D project termination decisions: Processes, communication, and personnel changes. *Journal of Product Innovation Management, 13*(3), 245–256.
4. Boehm, B., (2000). Project termination doesn't equal project failure. *Computer, 33*(9), 94–96.
5. Bowen, D. J., Kreuter, M., Spring, B., Cofta-Woerpel, L., Linnan, L., Weiner, D., &Fernandez, M., (2009). How we design feasibility studies. *American Journal of*

Preventive Medicine, 36(5), 452–457.

6. Caulder, D. L., & Raymond, K. N., (1999). Supermolecules by design. *Accounts of Chemical Research, 32*(11), 975–982.
7. Chernyshova, E., (2018). Explicitation sequences in conversation: Some considerations on formulations, candidate inferences and grounding. *Revue Tranel, 68*, 51–58.
8. Choquet-Bruhat, Y., DeWitt-Morette, C., De Witt, C., Dillard-Bleick, M., & Dillar-Bleick, M., (1982). *Analysis*. Gulf Professional Publishing.
9. De, P. K., (2001). Project termination practices in Indian industry: A statistical review. *International Journal of Project Management, 19*(2), 119–126.
10. Ferlie, E. B., & Shortell, S. M., (2001). Improving the quality of health care in the United Kingdom and the United States: A framework for change. *The Milbank Quarterly, 79*(2), 281–315.
11. Fitriati, A., & Mulyani, S., (2015). The influence of leadership style on accounting information system success and its impact on accounting information quality. *Research Journal of Finance and Accounting, 6*(11), 167–173.
12. Freud, S., (1937). Analysis terminable and interminable. *International Journal of Psycho-Analysis, 18*, 373–405.
13. Freud, S., (1964). Analysis terminable and interminable. In: *The Standard Edition of the Complete Psychological Works of Sigmund Freud, Volume XXIII (1937–1939): Moses and Monotheism, An Outline of Psycho-Analysis and Other Works* (pp. 209–254).
14. Frigo, M., & Johnson, S. G., (2005). The design and implementation of FFTW3. *Proceedings of the IEEE, 93*(2), 216–231.
15. Fryling, M., (2010). Estimating the impact of enterprise resource planning project management decisions on post-implementation maintenance costs: A case study using simulation modelling. *Enterprise Information Systems, 4*(4), 391–421.
16. Gemperle, F., Kasabach, C., Stivoric, J., Bauer, M., & Martin, R., (1998). Design for wearability. In: *Digest of Papers. Second International Symposium on Wearable Computers (Cat. No. 98EX215)* (pp. 116–122). IEEE.
17. Guide, Jr. V. D. R., (2000). Production planning and control for remanufacturing: Industry practice and research needs. *Journal of Operations Management, 18*(4), 467–483.
18. Henriksen, A. D., & Traynor, A. J., (1999). A practical R&D project-selection scoring tool. *IEEE Transactions on Engineering Management, 46*(2), 158–170.
19. Hung, M., Wong, T. J., & Zhang, T., (2012). Political considerations in the decision of Chinese SOEs to list in Hong Kong. *Journal of Accounting and Economics, 53*(1, 2), 435–449.
20. Isaias, P., & Issa, T., (2015). Information system development life cycle models. In: *High Level Models and Methodologies for Information Systems* (pp. 21–40). Springer, New York, NY.

21. Kelly, A. E., (2003). Research as design. *Educational Researcher, 32*(1), 3.
22. Kovoor-Misra, S., (2020). The impetus for resilience and change in business education and management research. *Journal of Management Inquiry, 29*(2), 128–133.
23. Love, A., (2004). Implementation evaluation. *Handbook of Practical Program Evaluation, 2*, 63–97.
24. Lucas, B. J., Berry, Z., Giurge, L. M., & Chugh, D., (2021). A longer shortlist increases the consideration of female candidates in male-dominant domains. *Nature Human Behavior, 5*(6), 736–742.
25. Lukas, C. V., Holmes, S. K., Cohen, A. B., Restuccia, J., Cramer, I. E., Shwartz, M., & Charns, M. P., (2007). Transformational change in health care systems: An organizational model. *Health Care Management Review, 32*(4), 309–320.
26. MacLean, P. S., Bergouignan, A., Cornier, M. A., & Jackman, M. R., (2011). Biology's response to dieting: The impetus for weight regain. *American Journal of Physiology-Regulatory, Integrative and Comparative Physiology, 301*(3), R581–R600.
27. Maskin, E., & Sjöström, T., (2002). Implementation theory. *Handbook of Social Choice and Welfare, 1*, 237–288.
28. McHugh, S., Droog, E., Foley, C., Boyce, M., Healy, O., & Browne, J. P., (2019). Understanding the impetus for major systems change: A multiple case study of decisions and non-decisions to reconfigure emergency and urgent care services. *Health Policy, 123*(8), 728–736.
29. McLaughlin, W. J., Schifman, R. B., Ryan, K. J., Manriquez, G. M., Bhattacharyya, A. K., Dunn, B. E., & Weinstein, R. S., (1998). Telemicrobiology: Feasibility study. *Telemedicine Journal, 4*(1), 11–17.
30. Meade, L. M., & Presley, A., (2002). R&D project selection using the analytic network process. *IEEE Transactions on Engineering Management, 49*(1), 59–66.
31. Migdadi, M. M., & Abu, Z. M. K. S., (2016). An empirical investigation of knowledge management competence for enterprise resource planning systems success: Insights from Jordan. *International Journal of Production Research, 54*(18), 5480–5498.
32. Mills, D. H., (1978). Medical insurance feasibility study: A technical summary. *Western Journal of Medicine, 128*(4), 360.
33. Moon, M. C., Greenberg, R. K., Morales, J. P., Martin, Z., Lu, Q., Dowdall, J. F., & Hernandez, A. V., (2011). Computed tomography-based anatomic characterization of proximal aortic dissection with consideration for endovascular candidacy. *Journal of Vascular Surgery, 53*(4), 942–949.
34. Oakes, J., (1992). Can tracking research inform practice? Technical, normative, and political considerations. *Educational Researcher, 21*(4), 12–21.
35. Orsmond, G. I., & Cohn, E. S., (2015). The distinctive features of a feasibility study: Objectives and guiding questions. *OTJR: Occupation, Participation and Health, 35*(3), 169–177.

36. Snee, R. D., & Rodenbaugh, Jr. W. F., (2002). The project selection process. *Quality Progress, 35*(9), 78.

37. Souder, W. E., & Mandakovic, T., (1986). R&D project selection models. *Research Management, 29*(4), 36–42.

38. Stonebraker, M., & Rowe, L. A., (1986). The design of postgres. *ACM SIGMOD Record, 15*(2), 340–355.

39. Tan, H., Li, W., Wang, T., Fang, J., & Feng, Z., (2015). The analysis on the candidate frequency bands of future mobile communication systems. *China Communications, 12*(Supplement), 140–149.

40. Tsai, W. H., Lee, P. L., Shen, Y. S., & Lin, H. L., (2012). A comprehensive study of the relationship between enterprise resource planning selection criteria and enterprise resource planning system success. *Information & Management, 49*(1), 36–46.

41. Unger, B. N., Kock, A., Gemünden, H. G., & Jonas, D., (2012). Enforcing strategic fit of project portfolios by project termination: An empirical study on senior management involvement. *International Journal of Project Management, 30*(6), 675–685.

42. Venkatraman, N., & Ramanujam, V., (1987). Planning system success: A conceptualization and an operational model. *Management Science, 33*(6), 687–705.

43. Verdecchia, A., Francisci, S., Brenner, H., Gatta, G., Micheli, A., Mangone, L., & EUROCARE-4 Working Group, (2007). Recent cancer survival in Europe: A 2000–02 period analysis of EUROCARE-4 data. *The Lancet Oncology, 8*(9), 784–796.

44. Weitzel, J. R., & Kerschberg, L., (1989). Developing knowledge-based systems: Reorganizing the system development life cycle. *Communications of the ACM, 32*(4), 482–488.

45. Wilk, G. D., Wallace, R. M., & Anthony, J., (2001). High-κ gate dielectrics: Current status and materials properties considerations. *Journal of Applied Physics, 89*(10), 5243–5275.

46. Wong, E. M., Li, S. S., Choi, T. H., & Lee, T. N., (2008). Insights into innovative classroom practices with ICT: Identifying the impetus for change. *Journal of Educational Technology & Society, 11*(1), 248–265.

47. Wong, P. H., (2014). Maintenance required: The ethics of geoengineering and post-implementation scenarios. *Ethics, Policy & Environment, 17*(2), 186–191.

CHAPTER 3

REQUIREMENTS MODELING

UNIT INTRODUCTION

Systems analysts apply techniques for needs modeling and procedures based on teams to visualize and document new platforms. These methods and approaches are described in this chapter. After that, the chapter goes on to talk about the needs of the system as well as the several methods for gathering information, such as conducting interviews, reviewing documents, observing, questionnaires, and surveys, testing, and research (Aguilar, 2004).

The difficulties associated with determining whether system requirements have been met are satirically depicted in the Dilbert cartoon in Figure 3.1. Customers frequently have a tough time describing in detail what they would like to be able to perform, and even when they do identify the needs, the outcome is frequently a prioritized set of features that conflict with one another. The paradigmatic example is one in which technology is requested to be "very useful" while still being "totally safe." No system can adequately meet both objectives. A completely safe system will have to be locked inside a vault, unconnected from the rest of the globe, and unavailable to the user; such a system would not be beneficial (Smith et al., 2008).

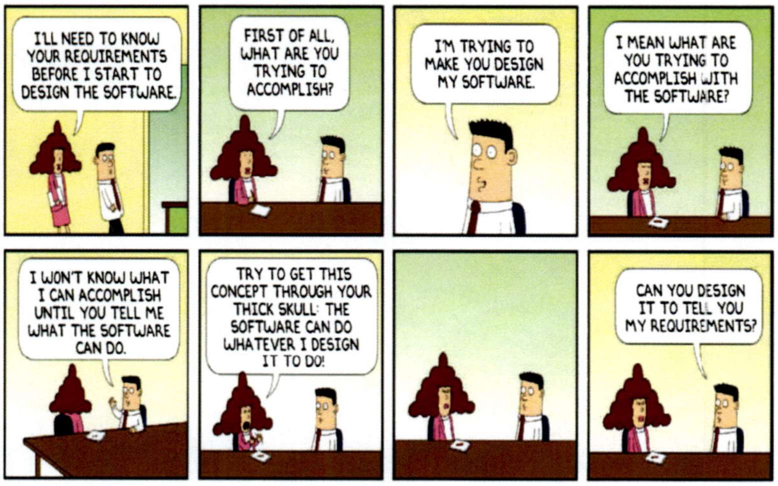

Figure 3.1. An example of difficulties that can arise while comprehending the system requirements.

Source: Dilbert, Commons Creative License.

Learning Objective

After studying this unit, you will be able to:

- Explain the systems analysis phase in the software development process;
- Describe the concept and process of joint application development;
- Understand the principles and techniques of rapid application development (RAD);
- Identify and explain agile development's key functions and benefits in software development.

Key Terms

- Requirements modeling
- System analysis phase
- Agile method
- Scalability
- System analysis skills
- System analysis activities
- Joint application development

3.1. SYSTEMS ANALYSIS PHASE

Understanding the planned project, ensuring this would fulfill business objectives, and laying a solid basis for developing the system are the main goals of the analysis phase. During this stage, the analyst describes and visualizes the suggested system using models and other documenting tools (Chen et al., 1991).

3.1.1. Systems Analysis Activities

The four critical tasks of a system analysis phase need modeling, information, and process mapping, modeling, and evaluation of strategic planning. These tasks are depicted in Figure 3.2. While the waterfall methodology describes the SDLC phases in such a sequential order, it is common for different stages (or specific tasks inside a degree) to communicate during the development phase, merely as they go into an adaptive approach. It happens, for instance, whenever during the model development, new information is discovered, or technical specifications start changing. The interactions between the three suggest process modeling, data, and procedure modeling, and object modeling are depicted in Figure 3.2 (Oleynik et al., 2017).

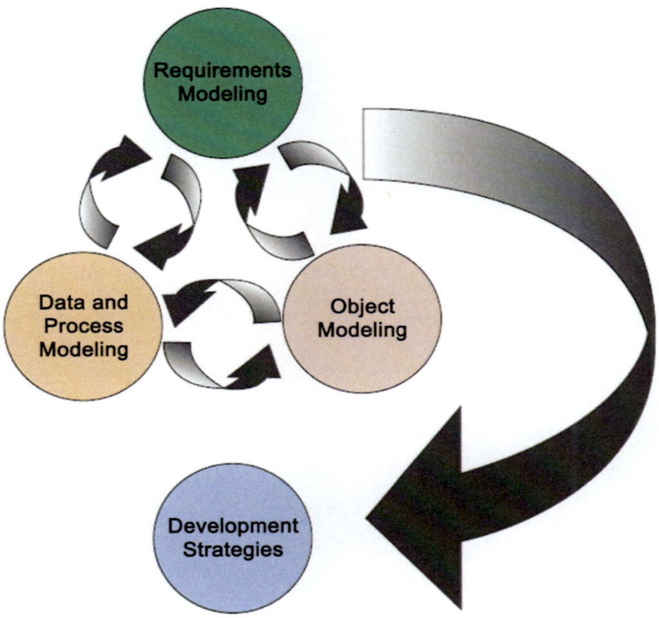

Figure 3.2. Requirements modeling, data modeling, and process modeling are all parts of the systems analysis phase.

Source: Slide player, Creative Commons License.

3.1.1.1. Requirements Modeling

The method of needs modeling, discussed in this chapter, entails gathering information to characterize the existing system and identifying the needs for such a new system, including those for outcomes, inputs, procedures, performances, and security:

1. **Output:** It refers to data generated by the system, whether printed or electronic (Ali et al., 2010).
2. **Input:** It refers to necessary information entered into the system, whether automatically or manually.
3. **Process:** It refers to the systematic principles used to convert the data into useful information that's also meaningful.
4. **Performance:** It describes system properties like velocity, volume, ability, reliability, and stability.
5. **Security:** It refers to hardware, and Software, including procedural safeguards that defend the system and its data against threats from within or the outside (dos Santos et al., 2011).

3.1.2. Systems Analysis Skills

A systems analyst requires solid analytical and communication abilities to produce an appropriate model for the new system. The analyst can recognize a problem, assess the essential components, and create a practical solution with the help of analytical capabilities. A systems analyst requires communication skills because they must interact with individuals at all levels of an organization, stable divergent user requirements, and communicate clearly. Team-oriented schemes must be considered at the beginning of a systems analysis phase, even though data systems impact people across the organization (Fortuin et al., 2013).

3.1.3. Team-Based Techniques: JAD, RAD, and Agile Methods

The IT department aims to deliver the best information management system at the lowest possible cost in the shortest amount of time. Software engineers must see customers as partners in the development phase if they are to produce the best results. More user participation generally translates to improved communication, quicker development timeframes, and more contented users.

An IT department that employs structured analysis but only contacts users if their input and permission are required for a typical system design model. Many IT managers encourage system users to proactively participate in various developmental chores, even though the IT team still plays a crucial role because the structured analysis is a popular technique for system design. Joint app development (JAD), a user-focused method for requirements modeling, including fact-finding, is a typical example. The developers used JAD wherever team input and participation were required since it is not connected to a single development process. Rapid application development (RAD) is another well-liked approach that prioritizes users (RAD). Users are involved at every stage of RAD, which resembles a streamlined version of an entire SDLC. While JAD generally only concentrates on gathering information and determining requirements, RAD offers a quick way to complete all systems engineering tasks, which include planning, designing, building, and implementing systems. Finally, agile methodologies are a current trend emphasizing close communication among system users and developers. Further sections explain JAD, RAD, and agile development (Van & Lane, 2003).

3.2. JOINT APPLICATION DEVELOPMENT

Joint Application Development is a well-liked fact-finding technique that actively incorporates users in the development process (JAD; Liou & Chen, 1993).

3.2.1. User Involvement

Users could also be active in a data system as they have a crucial stake. Several years ago, system development was typically the exclusive responsibility of the IT department, with users playing a largely passive role. The IT team would gather data from users during the development stage, specify the requirements of the system, as well as build a new scheme. The IT staff may ask customers to review the design, provide feedback, and submit variations throughout the procedure (Kujala, 2003).

Users typically play a significantly active role in the development of systems today. Modern IT professionals agree that user-centric systems should involve consumers at each system design phase, whether informally or formally. A JAD teamwork, which entails a working group of consumers, management staff, and IT specialists working together to collect information, explain business requirements, and define the exact new system requirements, has been one well-liked method for involving users (Ives & Olson, 1984).

3.2.2. JAD Participants and Roles

A JAD team typically meets for several days or weeks for an off-location or even in a designated conference hall. Members of the JAD must be shielded from everyday activities in any case. The three main goals are analysis of the current system, gathering user feedback and expectation, and documenting user needs for such a new system.

The JAD group typically consists of a project manager with good personal and intergroup abilities and one or more individuals who could record and document the outcomes. The usual JAD members and associated roles are shown in Figure 3.3. JAD project leads are frequently part of the IT staff; however, that is not always the situation. The JAD team's system designers participate in meetings, pose queries, take notes, and help. Analysts could create models and input JAD session documentation into tools if accessible (Yue et al., 2022).

JAD PARTICIPANT	ROLE
JAD project leader	Develops an agenda, acts as a facilitator, and leads the JAD session
Top management	Provides enterprise-level authorization and support for the project
Managers	Provide department-level support for the project and understanding of how the project must support business functions and requirements
Users	Provide operational-level input on current operations, desired changes, input and output requirements, user interface issues, and how the project will support day-to-day tasks
Systems analysts and other IT staff members	Provide technical assistance and resources for JAD team members on issues such as security, backup, hardware, software, and network capability
Recorder	Documents results of JAD sessions and works with systems analysts to build system models and develop CASE tool documentation

Figure 3.3. Participants and roles in a typical JAD.

Source: GeeksforGeeks, Creative Commons License.

Figure 3.4 depicts an agenda for a typical JAD session. All teams need to work extremely hard during the JAD procedure. Many businesses agree that the meaning of a new system produced by a JAD group is the best one that can make due to its wide range of input and continuous interaction among some participants (Zygouris et al., 2015).

3.2.3. JAD Advantages and Disadvantages

JAD is more expensive than traditional techniques and may not be accessible if the gathering is too big for the project's scope. However, most businesses discover that JAD enables significant users to contribute significantly to the demands modeling process (Anwar & Razali, 2014).

Project leader	• Introduce all JAD team members • Discuss ground rules, goals, and objectives for the JAD sessions • Explain methods of documentation and use of CASE tools, if any
Top management (sometimes called the project owner or sponsor)	• Explain the reason for the project and express top management authorization and support
Project leader	• Provide overview of the current system and proposed project scope and constraints • Present outline of specific topics and issues to be investigated
Open discussion session, moderated by project leader	• Review the main business processes, tasks, user roles, input, and output • Identify specific areas of agreement or disagreement • Break team into smaller groups to study specific issues and assign group leaders
JAD team members working in smaller group sessions, supported by IT staff	• Discuss and document all system requirements • Develop models and prototypes
Group leaders	• Report on results and assigned tasks and topics • Present issues that should be addressed by the overall JAD team
Open discussion session, moderated by project leader	• Review reports from small group sessions • Reach consensus on main issues • Document all topics
Project leader	• Present overall recap of JAD session • Prepare report that will be sent to JAD team members

Figure 3.4. Typical JAD session agenda.

Source: GeeksforGeeks, Creative Commons License.

If customers participate in the systems development process, they are significantly more likely to believe that they control the results and accept a new structure. When properly used, JAD may result in a more detailed description of the requirement analysis, a better grasp of common goals, and a more profound dedication to the success of such a new system (Moock, 2014).

3.3. RAPID APPLICATION DEVELOPMENT (RAD)

Rapid application development (RAD), a team-based method, speeds up the building of information systems and produces functional data systems. RAD employs follow these steps and creates like JAD system but goes even further. A requirement analysis model is the final product of JAD, whereas the new system is the end outcome of RAD. With a four-phase product lifecycle like the conventional SDLC phases, RAD is a complete technique. Businesses use RAD to cut costs, speed development, and improve success rates (Agarwal et al.,

2000). Prototyping and user participation are essential components of RAD. Users may evaluate a functional design as soon as feasible, decide if it fulfills their needs, also suggest necessary improvements thanks to the RAD process. The prototype is adjusted in response to user feedback, while the interaction process continues until the program is entirely created and consumers are happy. The development team builds the prototype that generates a steady stream of documents using CASE tools (Daud et al., 2010).

3.3.1. RAD Phases and Activities

According to Figure 3.5, the RAD theory includes four different stages: needs planning, user design, development, as well as cutover. Take note of the ongoing interaction between the phases of the construction and user design (Bakhsheshi et al., 2017).

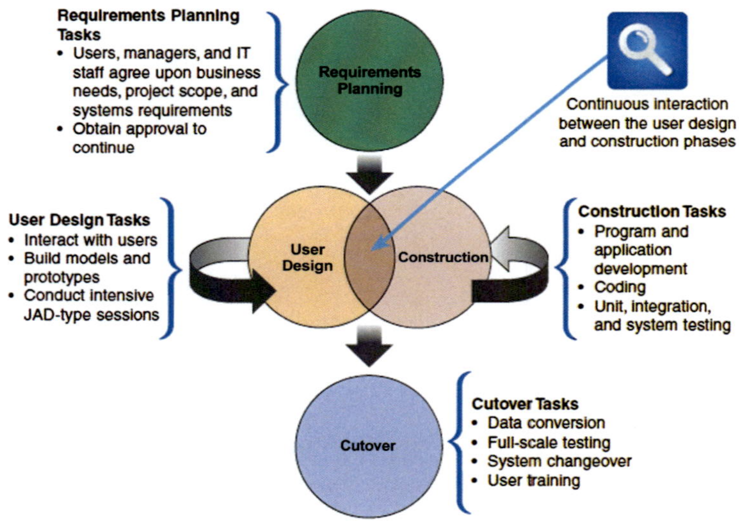

Source: Slide player, Creative Commons License.

Figure 3.5. The RAD model comprises requirements planning, user design, construction, and cutover stages. Be mindful of the continual relationship between the user-design process and the construction stages.

3.3.1.1. Requirements Planning

Systems planning of systems analysis components is combined in the requirement analysis stage of the SDLC. Business demands, project scope, limitations, and system requirements are discussed and decided upon by users, management, and IT professionals. Whenever the team reaches a consensus on the crucial points and receives management approval to move forward, the necessities planning phase is complete (Baker, 1993).

3.3.1.2. User Design

Customers and developers work together to construct models and prototypes that faithfully represent all system actions and outputs, including inputs throughout the designing process. The RAD workgroup or divisions often mix JAD techniques and CASE technology to translate users' requirements into usable models. Customers may perceive, modify, and eventually approve a functioning system model that fits their needs via a continuous, participatory process known as user designing (Redström, 2006).

Did you Know?

Requirements modeling in software engineering identifies the requirements that a software application or system must meet in order to solve the business problem.

3.3.1.3. Construction

The development of programs and applications is the primary focus of the building phase, which follows the SDLC. But once actual displays or results are created in RAD, users could still contribute and adjust or make improvements (Plotkin, 1976).

3.3.1.4. Cutover

The last responsibilities in the SDLC project implementation that are identical to those during the cutover phase include data analysis, testing, moving to a new network, and tech assistance. When compared to traditional methods, the whole process is simplified. As a result, the new system is built, delivered, and placed into use much quicker (González & Rochefort, 2014).

3.3.1.5. RAD Objectives

The primary goal of all RAD techniques is to reduce development costs and time by incorporating users in all phases of system development. Because it is such a continual process, RAD enables the developing team that makes essential design changes because it develops. In times of limited corporate resources, it is especially critical to reduce the expense of adjustments that generally occur inside an extended, drawn-out production timetable. A successful RAD team should have IT facilities, skills, managerial support, and customer interaction. RAD is incredibly beneficial when a corporation needs a data system that supports any new business functionality, as it is a dynamic consumer process. RAD also assists the development process in designing a system that needs a thoroughly engaging or complicated user interface (UI) by gathering input from the user from the start (Khanali et al., 2021).

3.3.2. RAD Advantages and Disadvantages

RAD offers both advantages and disadvantages in comparison to conventional structure analysis approaches. The main advantage would be systems could be created more quickly and cheaply. One drawback of RAD is that it concentrates on a system's technical details instead of the operational and commercial needs of the company. The risk is that a system could function effectively within the short term but might not have achieved its corporate and long-term goals. The faster time cycle may also have the drawback of giving less time to determine quality, consistency, and design standards. However, if a company is conscious of the potential hazards, RAD could be a desirable alternative (Masoudi et al., 2014).

3.4. AGILE METHODS

Agile approaches seek to incrementally construct a system by creating several prototypes and constantly modifying these to user needs. Developers change, enhance, and incorporate previous versions into the result as the rapid process progresses. An agile methodology stresses continual feedback, so each gradual step is influenced by what has been discovered in previous actions (Cohen et al., 2004).

Figure 3.6. Reinforcing the agile strategy: Simple, quick, adaptable, and user-centered.

Source: Sam Edwards, Creative Commons License.

As agile approaches gain popularity, a thriving community for agile-related services and Software has emerged. Most agile engineers choose not to utilize CASE tools, instead relying on whiteboard presentations and post-it notes layouts, as seen in Figure 3.6. They believe this method reinforces the agile philosophy of being simple, quick, flexible, and user oriented (Abrahamsson et al., 2003).

Scrum is yet another adaptable strategy. The word is derived from the rugby phrase *scrum,* in which team players lunge at one another and attain their goals, as illustrated in Figure 3.7. Scrum for system design has the same intense connection; however, it is more cerebral than physical. The agile team participates in a Scrum session (Reifer, 2002).

Figure 3.7. In a rugby scrum, teammates prepare to lunge at each other to achieve their goals.

Source: fotograf.lv, Creative Commons License.

Members take on specific duties, including colorful monikers like pigs or chickens. These characters are based on the famous joke about the pig and chicken discussing a restaurant that serves eggs and ham. But the pig declined since this function would necessitate absolute dedication, whereas the chicken could merely contribute something (Lindvall et al., 2002).

The pigs inside the agile world are the product owner, facilitator, and design team, whereas the chickens are consumers, certain interested parties, and managers. Scrum meetings follow strict guidelines that focus on time constraints, communication, and team-based actions that result in deliverable Software. An agile team uses a sequence of scrums to cease the activity and permits the team to repair the game plan, which remains in place until another scrum (Campanelli & Parreiras, 2015).

3.4.1. Agile Method Advantages and Disadvantages

Agile is a highly versatile and practical technique for managing changes. They seem to be popular since they emphasize teamwork and reflect community values. Furthermore, frequent outputs legitimize the project with reduced risks.

Remember

An effective requirements management process must involve all four requirements' processes defined above: Requirements planning, requirements development, requirements verification, and requirements change management.

3.5. MODELING TOOLS AND TECHNIQUES

Models aid in understanding a system's structure by consumers, management, and IT experts. Modeling entails using graphical methods and nontechnical terminology to portray a system in various phases of development. Various tools could be used by the analyst for uses a systematic approach to characterize business operations, needs, and user engagement with the system.

Systems analysts engage with modeling and fact-finding by first building fact-finding findings into modeling and studying the designs to decide whether more fact-finding is required. Analysts employ functional decomposition graphs, process management models, and data flow, including unified modeling language (UML) diagrams, to assist them in comprehending the system's requirements. Any of these diagrams can be created with CASE tools or stand-alone drawing tools if desired.

(Garny et al., 2008).

3.5.1. Functional Decomposition Diagrams (FDDs)

A top-down depiction of a function or procedure is a functional decomposition diagram (FDD). An analyst may use an FDD to display business operations and split these down into lower-level processes and functions. The method of creating an FDD is identical to that of developing an organizational chart. Begin from the top, then work your way down. FDDs may be applied at many phases of system design. Analysts utilize FDDs during use a systematic approach to model business operations and explain how they have been structured in lower-level procedures. In app development, these procedures are translated into software modules (Brimhall et al., 2016).

3.5.2. Business Process Modeling (BPM)

A business process model (BPM) represents one or even more business operations, including processing an airline ticket, completing a customer order, or maintaining account information. Analysts frequently build models during a systematic approach that utilizes a standard language called business process modeling notation (BPMN). To represent occurrences, procedures, and workflows, BPMN uses a variety of shapes with symbols (Indulska et al., 2009).

The diagram is immediately included in the estimated model when utilizing a CASE tool like Visible Analyst to build a business modeling approach. The entire graph is referred to as the pool in BPMN terminology, and the defined customer regions are referred to as swimmer lanes. Integrating business process management (BPM) into the CASE project development leads to quicker outcomes, fewer mistakes, and lower costs (Recker et al., 2009).

3.5.3. Unified Modeling Language (UML)

The unified modeling language (UML) is a popular tool to visualize and document software product development. UML employs object-oriented (O-O) design ideas, although it is not limited to any computer language but may be used to define business requirements and processes in general. UML includes several graphical tools, including use context diagrams and sequence diagrams. In needs modeling, a computer programmer might use UML to depict the information management system from the user's perspective (Booch et al., 1996).

KEYWORD

The unified modeling language (UML) is a general-purpose modeling language that is intended to provide a standard way to visualize the design of a system.

3.5.3.1. Use CASE Diagrams

Systems analysts and users collaborate to record needs and model system functionalities during requirements modeling. The communication between consumers and the data system is depicted graphically in some used context diagrams. In some use CASE models, the user takes on the role of an actor with a particular function that illustrates how they communicate with the system. System designers could use CASE tools that incorporate use-CASE graphical representations into the idea-generation process or create use-CASE diagrams by hand (Figure 3.8) (Al-Msie'deen et al., 2014).

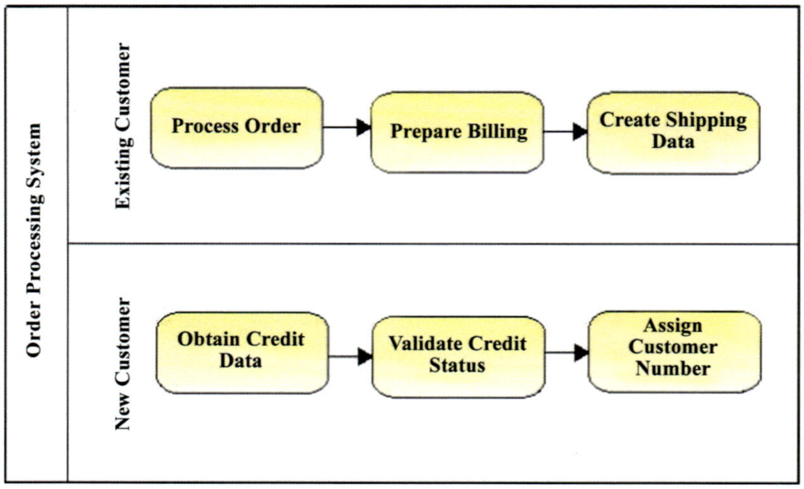

Figure 3.8. A business process diagram can be made by an analyst using the visible analyst CASE tool.

Source: Visible Systems Corporations, Creative Commons License.

3.6. SYSTEM REQUIREMENTS CHECKLIST

Systems developers should list and define each need for the system during the conditions modeling phase. A system need is a quality or function that must be present in an information system to meet business needs and user expectations. System requirements act as standards to assess the final system's general acceptability (Firesmith, 2005).

The five broad types of system requirements are inputs, outputs, procedures, efficiency, and controls. Further subsections includes typical illustrations of every category's requirement specification.

3.6.1. Output Examples

1. The website must report online traffic data every four hours, including hourly during peak times.
2. A daily report from the inventory management system should include the component number, descriptions, amount in stock, quantity allotted, quantity accessible, and the unit cost of each item, ordered by part number.
3. All sales representatives must get a daily reminders list from the contacts management system.
4. Current specifications must be made available to vendors through the buying system.
5. Every day, the sales monitoring system must provide a

brief report identifying all items that sell more than expected, broken down by style, color, and size, including reordering status.

6. The quarterly results from the customer review system are required, including comparisons to the preceding four quarters, to reflect differences in ordering trends or patterns (Feser et al., 2015).

3.6.2. Input Examples

1. Workers in the production company should swipe personal ID cards into machines that gather data online and track labor expenses and productivity improvement.
2. On a second screen, the head of the department should input extra hours.
3. Grades for students should be entered on computer-readable forms that the teacher has created.
4. The time, date, product id, consumer number, and quantity must all be entered on every input form.
5. All entering data screens should be consistent, except the backdrop color, which is user editable.
6. The medical group's invoicing system requires services to patients to be entered by a data input employee (Xie et al., 2019).

3.6.3. Process Examples

1. After every semester, the GPA should be calculated by the student records.
2. The pay system should modify staff wages and incentives, including benefits, to generate the IRS-required tax information as the last step in the year processes (Shadish, 1996).
3. The warehousing distribution network must examine each day's orders to develop a delivery van routing scheme that maximizes effectiveness and minimizes wasteful miles.
4. The equipment rental system must not process new rental transactions for clients who have past-due accounts.
5. The prescription management system should automatically create an insurance payout form (Atkinson & Renkl, 2007).

3.6.4. Performance Examples

1. The system should be able to accommodate 25 people online at once.
2. Four seconds is the maximum response time allowed.

3. The system should be available 24 hours a day, 365 days per year.
4. The receivables systems should create customer statements by the third business day after the month following (Hancock & Vasmatzidis, 1998).
5. The online inventory control system must identify all low-stock products within an hour of the number falling below a predefined minimum.

3.6.5. Control Examples

1. The system must provide both operating systems (OS) with application-level login security.
2. Only one representative of a human resources team is permitted to add, modify, or remove an employee profile (Caltagirone, 1981).
3. The system must keep the system superintendent's and users' security levels distinct.
4. Audit trails are required for every transaction.
5. The system should produce an issue log file with the error occurring, an explanation, and a time (Melander et al., 2005).

3.7. FUTURE GROWTH, COSTS, AND BENEFITS

Systems analysts should also consider adaptability, which determines how well a system would manage future growth and needs, and the total cost of ownership (TCO), which incorporates all future operating and maintenance expenses. These factors are in addition to a requirement specification (Arrow et al., 2013).

3.7.1. Scalability

The ability of a system to manage future increases in business volumes and volume of transactions is referred to as scalability. A scalable system delivers a more significant return on the original investment due to its extended usable life. Assessed scalability is necessary to know the anticipated volume of all outputs and inputs, including processes. For just a web-based order processing, for instance, one must be aware of the maximum predicted number of simultaneous clients, the peak online behavior times, the quantity and types of data items needed for every transaction, as well as the mechanism for obtaining and changing client files (Hill, 1990).

The analyst must know how many active accounts there are and have a projection for one, two, or five years because those numbers will affect future hardware choices, even for printing client statements. Furthermore, accurate cost estimations for associated expenditures like mailing and internet fees may be given with realistic quantity projections. Similarly, the analyst would have to forecast exercise levels over several years of business to verify that a web-based booking system is appropriately scalable. For instance, one may predict the number of online requests for accommodation and calculate the average responsiveness and the time needed for each request. The server transaction volume with network needs might be predicted using such data (Bondi, 2000).

Operating expenses are significantly influenced by transaction volume. Maintenance expenses spike whenever volume exceeds a system's capacity. A company's volume may alter significantly if it grows or joins a new industry. For instance, a new Online marketing campaign could need a second server and round-the-clock technical assistance. Another significant scaling problem is data storage. Depending on system usage and growth, the analyst should ascertain how much cloud hosting is now needed and forecast future requirements. These specifications have an impact on the hardware, Software, as well as network bandwidth required to keep the system functioning. Data retention regulations should also be considered to evaluate whether data could be erased or archived on a specific schedule (Jogalekar & Woodside, 2000).

3.7.2. Total Cost of Ownership (TCO)

Systems developers should recognize and record indirect costs that go toward the total ownership cost along with the direct costs (TCO). If a development team examines numerous options, TCO is crucial (Ellram & Siferd, 1998). A system that appears affordable at first glance could become the most expensive option when indirect expenses are considered, which is not usually obvious. One issue would be those cost projections frequently underestimate indirect expenses like user assistance and lost productivity due to outages. Systems analysts must try to locate indirect costs and incorporate them in TCO estimations, even if precise statistics are unavailable (Ellram, 1993). Vendors frequently assert that their goods or services would considerably lower the TCO since cost management is crucial. For instance, decreased TCO is among the most popular justifications for moving a traditional system into the cloud. Because capital investments and other expenses may be outsourced to a cloud in return for a pay-as-you-go price structure, there is the potential for cheaper operating costs (Figure 3.9) (Ferrin & Plank, 2002).

KEYWORD

Total cost of ownership is a financial estimate intended to help buyers and owners determine the direct and indirect costs of a product or service.

Figure 3.9. When moving to a cloud, the overall cost of ownership may be considerably lower than on existing computing systems.

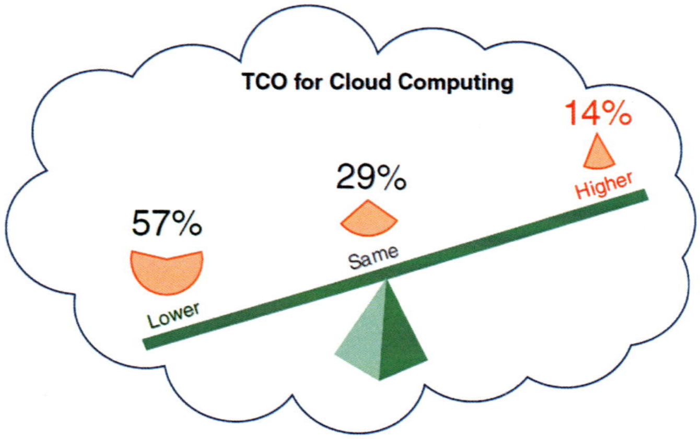

Source: Marc Walter Busch, Creative Commons License.

3.8. FACT FINDING

After understanding the divisions of system needs, scalability, and TCO, fact-finding is the following stage. An analyst would employ a variety of fact-finding approaches, such as interviews, documentary review, observation, survey, and questionnaires, sampling, and research, whether they are working alone or as a part of a JAD team, through a systematic approach. No program genuinely does fact-finding automatically, even though Software could assist in gathering and analyzing information. The information that is required must be first determined. Usually, this activity starts with a sequence of inquiries like these (Ehrmann & Stinson, 1999):

- Which business operations are the existing system capable of supporting?
- What are the suggested system's advantages and TCO (Larsen, 2012)?
- Which kind of transactions would the system handle?
- What data does the system need to provide users and management?
- Does the new system have to connect to existing systems (Faigman, 1990)?
- What processes of business reengineering eliminate?
- What security problems are there?
- How much danger is acceptable?
- What financial and scheduling restrictions impact system development (Orentlicher, 1990)?

The analyst creates a fact-finding strategy to locate the answers to such queries. This strategy may include asking additional questions like "who," "what," "where," "when," and "how," or it may take a more organized approach like the Zachman Framework. In any case, the analyst would create a plan, employ strategies for gathering information, record the outcomes, and create system specifications given to management (Borgmann, 2009).

3.8.1. Who, What, Where, When, How, and Why?

Answers to the five well-known questions of who, what, where, when, and how are part of fact-finding. One should also ask a further, very significant question for every one of those: why. These inquiries include, for instance (Kosciw et al., 2009):

1. **Who?** Each systemic process is carried out by who? Why? Are the right personnel carrying out the task? Could the studies be carried out more efficiently by others?
2. **What Steps are Taken?** What protocols are being adhered to? Why is that procedure required? Many times, protocols are followed for several years without anybody understanding why. Ask yourself why a method is even being followed (Pfaus et al., 2012).
3. **Where?** Where are the surgeries taking place? Why? Where may they take place? Could they be done more effectively somewhere else?
4. **When?** What time is the process carried out? What justifies performing it now? Is now the ideal time (Beltrame et al., 2016)?
5. **How?** How is a process carried out? Why is it carried out in that way? Could it be done differently for less money, more effectively, or both?

There's a distinction between questioning what is being performed and what might or should be done. The systems analyst should initially comprehend the existing circumstance (Figure 3.10).Only thencan he or she tackle the question of what should be done.(Sherrod et al., 2002).

CURRENT SYSTEM		PROPOSED SYSTEM
Who does it?	Why does this person do it?	Who should do it?
What is done?	Why is it done?	What should be done?
Where is it done?	Why is it done there?	Where should it be done?
When is it done?	Why is it done then?	When should it be done?
How is it done?	Why is it done this way?	How should it be done?

Figure 3.10. Examples of questions to ask when modeling requirements as the emphasis switches from the current system to the suggested system.

Source: Romolo Marcelli, Creative Commons License.

3.8.2. The Zachman Framework

John Zachman studied how complicated projects were managed in the construction and architectural sectors in the 1980s, and he proposed that the same concepts might be used to create data systems. His idea, *the Zachman Framework for Enterprise Architecture,* is a paradigm that poses customer inquiries about the truth inside the context of system design. A technique that is well-liked for modeling enterprise architecture is the Zachman Framework (Pereira & Sousa, 2004). It guarantees that overall corporate objectives translate into fruitful IT initiatives and aids managers and users in understanding the model. The system has changed over time, with graphical components being improved and the modeling language being clarified, but the core ideas have mostly remained the same (Zachman, 2003).

3.9. INTERVIEWS

Interviews are critical for gathering information, even during the analysis stage. A prearranged meeting is called an interview when the analyst collects data from a separate individual. It's crucial to comprehend the skills necessary to plan, conduct, record, and evaluate interviews correctly (Nunkoosing, 2005).

The interview method, which has seven steps for every interview, begins after determining the information required, as discussed previously in the chapter (Luo & Wildemuth, 2009):

- Determine the people to interview;
- Establish objectives for the interview;
- Develop interview questions;
- Prepare for the interview;
- Conduct the interview;
- Document the interview;
- Evaluate the interview (Hopf, 2004).

3.9.1. Step 1: Determine the People to Interview

The analyst should select the correct persons to interview and formulate the appropriate questions to obtain an accurate image. Most of the participants in the first investigation were management consultants or heads of departments. People from all levels within the company must now be interviewed during the systems analysis phase. Interviewing stakeholders who are not firm employees may be wise in specific circumstances since their insight is priceless (Huppert et al., 2021).

Although interview candidates could be chosen from the standard organizational charts we previously discussed, it is also essential to consider any unofficial structures the company may have (Oltmann, 2011).

Unofficial processes, geographic closeness, past job assignments, personal contacts, or social gatherings, like informal meetings, can all lead to the development of informal structures, which are typically built on interpersonal interactions. In a non-hierarchical framework, some persons may be more powerful or knowledgeable than they may be. The individuals to interview throughout the analysis phase are chosen with the analyst's understanding of the formal and informal processes of the firm in mind (Abrahamson et al., 2009).

Should multiple people be questioned simultaneously? The interview process could be time-efficient and allow you to watch how the participants interact. Problems arise during interview sessions as well.

Even though questions are specifically directed at other people, one person may dominate the conversation. Organizational-level issues could also occur because senior managers' appearance in such an interview may make it difficult for lower-level employees to express themselves honestly (Morse, 2000).

3.9.2. Step 2: Establish Objectives for the Interview

The goals for the sessions should be decided upon after selecting the interviewees. These facts which need to be obtained should be stated once the broad topics that will be covered have been determined.

It's also wise to get candidates' thoughts, comments, and opinions throughout the interview (Platt, 1980). The goals of the interview are based on the function of the interviewee.

Upper-level management may provide the large picture, which will aid in understanding the system world in general. It is preferable to gather specifics regarding business and operational processes from those who use the system regularly (Figure 3.11) (Dikko, 2016).

Interviews at the first phases of a system study are frequently generic. But as the process of gathering information progresses, the discussions get more specialized. The goals of the interviews also change depending on where the inquiry is located.

Because time is so essential to employees, especially managers, interviews must be as fast as possible (although if necessary). By establishing clear goals, an analyst may build a framework to help them choose possible questions and how to express them (Fishbein & Tyler, 1973).

Figure 3.11. An analyst should explore potential sources of information outside of the conventional organization chart while setting up interviews.

Source: Mamamart, Creative Commons License.

3.9.3. Step 3: Develop Interview Questions

The best way to avoid unnecessary detours and maintain focus during an interview is to prepare a consistent list of inquiries. Additionally, when interviewing many candidates for the same position, a uniform question list enables a comparison of the responses. Even though there might be a list of specified questions, the interviewee may opt to stray from that if the candidate's response raises a relevant point that merits further discussion. The new collection of questions for future interviews must incorporate that question or topic. It could be necessary to re-interview a former interviewee if the question is particularly crucial (Roberts, 2020).

Open-ended, closed-ended, or questioning with various possible answers should all be part of the interview. Avoid asking leading questions that promote or prefer a specific response. For instance, ask, "Do you notice any benefits in the proposed model?" instead of "What benefits do you perceive inside the proposed model (Castillo, 2016)?"

3.9.3.1. Open-Ended Questions

Open-ended inquiries foster unplanned and unexpected replies. Such questions can help you comprehend a more complex process or elicit the interviewee's thoughts, attitudes, or recommendations. Here are a few illustrations of open-ended queries (Kallio et al., 2016):

- What opinions do users have on the new system?
- How is this activity carried out?
- Why do you go about doing it that way?
- How are the checks reconciled?
- Would you prefer extra features within new billing (Pulakos & Schmitt, 1995)?

Additionally, you may utilize an open-ended inquiry to elicit more information by posing the query: Is there anything else you could tell me about this subject?

3.9.3.2. Closed-Ended Questions

The response is limited or constrained by closed-ended questions. Closed-ended inquiries are utilized when more information is required or when findings need to be confirmed—the illustrations of closed-ended questions (Maras et al., 2021):

- How many personal computers do you have in this department?
- Do you review the reports before they are sent out?
- How many hours of training does a clerk receive?
- Is the calculation procedure described in the manual?
- How many customers ordered products from the website last month (Carson et al., 2005)?

3.9.3.3. Range-of-Response Questions

Closed-ended questions with a range of replies encourage the respondent to rate something by giving only a few answers that can be categorized as either positive, negative, or quantitative. It is simpler to tabulate the responses and understand the findings using this approach. These examples of questions with a wide range of answers (Yeong et al., 2018):

- How successful was your training, on a scale of 1 to 10, with one being the lowest and 10 being the highest?
- How would you rate the severity of the problem: low, medium, or high (Wimpenny & Gass, 2000)?
- Is the shutdown of a system anything that happens never, occasionally, frequently, typically, or continuously (Wegmeyer et al., 2022)?

3.9.4. Step 4: Prepare for the Interview

The next step is to be available for the interview after establishing the goals and creating the questions. An interview is not simply a casual conversation; it is a crucial encounter that needs careful preparations. When the interview is set up, provide a precise time and date and inform the applicant of the anticipated meeting duration. The day before the interview, it's a great idea to phone or email as a reminder (Hardavella et al., 2016).

Remember that the interview will disrupt the other person's daily activities, so keep it to one hour. If the meeting must be postponed due to business obligations, make an alternative appointment immediately soon as possible. Don't forget to let department supervisors know about meetings with your personnel. An excellent technique to keep department managers updated is sending everyone a list of scheduled appointments. Such a message is seen in Figure 3–11.

The candidate is free to react and make any required revisions. One strategy is to be ready again for interviews and reduce any need for an obey meeting; a list of subjects must be supplied to the candidate many days before the appointment, especially when comprehensive information is required. The figure displays an example message that outlines specific queries and verifies the interview's scheduled time, place, reason, and length (Ackerley, 2015).

Ask the interviewer to bring samples of the papers if there are queries at the meeting. The list of items to be discussed should be included in the advance note (if it is known what they are). Also, even as the analyst indicated in the email depicted in figure, a generic request for materials might be issued. Regarding where to hold interviews, there are two camps of opinion. While some analysts think that interviews must be conducted just at the interviewee's office, others think a neutral setting, like a conference hall, is preferable (Lotz et al., 2017).

Supporters of in-person interviews contend that doing so in the candidate's workplace is ideal since it puts them at ease throughout the encounter. The fact that the interviewee has the quickest access to any supporting documentation that may be required during the conversation is the second factor in favor of having the interview in their workplace (Mills et al., 2017).

However, the candidate could bring the relevant materials to a conference hall or other venue if a thorough list of subjects is supplied in advance. Supporters of neutral venues emphasize how crucial it is to limit disruptions so both parties may focus entirely. Additionally, an uninterrupted interview goes more quickly. If such an interviewee's office is the location of the meeting, politely request that any calls be put on hold until after the interview (McLellan et al., 2003).

3.9.5. Step 5: Conduct the Interview

A clear meeting agenda should be created after selecting the interview subjects, establishing the meeting's goals, and composing the interview questions. When conducting an interview, start by introducing yourself, outlining the project, and outlining the purposes of the interview. Ask the interviewer the questions in the order they were presented and allow them enough time to consider their responses (Lloyd et al., 2006). Some responses will prompt follow-up inquiries, which must be made in a logical sequence. Getting along well with your interviewee is crucial, mainly when this is your first encounter. The other individual will likely give more thorough and frank responses if they are relaxed and at ease. The analyst's primary duty in an interview is to pay close attention to the responses. Sometimes, analysts hear what they desire to hear. Focus on what is being said while keeping an eye out for nonverbal cues. Engaging listening is what we do when we do this (Rabionet, 2011).

Give the adequate individual time to consider your query and come up with a response after you ask it. According to studies, a conversational pause should last no more than 3 to 5 seconds. After then, one individual will start speaking. To succeed, analysts must have patience and put their abilities to the test in several real-world interview settings. Once all queries have been answered, briefly review the key topics discussed during the interview and describe the next step. Mention, for instance, that a follow-up memo would be issued and that the interviewer must supply a specific piece of desired data following the meeting. After the interview, express your gratitude and invite the subject to get in touch if they have any more questions or remarks. Asking the interviewee if any different topics should be covered after the interview is over is also a good option (Melia, 2000).

After such an interview, sum up the conversation and ask another person whether they agree. They rephrased the interviewee's responses by outlining how the interviewer interpreted the conversation. For instance, the analyst may begin the interviewee's statement with, "*If I understand you right,* you are *stating that...*" and then restate it (Kortesluoma et al., 2003).

3.9.6. Step 6: Document the Interview

While taking notes in an interview can have benefits and drawbacks, it must be done sparingly. Writing down just a few comments is a bright idea to help you recall important information after interviews, but you should not record every word spoken. The other person becomes distracted by excessive writing, making building trust more challenging. Record the facts as soon as the interview is over. After the Conference, set aside some time to take notes and analyze the material. Try to avoid back-to-back scheduling interviews as a result. According to studies, after 30 minutes, 50% of a talk is forgotten. We are using the notes to record the information, so it won't be forgotten instantly. Write a narrative of what happened or list the responses to every question you provided to summarize the data (Owen, 2014). Although they are helpful tools during interviews, more minor, portable recordings can make some individuals uneasy. Talk to the candidate about using a recorder before you start recording. Reassure participants that the interview could be terminated at any moment at the interviewee's desire and that the recordings would be deleted after the contents have been converted into notes. Inform the interviewee that such a recorder could be switched off for a while if they wish to respond to a question privately or get a sensitive inquiry (Makady et al., 2017).

An interviewer could utilize the built-in voice (and even video) recording facilities on a laptop or mobile device instead of a conventional recording that draws attention to its usage. A vital information management tool, like Microsoft OneNote, may be used to interview, preserve the findings, and produce a search file for quick access. No method is utilized to record the discussion; everyone in attendance must be conscious that their words are being captured (Huntington, 1998). To offer insightful follow-up questions, pay close attention to a candidate's comments on whether or not the discussion is being recorded. If not, you may want to go back and ask about the inquiries you skipped the first time. Also, remember that every recorded interview costs twice as long to complete since the analyst must listen to or watch the discussion again after the interview has already been conducted. A note thanking the interviewee for their time and participation should be issued to them following the meeting. Make sure to include the date, time, place, reason for the interview, and critical issues mentioned in the memo so that the interviewer does have a concise explanation and may make any adjustments or additions (Vatnar et al., 2017).

3.9.7. Step 7: Evaluate the Interview

In addition to writing down the information collected from an interview, look for any potential biases. For instance, an interviewer who seeks to preserve his area or function may provide evasive or partial answers. Or a subject of an interview who has strong sentiments about the existing or prospective system could embellish the truth. Even if they lack the expertise to offer correct information, some interviewers may attempt to help by answering questions (Stiles, 1989).

3.9.7.1. Unsuccessful Interviews

Despite thorough preparation, specific interviews nonetheless fail. The interviewer and the participant not getting along might be one of the fundamental causes. Many things can lead to such a predicament. For instance, a miscommunication or personality clash might negatively impact the interview, or the applicant may be concerned that the new scheme would modify or remove their employment (Ljungman et al., 1999). Other times, the interviewee might provide cursory or terse answers to open-ended inquiries. If this is the case, switching to closed-ended questions and questions with such a range of answers may provide better results. If it doesn't work, find a diplomatic method to end the meeting (Kell et al., 2017).

It's challenging to keep on with an ineffective interview. Later, during the interview, the subject could cooperate more, or the analyst may uncover the needed data elsewhere. The supervisor must be told that failing to gather certain information would jeopardize the success of any project, so they may determine what to do. The manager may ask another network expert to interview the applicant, get in touch with the interviewee's manager, or identify another means to gather the required data (Rajesh & Asaad, 2021).

3.10. OTHER FACT-FINDING TECHNIQUES

Systems analysts employ fact-finding methods in addition to interviews, such as document examination, observation, surveys, questionnaires, samples, and research. These methods are applied before the interview to get a solid overview and assist in developing better questions (Wang et al., 2011).

3.10.1. Document Review

The analyst may better understand how the current system is designed to work by reading the documentation. Remember that sometimes system documentation may be pretty dated. Forms may be halted or altered, and recorded procedures are regularly updated or erased. It is recommended to get photocopies of actual service papers, including current forms in use, and evaluate blank forms and instances of finished documents. Interviewing both people who perform that process would allow examples of the papers to be acquired. If this system employs the program, review the instructions for the Software (Knopf, 2006).

3.10.2. Observation

Observing standards is another way to obtain information. Observing the system in action offers a different viewpoint and a greater understanding of system operations. Additionally, the professional analyst may corroborate interview answers and determine if described activities occur by firsthand observation (Korsheninnikov et al., 1994). The truth of the interview statements and the design papers may be revealed through observation. The personal view may prove to be quite beneficial as active learning develops. For example, recommendations based on an intimate knowledge of everyday operations are typically accepted more favorably. Additionally, observing may help establish relationships with the users of the new technologies and can provide the data needed to test or implement impending changes (Cowie, 2009).

Create a checklist of actions to observe and questions to ask to plan observation. When making a list, keep the following things in mind:

1. To completely understand how the present system works, ensure we have enough questions. A fundamental goal is to find answers to issues not handled by standard processes. What happens, for example, if a worker loses a timecard in such a payment service? What happens if a worker starts their shift 10 minutes late but works 20 minutes longer than expected? Because rules for circumstances like these are typically not established or documented, try to develop any means for handling exceptions (Cohen et al., 2017).
2. As you watch a transaction, note the documents, inputs, outputs, and processes employed at every stage.
3. Analyze each document, report, each form. Establish each piece of information's function (Chamberlain et al., 1955).
4. Consider the above inquiries, but for each user who uses the system: What information does the person pick up from others? Precisely what sort of information does this individual generate? How is the information displayed? How often do they occur? How long does the outage last? How much help is required either by the user or who provides it?
5. Ask those who receive recent reports if they are complete, delivered on time, accurate, and presented in a helpful format. Ascertain whether there is room for improvement or elimination of information, as well as interest in receiving more information (Ciesielska et al., 2018).

Examine the Hawthorne Effect while people are watched at work, as depicted in Figure 3.12. The term derived from well-known research conducted in the 1920s at the Western Electric Company's Hawthorne plant. The study's goal was to ascertain how various modifications to the workplace might impact worker productivity. Surprisingly, productivity increased throughout (Hanson, 2009).

Observe whether the situation has improved or gotten worse. Researchers concluded that productivity increased when employees were aware of being watched (Fodor, 1984).

Be careful that observation may and does affect routine operations, despite some recent research casting doubt on the initial findings. Considering this, always notify the relevant supervisor in advance. In some circumstances, it could be beneficial to inform the subjects of the observation of the visit's objective (Angrosino & Rosenberg, 2011).

Figure 3.12. According to the Hawthorne study, employee productivity increases while being observed.

Source: Monkey Business Images, Creative Commons License.

3.10.3. Questionnaires and Surveys

Questionnaires might be beneficial when several people's opinions are needed for an effort. Questionnaires or surveys would be a document that includes a collection of typical questions and may be disseminated to a large population. By using surveys, you might find more information about a range of topics, such as workloads, amounts of remarks received about the system level, job duties, difficulties, and recommendations concerning how the job could be performed more skillfully or better (Young, 2015).

The topic of this type of typical survey is followed by a brief explanation of its aim, the principal contact's location with phone number, the completion deadlines, and directions on how to contribute important information as well as return the form. Usually, the header is followed by comprehensive instructions that explain exactly how to reply to queries. Headings are used to start introducing each major section or industry of a survey and provide guidance whenever the type of inquiry or reaction modifications (de Leeuw & Hox, 2012). The conclusion of long and complex survey questions might thank the participants and include directions for returning to the form. Consider the problem of anonymity. Which is preferable: asking individuals to sign their survey or allowing anonymous responses? The answer will depend on two queries. First, when comparing or correlating data, is it necessary for an expert to be conscious of the respondents? For instance, while specific usernames might not be necessary, knowing the percentage of users who need a particular software function might be (Slattery et al., 2011). Second, are any delicate or debatable subjects included in the survey questions? Many employees would remain anonymous when asked how effectively their supervisor had described the system to them. Anonymous answers may offer more useful information in certain circumstances. The most crucial guideline when creating a questionnaire would be to ensure that the questions gather the appropriate information in a way that will help the fact-finding process. When creating the questionnaire, continue to keep extra considerations in mind (Duncan, 1979):

- Make the questionnaire simple to complete and concise.
- Give precise instructions that address all anticipated queries.
- Put the questions in a logical progression from easy to complex topics.
- Ask questions in clear, unambiguous terms to prevent misinterpretations.
- Avoid leading the response or asking questions that suggest the likely course of action.
- The minimum use of open-ended and challenging-to-tabulate questions.
- Avoid asking queries that can cause people to worry about job security or other unpleasant circumstances.
- Include a space for general remarks at the end of the questionnaire.
- Before finishing and sending it to a big group, test the survey whenever feasible on a short test group (Burgess, 2001).

3.10.4. Brainstorming

Another popular method for getting input is "brainstorming," which refers to a brief conversation about a subject, opportunity, or problem. This approach encourages original thought, fosters collaboration, and enables individuals to build on someone else's contributions and ideas. Thoughts may be organized or unstructured (Furnham, 2000). Every participant does so whenever it is their time to speak or pass during a structured brainstorming. During an open brainstorming process, anybody may speak at any time. The results are finally recorded as part of a reality documentation process (Camacho & Paulus, 1995).

3.10.5. Sampling

When examining a management information system, a simple random sample must gather examples of actual records. A good example might include documents, reports, required to operate logbooks, data input documents, complaint handling descriptions, application forms, and different matters. Sampling techniques include systematic, managed, and random methods. Suppose that 20 customers were chosen randomly from 200 respondents who reported inaccurate statements

(Acharya et al., 2013). A sampling process would select every 10th customer for assessment. To ensure that another specimen is physically balanced, a stratified sample might be used to select five customers, each of the four postal codes. Another application of sample selection is to obtain a specific percentage of transactions from each postal code, even though opposed to a set number. Finally, 20 clients are randomly selected as a sample. Its main objective is to ensure that such a chosen sample accurately represents the population. For example, when examining inventory transaction data, select a sampling of trades that accurately reflects the data input and remove anomalous or disconnected samples. For instance, if a firm is undertaking special processing on the final business of the month, sampling typical daily operating activities during that time is not intelligent. A sample must be large enough to accurately reflect the data (Maddison et al., 2014).

Suppose employing interviews or surveys, sampling is considered. A sample of respondents could be utilized in place of interviewing each person in the group or sending out a question to everybody. Sound sampling methods should be used to obtain an accurate image and represent the population (Berndt, 2020).

3.10.6. Research

Another essential technique for acquiring knowledge is research. You may research using the Web, IT publications, and textbooks to get background information, technical information, and news about industry trends with breakthroughs. Participating in networking events, training sessions, and discussions with other IT professionals may all be very helpful for problem-solving (Johnson & Onwuegbuzie, 2004). The Internet is a helpful resource. About national, state, and municipal governments, the analyzer may utilize the Internet to access data from foreign publications, universities, and libraries. Online discussion forums and newsgroups are helpful resources for connecting with other professionals, finding solutions to your difficulties, and staying up to date on subjects that concern you both (Liao et al., 2017).

3.11. DOCUMENTATION

For systems development to be effective, it is crucial to keep precise records of interviews, data, concepts, and observations. Effective systems analysts possess the capacity to handle information, making it a critical talent for all IT workers (Rinaldi, 2005).

3.11.1. The Need for Recording the Facts

As information is acquired, it's possible to forget the complexity of a system or the significance of a single piece. Writing it down is the fundamental guideline. An analyst must record their work following the following guidelines (Laughlin, 2004):

- As soon as you get information, immediately record it;
- Use the most basic recording technique you can;
- Make sure to document your findings so that others can understand them;
- Organize your documentation to make it simple to find pertinent information.

Systems analysts frequently utilize unique formats to describe systems, and document interviews, including summarizing papers. A narrative list containing straightforward explanations about what is happening, any apparent issues, and recommendations for change is one sort of documentation. This chapter also includes flowcharts, sampling forms, flow diagrams, screen grabs, and other types of documentation (Kane et al., 1981).

3.11.2. Software Tools

There are several software tools available to assist with capturing and documenting information. Here, a few instances are given (Cobo et al., 2011).

3.11.2.1. CASE Tools

Each stage of the development of such a system could utilize CASE tools. This chapter has several CASE tools examples (Kernighan & Plauger, 1976).

3.11.2.2. Productivity Software

Productivity software for collaborative, word processing, spreadsheets, databases, and presentation graphics. Other companies provide products in every one of these groups, while Microsoft Office provides the most well-known suite of productivity software tools.

The analyst could produce reports, summaries, tables, including forms using word processing programs like Microsoft Word. The tool may assist in arranging a presentation using templates, bookmarking, comments, versioning, an index, and essential document preparation. More details about these and many other features are available in the program's Help system. As mentioned in this chapter, fill-in forms could also be produced for surveys and questionnaires (Xiao et al., 2015).

3.12. INFORMATION MANAGEMENT SOFTWARE

Emails, text messages, personal connections, conferences, bookings, deadlines, and a lot more need to be managed by harried IT workers. They also need vital tools to record, arrange, and retrieve project documents and information. The Software, which is probably more suited for managing personal information and data management system created for the enormous quantity of information created by an IT project, has emerged, even though there is still a significant degree of overlap. The typical examples of both software kinds are described in subsections (Tyndale, 2002).

3.12.1. Personal Data Management

A personal information manager (PIM), including Microsoft Outlook, provides a personal calendar, a to-do list containing priority and the opportunity to check off finished tasks, and comprehensive contact management tools. Outlook allows for teamwork and project interaction, in addition to managing email as well as appointments. Novell's GroupWise is another famous PIM, and short research on the website will uncover many additional possibilities, including payware, shareware, and even free products (Straub & Collins, 1990).

ACTIVITY 3.1

Write the importance of interviews in system analysis.

3.12.2. Project Data Management

However, a PIM like Microsoft Outlook could manage daily chores, calendars, and activities, but it is not an ideal method for gathering and organizing massive volumes of data. Instead, analysts utilize data management tools like Microsoft OneNote, a robust, adaptable program that can handle a wide range (Hensley, 2011) of inputs, including text, handwritten notes, photos, video, and audio recordings, online connections, and many more. Several Office suite versions come with OneNote (Jennings & Wooldridge, 1996).

3.13. PREVIEW OF LOGICAL MODELING

Systems developers must have a comprehensive grasp of business operations, including system requirements, just at the end of using a systematic approach. Building a conceptual model of a system is the next phase. A structured analysis methodology is used in data processing modeling. A well-liked, time-tested method for describing a system's information and the activities that occur on it is called structured analysis. Object modeling is a substitute for structured analysis modeling. Object modeling combines information and procedures to create objects, which are entities that reflect natural persons, things, activities, and events. Systems analysts use object models to illustrate and record business activities and procedures (Rabinia et al., 2020). There are varying opinions among IT experts on systems development approaches, and there is no one acknowledged way. Researching structural analyzes and object-oriented (O-O) methodologies makes learning essential concepts, abilities, and viewpoints possible. With this knowledge, it will be possible to choose the appropriate method—or set of methods—for the many circumstances that all analysts will encounter during their careers (Gluck et al., 2006).

3.14. SUMMARY

Three tasks are included in the systems analysis phase: modeling of needs, modeling of data and processes, and thinking through development approaches. The primary goals are understanding the planned project, ensuring it will satisfy business objectives, and laying a solid basis for the systems design stage. The outcomes, inputs, procedures, performance, and controls for such a new information system are all identified throughout the demands modeling phase. Scalability ensures that the system can accommodate future development and expansion. All expenses, particularly indirect costs, are projected to be included in the TCO.

JAD, RAD, and agile techniques are a few common team-based strategies. Joint application development (JAD) is a well-liked team-based method for gathering information and modeling needs. JAD incorporates an interactive team of users, administrators, and IT specialists who take part in a systematic approach and get closer to a project and its shared objectives. A team-based approach called rapid application development (RAD) expedites the creation of information systems and results in a working information system. With a four-phase product lifecycle like the conventional SDLC phases, RAD is a complete approach.

Agile development practices aim to create systems progressively by creating several prototypes and iteratively tailoring them to user needs. Tools are frequently ignored to improve communication in favor of more basic ones like sticky notes and whiteboards. System requirements are modeled using various tools and approaches by systems analysts. A popular technique for visualizing and describing software architecture from the perspective of a business customer seems to be the unified modeling language (UML). Using CASE diagrams and sequence diagrams are two UML tools used to describe actors, their roles, and the order of transactions.

A representation of business processes and functions is called a functional decomposition diagram (FDD). Directly from such an FDD, a CASE tool may produce a set of information flow diagrams. Interviews, document reviews, observations, surveys, sampling, and research are all part of the fact-finding process. Proper planning, excellent communication, and interpersonal skills are necessary for a successful interview. The systems analyst should select the candidates for such interviews, establish the goals of the interview sessions, and plan, carry out, and evaluate the interviews. While gathering information, the analyst could also find it helpful to employ one or more software tools. As data is gathered, systems analysts must carefully capture and document it. Various software tools could assist analysts in visualizing and describing an information system. A sneak peeks of logical modeling was given as the chapter ended. A structured analysis method called information and process modeling looks at the systems regarding the information it contains and the procedures it uses to make decisions. A technique is known as "*object modeling*" looks at the system as a collection of information and the procedures that use that information.

REVIEW QUESTIONS

1. What are the best practices for requirements modeling in software development?
2. How do requirements modeling help to reduce development costs?
3. What are the advantages and disadvantages of using requirements modeling?
4. What techniques can be used to ensure the accuracy of requirements modeling?
5. How can requirements modeling help to ensure the success of a software project?

MULTIPLE CHOICE QUESTIONS

1. What is the primary goal of requirements modeling?

a. To identify and document the functional and non-functional requirements of a system
b. To design the user interface of a system
c. To create a detailed project plan
d. To test the system for bugs

2. Which of the following is NOT a common technique for gathering requirements?

a. Interviews
b. Surveys
c. Focus groups
d. Code reviews

3. What is the difference between functional and non-functional requirements?

a. Functional requirements define what the system should do, while non-functional requirements define how the system should do it
b. Functional requirements define how the system should do it, while non-functional requirements define what the system should do
c. Functional and non-functional requirements are the same thing
d. Functional and non-functional requirements are not related

4. What is the purpose of a use CASE in requirements modeling?

a. To describe a specific interaction between a user and the system
b. To document all of the functional requirements of the system
c. To describe how the system will be implemented
d. To describe the system's architecture

5. What is the primary goal of requirements validation?

a. To ensure that the requirements are complete and accurate
b. To ensure that the requirements are feasible and can be implemented

c. To ensure that the requirements are testable

d. All of the above

Answers to Multiple Choice Questions

1. (a) 2. (d) 3. (a) 4. (a) 5. (d)

REFERENCES

1. Abrahamson, V., Wolf, J., Lorenzoni, I., Fenn, B., Kovats, S., Wilkinson, P., &Raine, R., (2009). Perceptions of heatwave risks to health: Interview-based study of older people in London and Norwich, UK. *Journal of Public Health, 31*(1), 119–126.
2. Abrahamsson, P., Warsta, J., Siponen, M. T., & Ronkainen, J., (2003). New directions on agile methods: A comparative analysis. In: *25th International Conference on Software Engineering, 2003; Proceedings.* (pp. 244–254). IEEE.
3. Acharya, A. S., Prakash, A., Saxena, P., & Nigam, A., (2013). Sampling: Why and how of it. *Indian Journal of Medical Specialties, 4*(2), 330–333.
4. Ackerley, N., (2015). Prepare for your interview. *Veterinary Nursing Journal, 30*(10), 282–283.
5. Agarwal, R., Prasad, J., Tanniru, M., & Lynch, J., (2000). Risks of rapid application development. *Communications of the ACM, 43*(11es), 1-es.
6. Aguilar-Saven, R. S., (2004). Business process modeling: Review and framework. *International Journal of Production Economics, 90*(2), 129–149.
7. Ali, R., Dalpiaz, F., & Giorgini, P., (2010). A goal-based framework for contextual requirements modeling and analysis. *Requirements Engineering, 15*(4), 439–458.
8. Al-Msie'deen, R., Huchard, M., Seriai, A. D., Urtado, C., & Vauttier, S., (2014). Automatic documentation of [mined] feature implementations from source code elements and use-CASE diagrams with the REVPLINE approach. *International Journal of Software Engineering and Knowledge Engineering, 24*(10), 1413–1438.
9. Angrosino, M., & Rosenberg, J., (2011). Observations on observation. *The Sage Handbook of Qualitative Research, 4*, 467–478.
10. Anwar, F., & Razali, R., (2014). Requirements elicitation techniques selection survey. In: *SoMeT* (pp. 280–294).
11. Arrow, K. J., Cropper, M., Gollier, C., Groom, B., Heal, G. M., Newell, R. G., & Weitzman, M., (2013). How should benefits and costs be discounted in an intergenerational context? The views of an expert panel. *The Views of an Expert Panel (December 19, 2013). Resources for the Future Discussion Paper* (pp. 12–53).
12. Atkinson, R. K., & Renkl, A., (2007). Interactive example-based learning environments: Using interactive elements to encourage effective processing of worked examples. *Educational Psychology Review, 19*(3), 375–386.

13. Baker, K. R., (1993). Requirements planning. *Handbooks in Operations Research and Management Science, 4*, 571–627.
14. Bakhsheshi-Rad, H. R., Hamzah, E., Low, H. T., Kasiri-Asgarani, M., Farahany, S., Akbari, E., & Cho, M. H., (2017). Fabrication of biodegradable Zn-Al-Mg alloy: Mechanical properties, corrosion behavior, cytotoxicity and antibacterial activities. *Materials Science and Engineering: C, 73*, 215–219.
15. Beltrame, J. F., Crea, F., Kaski, J. C., Ogawa, H., Ong, P., Sechtem, U., & Coronary Vasomotion Disorders International Study Group, (2016). The who, what, why, when, how and where of vasospastic angina. *Circulation Journal, 80*(2), 289–298.
16. Berndt, A. E., (2020). Sampling methods. *Journal of Human Lactation, 36*(2), 224–226.
17. Bondi, A. B., (2000). Characteristics of scalability and their impact on performance. In: *Proceedings of the 2nd International Workshop on Software and Performance* (pp. 195–203).
18. Booch, G., Jacobson, I., & Rumbaugh, J., (1996). The unified modeling language. *Unix Review, 14*(13), 5.
19. Borgmann, C. E., (2009). Rethinking judicial deference to legislative fact-finding. *Ind. LJ, 84*, 1.
20. Brimhall, E., Wise, R., Simko, R., Huggins, J., & Matteson, W., (2016). A systematic process for functional decomposition in the absence of formal requirements. In: *INCOSE International Symposium* (Vol. 26, No. 1, pp. 1204–1218).
21. Burgess, T. F., (2001). Guide to the design of questionnaires. *A General Introduction to the Design of Questionnaires for Survey Research, 30*(4), 411–432.
22. Caltagirone, L. E., (1981). Landmark examples in classical biological control. *Annual Review of Entomology, 26*(1), 213–232.
23. Camacho, L. M., & Paulus, P. B., (1995). The role of social anxiousness in group brainstorming. *Journal of Personality and Social Psychology, 68*(6), 1071.
24. Campanelli, A. S., & Parreiras, F. S., (2015). Agile methods tailoring–a systematic literature review. *Journal of Systems and Software, 110*, 85–100.
25. Carson, K. D., Carson, P. P., Fontenot, G., & Burdin, Jr. J. J., (2005). Structured interview questions for selecting productive, emotionally mature, and helpful employees. *The Health Care Manager, 24*(3), 209–215.
26. Castillo-Montoya, M., (2016). Preparing for interview research: The interview protocol refinement framework. *The Qualitative Report, 21*(5), 811–831.
27. Chamberlain, O., Segrè, E., Wiegand, C., & Ypsilantis, T., (1955). Observation of antiprotons. *Physical Review, 100*(3), 947.
28. Chen, T. H., Chen, M. S., Inoue, T., Kotas, P., & Chebli, E. A., (1991). Three-phase cogenerator and transformer models for distribution system analysis. *IEEE Transactions on Power Delivery, 6*(4), 1671–1681.
29. Ciesielska, M., Boström, K. W., & Öhlander, M., (2018). Observation methods. In:

Qualitative Methodologies in Organization Studies (pp. 33–52). Palgrave Macmillan, Cham.

30. Cobo, M. J., López-Herrera, A. G., Herrera-Viedma, E., & Herrera, F., (2011). Science mapping software tools: Review, analysis, and cooperative study among tools. *Journal of the American Society for Information Science and Technology, 62*(7), 1382–1402.
31. Cohen, D., Lindvall, M., & Costa, P., (2004). An introduction to agile methods. *Adv. Comput., 62*(03), 1–66.
32. Cohen, L., Manion, L., & Morrison, K., (2017). Observation. In: *Research Methods in Education* (pp. 542–562). Routledge.
33. Cowie, N., (2009). Observation. In: *Qualitative Research in Applied Linguistics* (pp. 165–181). Palgrave Macmillan, London.
34. Daud, N. M. N., Bakar, N. A. A. A., & Rusli, H. M., (2010). Implementing rapid application development (RAD) methodology in developing practical training application system. In: *2010 International Symposium on Information Technology* (Vol. 3, pp. 1664–1667). IEEE.
35. De Leeuw, E. D., & Hox, J. J., (2012). Self-administered questionnaires: Mail surveys and other applications. In: *International Handbook of Survey Methodology* (pp. 239–263). Routledge.
36. Dikko, M., (2016). Establishing construct validity and reliability: Pilot testing of a qualitative interview for research in Takaful (Islamic insurance). *The Qualitative Report, 21*(3), 521–529.
37. Dos Santos, S. M., Vrancken, J., & Verbraeck, A., (2011). User requirements modeling and analysis of software-intensive systems. *Journal of Systems and Software, 84*(2), 328–339.
38. Duncan, W. J., (1979). Mail questionnaires in survey research: A review of response inducement techniques. *Journal of Management, 5*(1), 39–55.
39. Ehrmann, J. R., & Stinson, B. L., (1999). Joint fact-finding and the use of technical experts. *The Consensus Building Handbook,* 375–399.
40. Ellram, L. M., & Siferd, S. P., (1998). Total cost of ownership: A key concept in strategic cost management decisions. *Materials Engineering, 19*(1), 55–84.
41. Ellram, L., (1993). Total cost of ownership: Elements and implementation. *International Journal of Purchasing and Materials Management, 29*(3), 2–11.
42. Faigman, D. L., (1990). Normative constitutional fact-finding: Exploring the empirical component of constitutional interpretation. *U. Pa. L. Rev., 139*, 541.
43. Ferrin, B. G., & Plank, R. E., (2002). Total cost of ownership models: An exploratory study. *Journal of Supply Chain Management, 38*(2), 18–29.
44. Feser, J. K., Chaudhuri, S., & Dillig, I., (2015). Synthesizing data structure transformations from input-output examples. *ACM SIGPLAN Notices, 50*(6), 229–239.
45. Firesmith, D., (2005). Quality requirements checklist. *J. Object Technol., 4*(9), 31–38).

46. Fishbein, J. M., & Tyler, R., (1973). "Kappan" interview: The father of behavioral objectives criticizes them: An interview with ralph Tyler. *The Phi Delta Kappan, 55*(1), 55–57.
47. Fodor, J., (1984). Observation reconsidered. *Philosophy of Science, 51*(1), 23–43.
48. Fortuin, K. P. J., Van, K. C. S. A., & Kroeze, C., (2013). The contribution of systems analysis to training students in cognitive interdisciplinary skills in environmental science education. *Journal of Environmental Studies and Sciences, 3*(2), 139–152.
49. Furnham, A., (2000). The brainstorming myth. *Business Strategy Review, 11*(4), 21–28.
50. Garny, A., Nickerson, D. P., Cooper, J., Santos, R. W. D., Miller, A. K., McKeever, S., & Hunter, P. J., (2008). CellML and associated tools and techniques. *Philosophical Transactions of the Royal Society A: Mathematical, Physical and Engineering Sciences, 366*(1878), 3017–3043.
51. Gluck, K. A., Pew, R. W., & Young, M. J., (2006). Background, structure, and preview of the model comparison. In: *Modeling Human Behavior with Integrated Cognitive Architectures* (pp. 21–30). Psychology Press.
52. González, E., & Rochefort, L., (2014). Drivers of success in 53 cutover bogs restored by a moss layer transfer technique. *Ecological Engineering, 68*, 279–290.
53. Hancock, P. A., & Vasmatzidis, I., (1998). Human occupational and performance limits under stress: The thermal environment as a prototypical example. *Ergonomics, 41*(8), 1169–1191.
54. Hanson, N. R., (2009). On observation. *Philosophy of Science: An Historical Anthology, 14*, 432.
55. Hardavella, G., Gagnat, A. A., Xhamalaj, D., & Saad, N., (2016). How to prepare for an interview. *Breathe, 12*(3), e86–e90.
56. Hensley, M. K., (2011). Citation management software: Features and futures. *Reference & User Services Quarterly, 50*(3), 204–208.
57. Hill, M. D., (1990). What is scalability? *ACM SIGARCH Computer Architecture News, 18*(4), 18–21.
58. Hopf, C., (2004). Qualitative interviews: An overview. *A Companion to Qualitative Research, 203*(8).
59. Huntington, H. P., (1998). Observations on the utility of the semi-directive interview for documenting traditional ecological knowledge. *Arctic*, 237–242.
60. Huppert, L. A., Hsiao, E. C., Cho, K. C., Marquez, C., Chaudhry, R. I., Frank, J., & Babik, J. M., (2021). Virtual interviews at graduate medical education training programs: Determining evidence-based best practices. *Academic Medicine, 96*(8), 1137–1145.
61. Indulska, M., Recker, J., Rosemann, M., & Green, P., (2009). Business process modeling: Current issues and future challenges. In: *International Conference on Advanced Information Systems Engineering* (pp. 501–514). Springer, Berlin, Heidelberg.

62. Ives, B., & Olson, M. H., (1984). User involvement and MIS success: A review of research. *Management Science, 30*(5), 586–603.
63. Jennings, N., & Wooldridge, M., (1996). Software agents. *IEE Review, 42*(1), 17–20.
64. Jogalekar, P., & Woodside, M., (2000). Evaluating the scalability of distributed systems. *IEEE Transactions on Parallel and Distributed Systems, 11*(6), 589–603.
65. Johnson, R. B., & Onwuegbuzie, A. J., (2004). Mixed methods research: A research paradigm whose time has come. *Educational Researcher, 33*(7), 14–26.
66. Kallio, H., Pietilä, A. M., Johnson, M., & Kangasniemi, M., (2016). Systematic methodological review: Developing a framework for a qualitative semi-structured interview guide. *Journal of Advanced Nursing, 72*(12), 2954–2965.
67. Kane, J. N., Anzovin, S., & Podell, J., (1981). *Famous First Facts: A Record of First Happenings, Discoveries, and Inventions in American History* (Vol. 38, No. 3, p. 5). NY: HW Wilson.
68. Kell, H. J., Martin-Raugh, M. P., Carney, L. M., Inglese, P. A., Chen, L., & Feng, G., (2017). Exploring methods for developing behaviorally anchored rating scales for evaluating structured interview performance. *ETS Research Report Series, 2017*(1), 1–26.
69. Kernighan, B. W., & Plauger, P. J., (1976). Software tools. *ACM SIGSOFT Software Engineering Notes, 1*(1), 15–20.
70. Khanali, M., Akram, A., Behzadi, J., Mostashari-Rad, F., Saber, Z., Chau, K. W., & Nabavi-Pelesaraei, A., (2021). Multi-objective optimization of energy use and environmental emissions for walnut production using imperialist competitive algorithm. *Applied Energy, 284*, 116342.
71. Knopf, J. W., (2006). Doing a literature review. *PS: Political Science & Politics, 39*(1), 127–132.
72. Korsheninnikov, A. A., Yoshida, K., Aleksandrov, D. V., Aoi, N., Doki, Y., Inabe, N., & Yanokura, M., (1994). Observation of 10He. *Physics Letters B, 326*(1, 2), 31–36.
73. Kortesluoma, R. L., Hentinen, M., & Nikkonen, M., (2003). Conducting a qualitative child interview: Methodological considerations. *Journal of Advanced Nursing, 42*(5), 434–441.
74. Kosciw, J. G., Greytak, E. A., & Diaz, E. M., (2009). Who, what, where, when, and why: Demographic and ecological factors contributing to hostile school climate for lesbian, gay, bisexual, and transgender youth. *Journal of Youth and Adolescence, 38*(7), 976–988.
75. Kujala, S., (2003). User involvement: A review of the benefits and challenges. *Behavior & Information Technology, 22*(1), 1–16.
76. Larsen, A. O., (2012). Confronting supreme court fact finding. *Virginia Law Review*, 1255–1312.
77. Laughlin, R., (2004). Putting the record straight: A critique of 'methodology choices and the construction of facts: Some implications from the sociology of knowledge'.

Critical Perspectives on Accounting, 15(2), 261–277.

78. Leppink, J., Paas, F., Van, G. T., Van, D. V. C. P., & Van, M. J. J., (2014). Effects of pairs of problems and examples on task performance and different types of cognitive load. *Learning and Instruction, 30*, 32–42.
79. Liao, Y., Deschamps, F., Loures, E. D. F. R., & Ramos, L. F. P., (2017). Past, present and future of industry 4.0-a systematic literature review and research agenda proposal. *International Journal of Production Research, 55*(12), 3609–3629.
80. Lindvall, M., Basili, V., Boehm, B., Costa, P., Dangle, K., Shull, F., & Zelkowitz, M., (2002). Empirical findings in agile methods. In: *Conference on Extreme Programming and Agile Methods* (pp. 197–207). Springer, Berlin, Heidelberg.
81. Liou, Y. I., & Chen, M., (1993). Using group support systems and joint application development for requirements specification. *Journal of Management Information Systems, 10*(3), 25–41.
82. Ljungman, G., Gordh, T., Sörensen, S., & Kreuger, A., (1999). Pain in paediatric oncology: Interviews with children, adolescents and their parents. *Acta Paediatrica, 88*(6), 623–630.
83. Lloyd, V., Gatherer, A., & Kalsy, S., (2006). Conducting qualitative interview research with people with expressive language difficulties. *Qualitative Health Research, 16*(10), 1386–1404.
84. Lotz, J. D., Daxer, M., Jox, R. J., Borasio, G. D., & Führer, M., (2017). "Hope for the best, prepare for the worst": A qualitative interview study on parents' needs and fears in pediatric advance care planning. *Palliative Medicine, 31*(8), 764–771.
85. Luo, L., & Wildemuth, B. M., (2009). Semi-structured interviews. *Applications of Social Research Methods to Questions in Information and Library Science, 232*.
86. Maddison, C. J., Tarlow, D., & Minka, T., (2014). A* sampling. *Advances in Neural Information Processing Systems, 27*.
87. Makady, A., De Boer, A., Hillege, H., Klungel, O., & Goettsch, W., (2017). What is real-world data? A review of definitions based on literature and stakeholder interviews. *Value in Health, 20*(7), 858–865.
88. Maras, K., Norris, J. E., Nicholson, J., Heasman, B., Remington, A., & Crane, L., (2021). Ameliorating the disadvantage for autistic job seekers: An initial evaluation of adapted employment interview questions. *Autism, 25*(4), 1060–1075.
89. Masoudi, R. H., Rabiei, M., Sobhani, A., Sadegh, K. M., Rahbar, T. M., & Kazemnezhad, L. E., (2014). Free amino acids in stimulated and unstimulated whole saliva: Advantages or disadvantages. *Journal of Oral Rehabilitation, 41*(10), 759–767.
90. McLellan, E., MacQueen, K. M., & Neidig, J. L., (2003). Beyond the qualitative interview: Data preparation and transcription. *Field Methods, 15*(1), 63–84.
91. Melander, B., Rasmussen, I. A., & Bàrberi, P., (2005). Integrating physical and cultural methods of weed control—Examples from European research. *Weed Science, 53*(3), 369–381.

92. Melia, K., (2000). Conducting an interview. *Nurse Researcher, 7*(4), 75–89.
93. Mills, S., White, M., Wrieden, W., Brown, H., Stead, M., & Adams, J., (2017). Home food preparation practices, experiences and perceptions: A qualitative interview study with photo-elicitation. *PloS One, 12*(8), e0182842.
94. Moock, J., (2014). Support from the internet for individuals with mental disorders: Advantages and disadvantages of e-mental health service delivery. *Frontiers in Public Health, 2*, 65.
95. Morse, J. M., (2000). Determining sample size. *Qualitative Health Research, 10*(1), 3–5.
96. Nunkoosing, K., (2005). The problems with interviews. *Qualitative Health Research, 15*(5), 698–706.
97. Oleynik, A., Lomov, P., Shemyakin, A., & Avdeev, A., (2017). Solutions for system analysis and information support of the various activities in the arctic. *Czech Polar Reports, 7*(2), 280–289.
98. Oltmann, S. M., (2011). Telephone & email interviews: Using the respondents' context to determine the best interview mode. In: *Proceedings of the 2011 iConference* (pp. 734, 735).
99. Orentlicher, D. F., (1990). Bearing witness: The art and science of human rights fact-finding. *Harv. Hum. Rts. J., 3*, 83.
100. Owen, G. T., (2014). Qualitative methods in higher education policy analysis: Using interviews and document analysis. *The Qualitative Report, 19*(26), 1.
101. Pereira, C. M., & Sousa, P., (2004). A method to define an enterprise architecture using the Zachman framework. In: *Proceedings of the 2004 ACM Symposium on Applied Computing* (pp. 1366–1371).
102. Pfaus, J. G., Kippin, T. E., Coria-Avila, G. A., Gelez, H., Afonso, V. M., Ismail, N., & Parada, M., (2012). Who, what, where, when (and maybe even why)? How the experience of sexual reward connects sexual desire, preference, and performance. *Archives of Sexual Behavior, 41*(1), 31–62.
103. Platt, S., (1980). On establishing the validity of 'objective' data: Can we rely on cross-interview agreement? 1. *Psychological Medicine, 10*(3), 573–581.
104. Plotkin, G. D., (1976). A power domain construction. *SIAM Journal on Computing, 5*(3), 452–487.
105. Pulakos, E. D., & Schmitt, N., (1995). Experience-based and situational interview questions: Studies of validity. *Personnel Psychology, 48*(2), 289–308.
106. Rabinia, A., Ghanavati, S., Humphreys, L., & Hahmann, T., (2020). A methodology for implementing the formal legal-GRL framework: A research preview. In: *International Working Conference on Requirements Engineering: Foundation for Software Quality* (pp. 124–131). Springer, Cham.
107. Rabionet, S. E., (2011). How I learned to design and conduct semi-structured interviews: An ongoing and continuous journey. *Qualitative Report, 16*(2), 563–566.

108. Rajesh, A., & Asaad, M., (2021). Alternative strategies for evaluating general surgery residency applicants and an interview limit for MATCH 2021: An impending necessity. *Annals of Surgery, 273*(1), 109–111.

109. Recker, J., Rosemann, M., Indulska, M., & Green, P., (2009). Business process modeling-a comparative analysis. *Journal of the Association for Information Systems, 10*(4), 1.

110. Redström, J., (2006). Towards user design? On the shift from object to user as the subject of design. *Design Studies, 27*(2), 123–139.

111. Reifer, D. J., (2002). How good are agile methods? *IEEE Software, 19*(4), 16–18.

112. Rinaldi, C., (2005). Documentation and assessment: What is the relationship.*Beyond Listening: Children's Perspectives on Early Childhood Services,* 17–28.

113. Roberts, R. E., (2020). Qualitative interview questions: Guidance for novice researchers. *Qualitative Report, 25*(9).

114. Shadish, W. R., (1996). Meta-analysis and the exploration of causal mediating processes: A primer of examples, methods, and issues. *Psychological Methods, 1*(1), 47.

115. Sharma, S., Sarkar, D., & Gupta, D., (2012). Agile processes and methodologies: A conceptual study. *International Journal on Computer Science and Engineering, 4*(5), 892.

116. Sherrod, L. R., Flanagan, C., & Youniss, J., (2002). Dimensions of citizenship and opportunities for youth development: The what, why, when, where, and who of citizenship development. *Applied Developmental Science, 6*(4), 264–272.

117. Slattery, E. L., Voelker, C. C., Nussenbaum, B., Rich, J. T., Paniello, R. C., & Neely, J. G., (2011). A practical guide to surveys and questionnaires. *Otolaryngology--Head and Neck Surgery, 144*(6), 831–837.

118. Smith, B., Knorr, W., Widlowski, J. L., Pinty, B., & Gobron, N., (2008). Combining remote sensing data with process modelling to monitor boreal conifer forest carbon balances. *Forest Ecology and Management, 255*(12), 3985–3994.

119. Stiles, W. B., (1989). Evaluating medical interview process components: Null correlations with outcomes may be misleading. *Medical Care,* 212–220.

120. Straub, Jr. D. W., & Collins, R. W., (1990). Key information liability issues facing managers: Software piracy, proprietary databases, and individual WSprivacy rights. *MIS Quarterly,* 143–156.

121. Tyndale, P., (2002). A taxonomy of knowledge management software tools: Origins and applications. *Evaluation and Program Planning, 25*(2), 183–190.

122. Van, D. V. G., & Lane, M. S., (2003). Using the new generation of IS development techniques in effective group learning: A pilot study of a team-based approach in an IT Course. In: *Proceedings of the 2003 Informing Science+ Information Technology Education Joint Conference 2003 (InSITE 2003)* (pp. 1361–1373). Informing Science Institute.

123. Vatnar, S. K. B., Friestad, C., & Bjørkly, S., (2017). Intimate partner homicide in Norway 1990–2012: Identifying risk factors through structured risk assessment, court documents, and interviews with bereaved. *Psychology of Violence, 7*(3), 395.

124. Wang, D., Abdelzaher, T., Ahmadi, H., Pasternack, J., Roth, D., Gupta, M., & Aggarwal, C. C., (2011). On Bayesian interpretation of fact-finding in information networks. In: *14th International Conference on Information Fusion* (pp. 1–8). IEEE.

125. Wegmeyer, L. J., Tenbrink, A. P., Delacruz, A. Y., Salim, R., & Speer, A. B., (2022). Interviews from scratch: Individual differences in writing interview questions. *Personnel Assessment and Decisions, 8*(1), 2.

126. Wimpenny, P., & Gass, J., (2000). Interviewing in phenomenology and grounded theory: Is there a difference? *Journal of Advanced Nursing, 31*(6), 1485–1492.

127. Xiao, J., Zhang, Z., Wu, J., & Yu, J., (2015). A brief review of software tools for pangenomics. *Genomics, Proteomics & Bioinformatics, 13*(1), 73–76.

128. Xie, C., Zhang, Z., Zhou, Y., Bai, S., Wang, J., Ren, Z., & Yuille, A. L., (2019). Improving transferability of adversarial examples with input diversity. In: *Proceedings of the IEEE/CVF Conference on Computer Vision and Pattern Recognition* (pp. 2730–2739).

129. Yeong, M. L., Ismail, R., Ismail, N. H., & Hamzah, M., (2018). Interview protocol refinement: Fine-tuning qualitative research interview questions for multi-racial populations in Malaysia. *Qualitative Report, 23*(11).

130. Young, T. J., (2015). Questionnaires and surveys. *Research Methods in Intercultural Communication: A Practical Guide*,163–180.

131. Yue, Z., Liang, H., Gao, X., Qin, X., Li, H., Xiang, N., & Liu, E., (2022). The association between falls and anxiety among elderly Chinese individuals: The mediating roles of functional ability and social participation. *Journal of Affective Disorders, 301*, 300–306.

132. Zachman, J. A., (2003). The Zachman framework for enterprise architecture. *Primer for Enterprise Engineering and Manufacturing [SI]: Zachman International.*

133. Zygouris, S., Giakoumis, D., Votis, K., Doumpoulakis, S., Ntovas, K., Segkouli, S., & Tsolaki, M., (2015). Can a virtual reality cognitive training application fulfill a dual role? Using the virtual supermarket cognitive training application as a screening tool for mild cognitive impairment. *Journal of Alzheimer's Disease, 44*(4), 1333–1347.

CHAPTER 4

DATA AND PROCESS MODELING

UNIT INTRODUCTION

To illustrate a data system, systems analysts commonly utilize graphical tools. A frequent strategy is to generate many data flow diagrams (DFDs). A DFD depicts how a system translates incoming data into useful information using several symbols, as demonstrated in Chapter 3 (Kurgan & Musilek, 2006). The current system was investigated, and user requirements were found using fact-finding approaches during the demands modeling process discussed in Chapter 3 (Kurgan & Musilek, 2006).Chapter 4 covers the steps necessary to develop a logical model of the proposed system and collect the system requirements (Mariscal et al., 2010).A logical model shows what a system must do, independent of how it is built. Afterward, a physical model is created during the systems designing stage to explain the system's structure. Data and process modeling makes use of three primary tools: a data dictionary, DFDs, and descriptions of the process (Leoni et al., 2014).

Learning Objective

After studying this unit, you will be able to:

- Identify and describe the various processes in the system development life cycle;
- Analyze and explain the factors that cause consumers to alter their requests;

- Identify and describe the various elements of a feasibility study;
- Construct a computer-based information system using appropriate tools and methods;
- Evaluate and consider important aspects of a potential system in planning and development;
- Develop strategies for organizing and maintaining a system for success, including ongoing maintenance and updates.

Key Terms

- Data processing
- Data modeling
- Data dictionary
- Modeling design
- Data element
- Data flow
- Process description tools
- Modular design

4.1. DATA FLOW DIAGRAMS (DFDS)

During the systems analysis phase of the software development life cycle (SDLC), the systems analyst creates a visual depiction of the data system by combining many data flow diagrams (DFDs). Author and eminent professor Edward Tufte offers advice on drawing powerful diagrams to communicate complicated data in his famous work, the Graphical Display of Quantitative Data. This kind of visual illustration of system activity is a DFD (Butler et al., 1995).

Whereas a DFD does not show the logic of a program, or the steps used to analyze data, it does show the flow of information inside a system. Rather than focusing on the mechanics of a system's work, DFDs provide a high-level conceptual model of its output. Important as it may seem, this distinction is necessary since concentrating on implementation issues now will restrict the search for the most effective system design (Batini et al., 1986).

4.1.1. DFD Symbols

The four symbols used in DFDs indicate processes, data flows, data storage, and entities. DFD symbols come in various forms but always have the same function (Li & Chen, 2009). The Sarson and Gane symbol set is used in the DFD instances in this book. The Yourdon symbol set is an additional well-liked symbol set. Instances of both versions are shown in Figure 4.1. Symbol names are referred to in this text utilizing all capital letters (Yampolskiy et al., 2012).

4.1.1.1. Process Symbol

When a process gets information as input, the output may have various content, form, or both. For instance, payment is calculated by adding the number of hours worked per pay rate (total pay). The intricacy or ease of a process may range widely (Whittington, 2008). Processes are used in most businesses for tasks like validating customer email addresses, calculating sales trends, filing insurance claims online, and ordering products from a supplier's system. As the name implies, processes are where the "business logic" (or "business rules") are stored that perform the necessary data transformations and provide the desired outputs (Turner, 1977).

A rectangle having rounded corners serves as the representation of a process. The process's name can be seen inside the rectangle. The procedure name identifies a specific operation by starting with a singular noun and ending with a verb (and an adjective, whenever required). Examples of process names are APPLY RENT PAYMENT, CALCULATE COMMISSION, ASSIGN FINAL GRADE, VERIFY ORDER, and FILL ORDER. In a DFD, processing information is not displayed. There can be a procedure called DEPOSIT PAYMENT, for instance

(Anderson et al., 2003). The process symbol for the DEPOSIT PAYMENT method does not adequately convey the underlying business logic. An explanation of the process description, generated to record the logic, is discussed later in this chapter. Because its internal workings and logic are hidden, a procedure symbol in DFDs is often known as a "black box," even though its inputs, outputs, and fundamental functions are all well understood. By representing operations as "black boxes," an analyst may generate DFDs that represent how the system functions without adding unnecessary complexity or clutter (Nilsson, 2007). The analyst may focus on a procedure symbol to make a more detailed DFD that displays the process' underlying workings to display higher degrees of detail. This may disclose other processes, the flow of data, and data stores. This allows the data system to be represented as a sequence of progressively more detailed images (Figl et al., 2013).

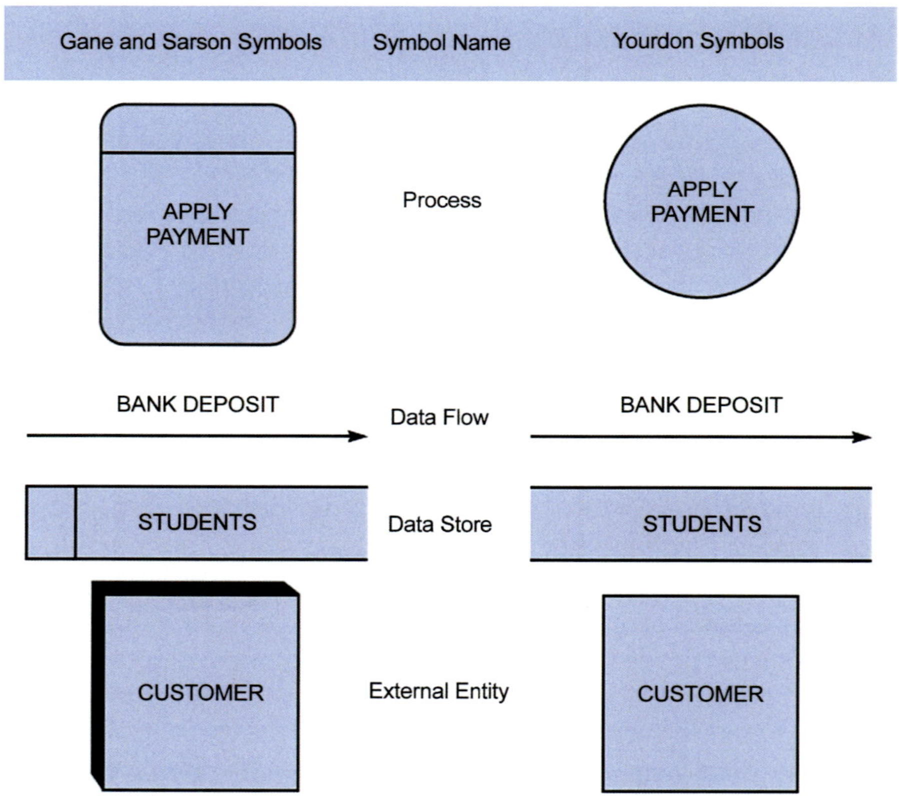

Figure 4.1. Symbols, names, and instances from the Gane and Sarson, Yourdon, and symbol sets used in data flow diagrams.

Source: Visual Paradigm, Creative Commons License.

Figure 4.2 depicts a mysterious black object that serves as a network router. While an outsider may be able to see a router's input and output ports, they will not be able to see inside the router itself (Hinton, 1990).

4.1.1.2. Data Flow Symbol

Information travels along a data flow as it is transferred from one location to another. One or several data items comprise a data flow in a DFD. One data item in a data flow could be an individual student ID number. In contrast, another data flow could comprise a list of student names, ID numbers, and registration dates for a particular class. The data dictionary, which is explained in the following section, provides this information even if the DFD does not fully show the components of a flow of information (Sagiv et al., 1995).

Figure 4.2. For network data, a router functions as a black box.

Source: John F. Buford, Creative Commons License.

Single or double arrows on a line denote the direction of data transfer. Above, below, or adjacent to the line, the data flow's label might be displayed. A data flow name comprises a singular noun and an optional adjective. DEPOSIT, STUDENT GRADE, INVOICE PAYMENT, and COMMISSION ORDER are a few instances of data flow names. Data flow names, like GRADING PARAMETERS, are an exception to the rule of using singular names since they may lead analysts to believe that there is just one parameter or one piece of data (Reps et al., 1995). Correct illustrations of the flow of data and process symbol linkages are shown in Figure 4.2. A single minimum flow of data should enter, and a single flow of data should exit every process symbol since a process alters the data format or content, such as in the CREATE INVOICE procedure. Multiple data flows may be present in a procedure symbol, as seen in the GRADE STUDENT WORK procedure, or multiple data flows may be present in the CALCULATE GROSS PAY procedure (Amamiya et al., 1987).

As seen by the link in figure between the symbols for VERIFY ORDER and ASSEMBLE ORDER, a procedure may also link to every sign, including another process symbol. Thus, a process symbol should be present on at least one data flow side (Figure 4.3) (Dennis, 1974).

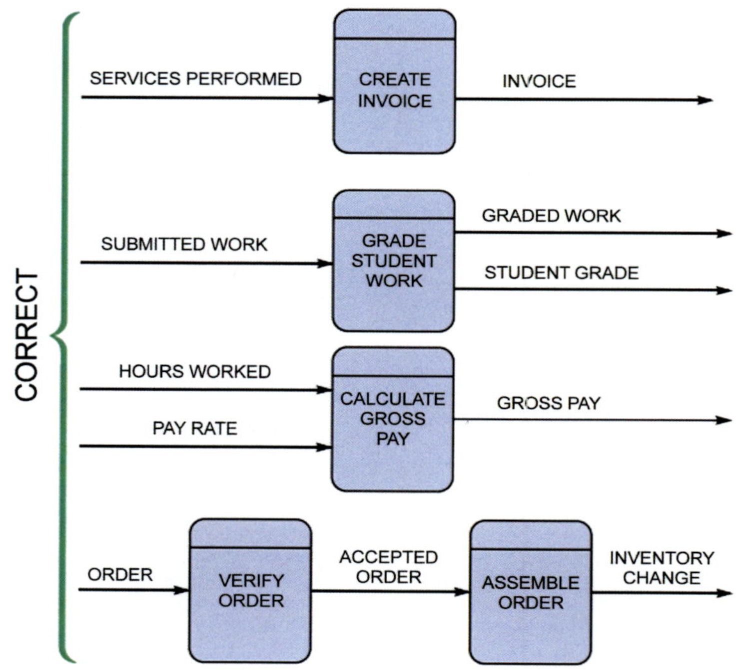

Figure 4.3. Illustrations of how the symbols for data transfer and procedures could be used effectively together.

Source: Edraw Soft, Creative Commons License.

Figure 4.4 depicts three data flow and procedure combinations to avoid:

1. **Spontaneous Generation:** For example, however, there is no input data flow to the APPLY INSURANCE PREMIUM procedure, which only produces output. We call this process "spontaneous generation" since it takes no external input.

2. **Black Hole:** The procedure of CALCULATE GROSS PAY has been known as a black hole since it receives input but provides no output (Wadge & Ashcroft, 1985).
3. **Grey Hole:** A "gray hole" exists in a process with at least one output and one input, but the input is inadequate to produce the output as specified. To give just one example, in the CALCULATE GRADE process, the date of birth input is inadequate to generate a final grade output. DFDs require processes to take in information, as illustrated by incoming data flows, and turn that information into something new, as demonstrated by outgoing data flows (Buck & Lee, 1993).

4.1.1.3. Data Store Symbol

Whereas one or more procedures require the usage of the data later, a data store is employed in a DFD to depict the information the system stores. For instance, to issue final marks after the term, teachers must keep track of students' performance on examinations and assignments throughout the semester. Likewise, a business keeps track of employee salaries and deductions throughout the year to generate W-2 forms that show total earnings and deductions after the year. The data dictionary, which will be discussed in more detail later in this chapter, details the data store's unique architecture and constituent data items. Data is not shown in their exact form in a DFD (Takabayashi et al., 2011).

The physical features of a data store are currently insignificant since the logical model is all that matters. Likewise, it makes no difference how long the data has been stored; it could require as little as a few seconds to carry out a transaction or several months to gather information for end-of-year processing. What's important is that the information will be needed for a process (Lin & Tzeng, 2011). According to the DFD notation introduced by Gane and Sarson, data storage is depicted by a two-dimensional rectangle with a hole on its right side and a wall on its left. Reading between the lines, one can learn crucial details about the data repository, such as its actual name. The name of a data warehouse is always in the plural, and it is formed by adding the noun it stores to relevant adjectives. Students, Purchase Orders, Receivable Accounts, Products, Outstanding Checks, Daily Payments, Insurance Policies, and Workers are a few instances of data store names. Collective nouns that denote several instances of an object are an exception to the rule against using plural names. GRADEBOOK, as an illustration, shows a group of students and their grades (Xu et al., 2021).

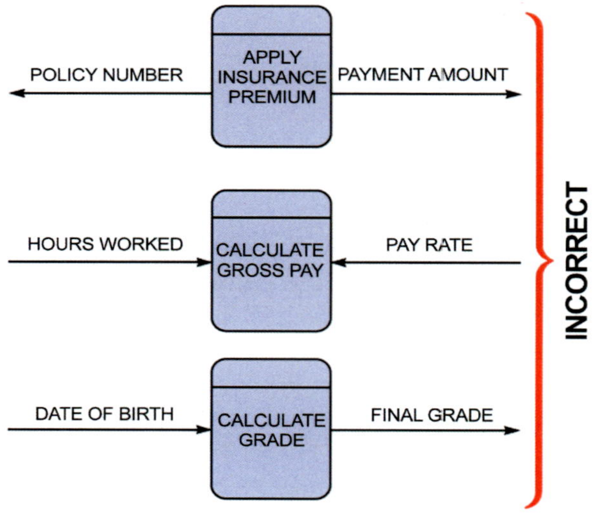

Figure 4.4. Examples of wrong data flow and process symbol combinations.

Source: Edraw Soft, Creative Commons License.

A data repository should be linked to a process utilizing a data flow. Examples of common data archives are shown in Figure 4.5. As data stores represent data storing for later usage by another process, they all have at least one outgoing and one entering data flow and are coupled to a procedure symbol through the flow of data (Liu et al., 2003).

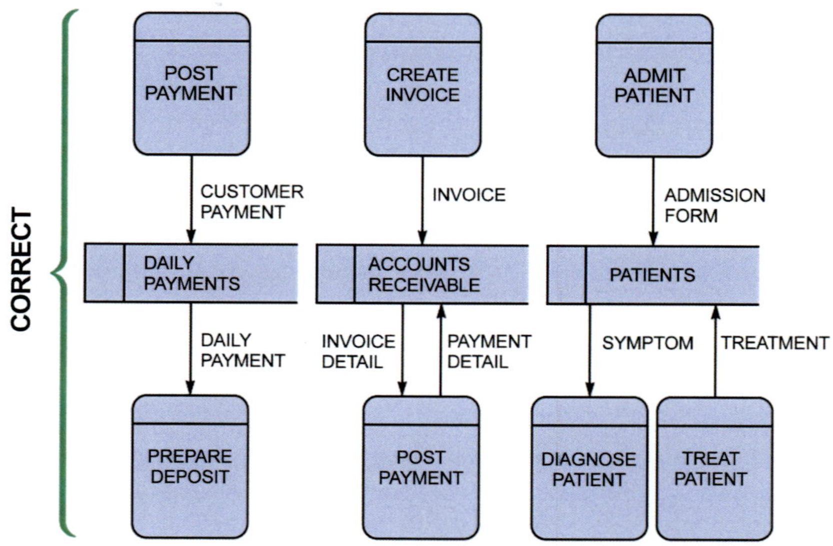

Figure 4.5. Examples of using data storage symbols in a data flow diagram.

Source: Edraw Soft, Creative Commons License.

Figure 4.6 displays instances of how a data store's requirement for at least one outgoing and one incoming data flow has been broken. Since there is no process between the two data stores in the initial case, their connection is wrong. Additionally, there is no incoming data flow for COURSES and no outgoing data flow for students. The data storage in the 2nd and 3rd instances do not have an incoming or outgoing data flow, respectively (Jeong & Lee, 2015).

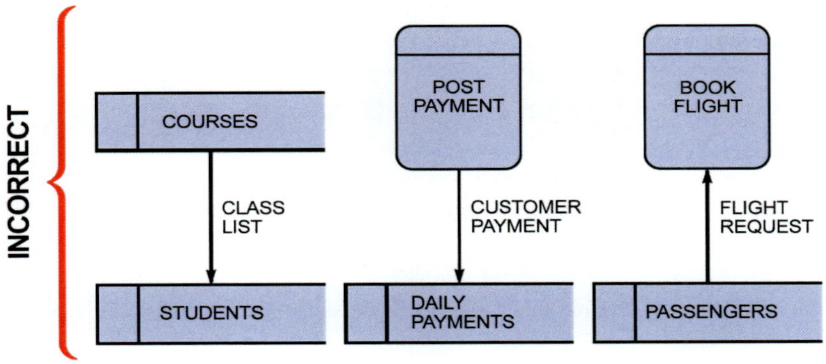

Figure 4.6. Examples of how data store symbols have been used incorrectly in data flow diagrams.

Source: Edraw Soft, Creative Commons License.

If a database only stores reference data that is never updated, then there is no need for data to enter the system. For instance, a company can keep track of the withholding tax data it obtains from the IRS in a TAX TABLE database. The CALCULATE WITHHOLDING procedure uses the data in this repository to calculate employee tax withholdings. On a DFD, this will look like an outbound data flow from the TAX TABLE data store to the CALCULATE WITHHOLDING procedure (Gopalan et al., 2012).

4.1.1.4. Entity Symbol

Instead of using actual 3D models, flat rectangles that can be colored to make them seem more 3D are used to represent creatures. The symbol represents the entity whose name it represents. Only the entities outside of the system involved in the system's input or output are depicted in a DFD. A DFD illustrates the system's boundaries and how they interact with its environment (Barsalou, 2019). For instance, an order management system might receive a submission from a customer entity. Another instance of an entity is a patient who provides information to a patient record system, an owner of the home who obtains a bill from a system of city property tax, or a system of accounts payable which receives information from a business's purchasing system (Jiang et al., 2022).

DFD objects, originators, or data destinations are also referred to as terminators. For those stated in the language of systems analysis, a source feeds information into the system, while a sink takes information out of the system. An entity name is a unique label given to a department, outside group, other information systems, or individual (Zhang & Zhu, 2015). Each object in the process needs to be connected to the procedure through a data flow, regardless of whether the entity is a sink, source, or both. The next stage is to create diagrams using DFD symbols after understanding how to utilize them correctly. An overview of the guidelines for employing DFD symbols is shown in Figure 4.7 (Harel & Kaput, 2002).

Figure 4.7. Instances of both appropriate and inappropriate data flow usage.

Source: Uwe Aickelin, Creative Commons License.

4.2. CREATING A SET OF DFDS

When creating the requirements model, information about the system was gathered through questionnaires, interviews, and other methods. It also stated how the different stakeholder's people, data, departments, and processes fit together to assist business operations. Depending on the fact-finding findings, an information system graphical model is now developed (Abedjan et al., 2014).

Two information system instances will be presented to demonstrate how to build DFDs. The first illustration shows a grading scheme used by teachers to determine final marks for students based on their performance during the term. The second instance is a firm's order system for entering orders and applying payments to a client's account balance. Review a list of instructions for drawing DFDs first. Then, discover how to implement these recommendations and produce a set of DFDs utilizing a 3-step procedure (Seifermann et al., 2022).

Did you Know?

Process modeling is the study of what the business does now and of what it should be doing. Data modeling is the study of what data the business needs to enable these activities to be complete. Business modeling is used during strategy studies, tactical studies, and detailed systems/operational studies.

4.3. GUIDELINES FOR DRAWING DFDS

The following principles ought to be adhered to while creating context diagrams and other DFDs:

i. Construct the context diagram to fit on a single page.

ii. As the procedure's name in the context diagram, use the name of the data system. For instance, the GRADING SYSTEM is the procedure's name in Figure 4.8. Keep in mind that the system name and the process name are the same. The context diagram, which shows the complete IT infrastructure as one seamless process, is helpful here. DFDs at a lower level describe actions by a verb followed by a word, like ASSIGN FINAL GRADE, ESTABLISH GRADEBOOK, or CREATE GRADE REPORT (Tavakoli et al., 2003).

iii. Make use of unique names for each set of symbols. Figure 4.8, for instance, simply shows one entity (STUDENT) and one data flow (FINAL GRADE). The word "STUDENT" denotes the same entity when it shows on any other DFD in the grading scheme. The FINAL GRADE data flow denotes the same flow every time it appears. The same naming pattern is used for data stores (Cruzes et al., 2018).

iv. Never cross a line. Reducing the number of symbols used in each DFD is one approach to achieving this goal. No more than nine process symbols may be used on low-level diagrams with multiple processes. The presence of more than nine symbols typically indicates that the diagram is particularly complicated and that the analysis must be reevaluated. Duplicating an object or data storage is another method for avoiding line crossings. It is important to keep track of each iteration to avoid making a mistake when duplicating a symbol on a diagram. To show that something has been duplicated on the diagram, a special symbol (like an asterisk) is placed after the symbol name and within the repeated symbols (Sullivan, 1989).

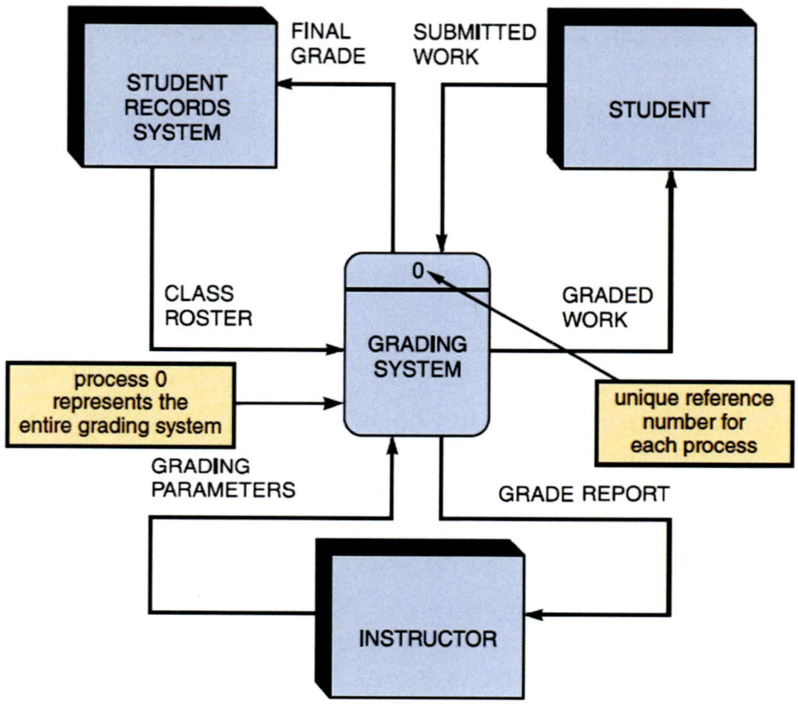

Figure 4.8. For a grading system, create a DFD context diagram.

Source: Uwe Aickelin, Creative Commons License.

v. Assign a unique name and number to each procedure. As the higher-level DFD, process 0 in the context diagram is a symbol for the entire IS without showing its internals. For the next level of detail inside procedure 0, which would indicate further processes that need to be named and numbered, you can draw them in a DFD with the name diagram 0. After developing lower-level DFDs, complete the logical model by assigning unique identifiers and references to each process (Güngör, 2006).

vi. Get as much input and feedback from users as possible. The primary objective is to ensure the model's accuracy, readability, and suitability to user needs (Protsko et al., 1984).

4.3.1. Step 1: Draw a Context Diagram

The first step in developing a DFD library is developing a context diagram. In a context diagram, which provides a bird's-eye view of an information system, its boundaries and scope are laid out for inspection. To begin making a context diagram, place a single procedure symbol in the center of the page. The process 0 (the numeral zero, not the letter O) symbol symbolizes the complete information system (Poranen et al., 2003). Afterward, utilize data flow to link the system entities to the primary process after placing them around the page's edge. Since data stores are internal to the system and are hidden until further in-depth diagrams are generated, they are not displayed in the context diagram (Wille, 1989).

After identifying all external sources of information and destinations, assess the system's requirements to decide which objects and data flows to include in the context diagram. The process of accomplishing this involves identifying the items, the information flow's name and type, and the direction in which it moves. Drawing the context diagram must be simple if it is completed properly and the investigative task was completed successfully in the earlier phase. Review the instances of the context diagrams below now (Ellis et al., 2012).

- **Example: Context Diagram for a Grading System:** A grading system's context diagram is shown in Figure 4.8. The central portion of the diagram represents the process of the GRADING SYSTEM. Three sub-processes surround the main process (INSTRUCTOR, STUDENT, and STUDENT RECORDS SYSTEM). Six data streams are at play in the dialog between the objects and the main procedure (Sparrow et al., 2000). The STUDENT RECORDS SYSTEM entity receives data from the CLASS ROSTER data flow and supplies data to the FINAL GRADE data flow. The STUDENT entity sends data via the SUBMITTED WORK data flow and receives data via the GRADED WORK data flow. Additionally, the entity INSTRUCTOR participates in the GRADE REPORT, and GRADING PARAMETER data flows, receiving, and contributing information as appropriate (Echauz & Vachtsevanos, 1995).
- **Example: Context Diagram for an Order System:** Figure 4.9 depicts the context diagram for an order system. The ORDER SYSTEM process is located in the diagram's center, while five other components surround it. For the incoming data flows of "BANK DEPOSIT," "COMMISSION," and "CASH RECEIPTS ENTRY," three of the entities, namely "BANK," "SALES REP," and "ACCOUNTING," share a common point of entry (Ibrahim, 2010). The PICKING LIST report, which lists the ordered products together with their amount, location, and picking order from the warehouse, is the only incoming data flow for the WAREHOUSE entity. The COMPLETED ORDER data flow is the only one that leaves

the WAREHOUSE entity. Two information flows (INVOICE and ORDER REJECT NOTICE) come into and leave out of the CUSTOMER entity, and vice versa (PAYMENT and ORDER; Bleistein et al., 2006).

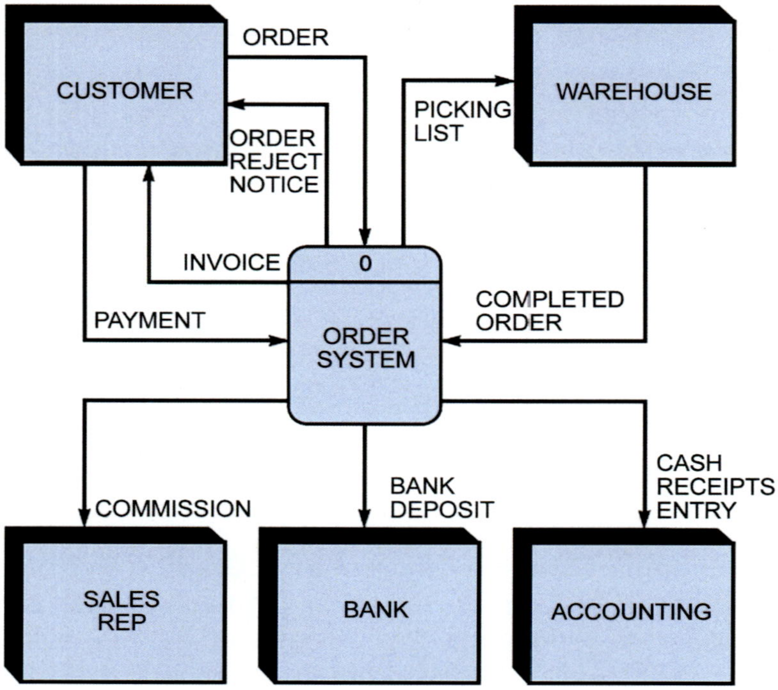

Figure 4.9. DFD context diagram for a system of orders.

Source: Geeks for Geeks, Creative Commons License.

Due to the addition of two extra entities and three extra data flows. At the same time, the grading system's context diagram was rather straightforward; the order system's diagram appears to be more intricate. The number of parts, the number of levels, and the degree of interaction among a system's operations, data stores, individuals, and data flow indicate how complicated something is relative to other systems (Akundi et al., 2018).

4.4. DATA DICTIONARY

The first part of the structured analysis is a group of DFDs, which together form a logical model of the system; the 2nd part, a data dictionary, documents the specifics of the DFDs themselves. A data repository, sometimes known as a data dictionary, is a central database for storing and retrieving data about a system's data (Uhrowczik, 1973). Data flows, data storage, entities, and procedures are just some of the many aspects of a system that can be documented and organized using a data dictionary. All data elements and logical pairings of data components have definitions and descriptions in the data dictionary. Data elements, fields, or items are the smallest meaningful information units in any database or other information system (Alvarado, 1999).

Examples of data items include account balance, firm name, student grade, Social Security number, and salary. Records, usually referred to as data structures, and are made up of data elements. A record is a purposeful grouping of pertinent data pieces kept in a data store or flown with a data flow. As an illustration, the inventory record for an auto parts store would include the component number, supplier code, description, cost, maximum, and minimum stock levels, and list price (Rashid et al., 2020).

There are significant connections between the elements in a data dictionary. Data structures of data pieces provide the foundation for data repositories and data flows. Data stores, entities, and processes are all connected through data flows. This is essential to accurately describe these relationships so that the data dictionary and DFDs are compatible. The design may be documented with CASE tools (Fanti et al., 2015).

4.4.1. Using CASE Tools for Documentation

This is harder to manage full and precise documentation the more complicated the system is. However, contemporary CASE systems make the process easier by automatically transferring documentation from modeling diagrams into the centralized source together with data input by the user important when many systems require the same information; a CASE repository guarantees data consistency (Lederer & Mahaney, 1996). In a large organization, for instance, the CUSTOMER NUMBER may be used by the shipping, accounting, and sales systems. After the CUSTOMER NUMBER has been defined in the repository, it can be used in several different ways across several processes, data flows, and data stores. As a result, current and consistent data may be shared among all systems throughout the company (Kusters & Wijers, 1993).

4.4.2. Data Element Documentation

Data items in the data dictionary should have supporting documentation. Some analysts choose to keep notes in the form of paper or web-based questionnaires. Sometimes, users prefer to start using a CASE tool and enter the data there. Whatever CASE tool is employed, the ultimate goal is to provide detailed, comprehensible information on the system's data and processes (Carney et al., 2002).

1. **Data Element Name or Label:** The common name of the data element ought to make sense to consumers (Zhu et al., 2006).
2. **Aliases:** These are alternative names for a data element that is not its primary name. Users may utilize different names for a data element with the name CURRENT BALANCE, for instance, CUSTOMER BALANCE, OUTSTANDING BALANCE, AMOUNT OWED, or RECEIVABLE BALANCE (Aldrich et al., 2002).
3. **Type and Length:** Depending on the type, a data item may have character, alphabetic, or numeric values. The maximum number of characters that may be utilized in a character data element, or the maximum number of digits and decimal places that may be utilized in a numeric data element, is the length of the data element. Images, sounds, and text may all be saved digitally in addition to numbers and text. Such binary data objects may be handled and processed similarly to conventional data components in certain systems. For instance, a digital photo image of a person may be included in an employee record (Sansone et al., 2017).
4. **Default Value:** The default value will be used if no alternative value is given for the data element. For instance, the default value for the CREDIT LIMIT data item can be $500 for all brand-new clients.
5. **Acceptable Values:** The domain of the data element and the values that can be assigned to it are described. Such values may either be chosen from a predetermined range of values or maybe precisely listed or referred to in a table. Also, mention if the data element's value is optional. Further validity requirements apply to some data items. An employee's salary, for instance, must be within the range determined for the individual's job classification (Cooper et al., 2001).
6. **Source:** The description of the location from which the data element values were derived. A particular form, a division or outside the organization, another data system, or the outcome of a calculation might all serve as the source.
7. **Security:** Identify the person or group granted access to or update rights for every data element. For instance, sales representatives can view data in a read-only mode, but only a credit manager has the right to adjust a credit limit (Byun & Li, 2008).
8. **Responsible User(s):** The data item's primary contributor or the user in charge of editing the item's values.
9. **Description and Comments:** It is possible to enter extra remarks in this documentation section (Turcu et al., 2009).

4.4.3. The Data Flows Documentation

All data should be documented, and every data element in the data dictionary. Though definitions may shift, typically, they share the following characteristics:

1. **Data Flow Label or Name:** The name of the data flow is shown on DFDs.
2. **Description:** Discuss the data flow as well as its purpose for it.
3. **Alternate Name(s):** Alternative names for the DFD flow of data.
4. **Origin:** The procedure, data store, or entity that started the data flow, or source, according to DFD (Koren & Klamma, 2018).
5. **Destination:** The DFD destination of data flow may be a procedure, a data store, or an entity.
6. **Record:** Every data flow depicts a record or data format, which is a collection of connected data pieces. Most data dictionaries define records independently of the flow of data and data repositories. Once records have been created, they may be referenced by other data streams or storage places (Osterweil & Fosdick, 1976).
7. **Volume and Frequency:** Specifies the anticipated number of data flow occurrences per unit of time. For instance, a TIME CARD data flow might contain 300 transactions and records weekly when workers submitted their work hour data when a company had 300 employees (Wang & Kumar, 2005).

4.4.4. The Data Stores Documentation

The data dictionary is recommended to include documentation for every DFD data saved there. The following are some examples of the typical qualities that data storage has:

1. **Data Store Label or Name:** The name of the data store as it displays on DFDs.
2. **Description:** Explains the data store's function and purpose (Cattell, 2011).
3. **Alternate Name(s):** Alternative names for the DFD data storage.
4. **Attributes:** Names of ordinary DFDs that are either added to or removed from the data store.
5. **Volume and Frequency:** Specify the anticipated number of records in the data repository and the frequency with which they are updated (Grolinger et al., 2013).

4.4.5. Documenting the Processes

Each procedure needs to be documented. The documentation details the process's properties, and, for functional components, a model of the processing stages and business logic known as a process description (Ciolfi et al., 2018).

The following traits of a process are typical:

1. **Process Name or Label:** The name of the process is written on the DFDs.
2. **Description:** A simple and concise description of the purpose of the process.
3. **Process Number:** A reference number is used to indicate the procedure, and it also serves to illustrate the interconnectedness of the system's many levels.
4. **Process Description:** In this section, you will find both the entry and exit flow for the data. In addition, the processing phases and the business logic for functional primitives are broken down in depth in the process description. The next part of this chapter will walk you through the steps of writing the process descriptions (Guthrie et al., 1993).

4.4.6. The Entities Documentation

The data dictionary can describe any external entity communicating with the system because it catalogs all entities. The following are examples of an entity's typical traits:

1. **Entity Name:** The name of the entity is written on the DFDs.
2. **Description:** Explain the organization and its goal (Yang & Mitchell, 2016).
3. **Alternate Name(s):** The entity name is the alternate name.
4. **Input Data Flows:** Standard DFD names are used to label the entity's incoming data flows.
5. **Output Data Flows:** The data flow exiting the entity is given the normal DFD names (Grulich et al., 2010).

4.4.7. The Records Documentation

An example of a data structure is a record that consists of a collection of related data items that are stored and processed as a whole. The data dictionary should describe records from data flow and data repositories. Additionally, every record's characteristic should be defined (Roberts, 1994).

Specific characteristics of records include:

1. **Record or Data Structure Name:** The name of the record as it appears in the data dictionary components of the associated data flow and data store.
2. **Definition or Description:** A brief analysis of the data.
3. **Alternate Name(s):** Variations on the record's official name.
4. **Attributes:** A collection of all the fields or data components present in the record. The data component names should match the data dictionary entries exactly (Martin, 2008).

4.4.8. Data Dictionary Reports

A data dictionary is the main hub of any information system's reference material. A data dictionary has been established during system development and is continuously updated during system implementation, operation, and maintenance (Sakamoto & Ball, 1982). The data dictionary also documents the associations among every data element, data flow, data repository, record, entity, and process. A data dictionary provides access to numerous useful reports, such as the following:

- A list of all data components alphabetized by name.
- A report that describes every data item and identifies the client or department accountable for information entry, modification, or removal (Ehrensberger, 1977).
- A summary of all the data flow and repositories employing a specific data element.
- Comprehensive reports display all attributes of data components, records, information flow, processes, and any other specified item in the data dictionary (Kahn & Lumsden, 1983).

Remember

Data modeling is the procedure of documenting a complex software design as an easily understood diagram to explain the way data need to flow. On the other hand, process modeling is the procedure of classifying the processes of the same nature together in to a model.

4.5. PROCESS DESCRIPTION TOOLS

The details of a functional primitive can be found in a process description, which represents a unique set of processing steps and business logic. With the use of several methods for describing processes, a precise, exhaustive, and understandable model can be developed (Kettinger et al., 1997).

Common approaches to describing processes include structured English, decision trees, and decision tables. Modular design is a method wherein a functional primitive's processing steps are broken down into smaller, more manageable chunks. It ought to be emphasized that although this chapter discusses structured analysis, object-oriented (O-O) programming may also employ process description tools (Bal, 1998).

As previously mentioned, O-O the analysis integrates information with the processes that operate on the data to create objects, which can then be categorized into classes. O-O processes have been referred to as methods. The procedures, or methods, are contained inside the objects instead of being independent components, even though O-O programmers use alternative nomenclature to produce similar modular coding structures (Gorla et al., 1995).

4.5.1. Modular Design

Modular architecture has three fundamental tenets, or "building blocks" (Often called control structures). Each logical framework needs only one point of entry and one point of departure.

The three types of organization are called sequence, choice, and repetition. A diamond-shaped condition or option is represented by a rectangle in conditional logic, with the logic proceeding along the lines in the direction of the arrows (Lawson & Richards, 2010).

1. **Sequence:** The result of a series of steps taken in a straight line, as depicted in Figure 4.10. A certain number of the phases may represent a more complex process with extra logical structures (Shen et al., 2019).

Figure 4.10. Sequence structure.

Source: Control Structures, Creative Commons License.

2. **Selection:** The completion of one of two or more phases of the process is conditional on the result of a test or condition. If the number of hours worked exceeds 40, as shown in Figure 4.11, the system initiates the Evaluate OVERTIME PAY function (Salama et al., 2017).

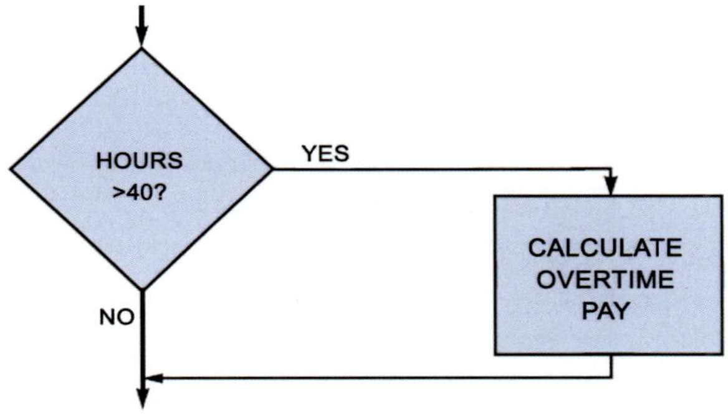

Figure 4.11. Selection structure.

Source: Control Structures, Creative Commons License.

3. **Iteration:** Performing a process step, after which it is repeated until a particular condition changes, as depicted in Figure 4.12. An instance of iteration is a procedure that keeps printing paychecks until they arrive at the end of the payroll file. Another name for iteration is looping. Processing logic may be characterized in various ways by combining sequence, selection, and repetition structures (Guo & Gershenson, 2004).

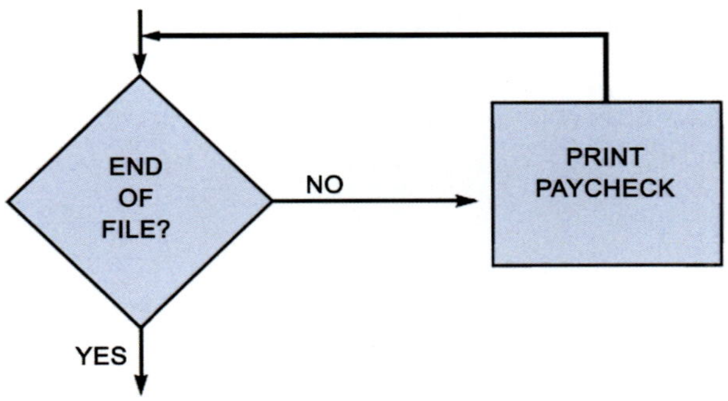

Figure 4.12. Iteration structure.

Source: Control Structures, Creative Commons License.

4.5.2. Structured English

Structured English seems to be a subset of normal English that precisely and concisely describes logical processes (Flake et al., 2000). The following principles should be kept in mind when utilizing structured English:

i. Utilize only the sequence, selection, and repetition building blocks.

ii. Use indents to increase readability.

iii. Use only a few words, such as those found in the data dictionary and the words specifically used to explain the processing rules (Chamberlin & Boyce, 1974).

An illustration of structured English that demonstrates the VERIFY ORDER procedure that was previously described. Be aware that the real logic that would be coded into the system is documented in the structured English version. Process descriptions can be more precise and clearer for users and system engineers using structured English (Astrahan & Chamberlin, 1975). Students studying programming may recognize structured English since it looks like pseudocode, a language utilized in computer design. Even though the approaches are comparable, programmers who seem concerned with coding primarily employ pseudocode as a shortcut representation for the real code. In contrast, structured English's major usage is to convey fundamental business logic. By adhering to structured English principles, process descriptions are made clear for consumers, who should validate the process' accuracy, and other analysts and programmers, who should use the descriptions to create the information system (Baker, 1998).

4.5.3. Decision Tables

All conceivable permutations of conditions and outcomes can be shown in a decision table. Analysts typically utilize decision tables to establish a process and check that they have considered all possible outcomes. Software packages such as Microsoft Excel, Word, and PowerPoint can be used to create decision tables (Kohavi, 1995).

4.5.3.1. Tables with One Condition

There are only two options when a procedure has a single condition: yes, or no. There have only been two rules because the condition is either true or false. The process criterion for starting an overtime computation could be: *Are there more than 40 hours?* In that case, a calculation is done. If not, it is not (Arnold et al., 2018).

4.5.3.2. Tables with Two Conditions

A decision table that depends upon the VERIFY ORDER business procedure needs to be created. It is crucial to ensure every alternative is mentioned while documenting a procedure. Two conditions are present in this example's process description: the product's availability and the consumer's *creditworthiness* (Pooch, 1974). The order has been accepted if both requirements are satisfied. If not, the order is declined. Making a decision table is the next step once all the criteria and outcomes are defined. Because there are two different outcomes for each condition, there are two times as many rules as conditions. One condition, for instance, generates two rules; 2 conditions, 4 rules; 3 conditions, 8 rules; and so forth. There are four possible outcomes in the two-condition instance, but only Rule 1 in combination would permit an order (Qian et al., 2008).

4.5.3.3. Tables with Three Conditions

As seen in Figure 4–12, let's say the business now chooses the credit manager may waive the customer credit criteria. There are now three conditions created by that, making a total of eight rules imaginable. The Y-N patterns must be filled in first (Huang et al., 2019). Using patterns like this is the best approach to ensure that all options are shown. In the 1st condition, a pattern of Y-Y-Y-Y accompanied by N-N-N-N is used; in the 2nd, a pattern of Y-Y-N-N is repeated; and in the third, a pattern of Y-Ns is used. No matter how many circumstances there are, the next step is essential. Each column's number indicates specific guidelines. Every rule's result should be shown, and the reasoning should be carefully examined (Huysmans et al., 2011).

Simplifying the table follows next after all the outcomes are decided. Certain rules in a multi-condition table could be redundant, duplicated, or impractical.

Take the following actions to streamline the table:

- Analyze every confluence of circumstances and results. If a rule has three circumstances, just one or two can determine the result, and the other circumstances are irrelevant.
- Mark any conditions with a dash (-), like in the first table, if they have no bearing on the conclusion.
- Combining and renumbering the rules (Miao et al., 2009).
- After completing these processes, Rules 1 and 2 may be combined, as the credit status has been acceptable under both; hence, the waiver is irrelevant. Rules 3, 4, 7, and 8 have also been combined if the product is out of supply and other requirements are irrelevant. As a result, 4 logical rules rather than 8 alternatives govern the Verify Order procedure (Vanthienen & Wets, 1994).

4.5.3.4. Multiple Outcomes

Decision tables may include greater than 2 possible outcomes in addition to several conditions. For instance, the sales promotion policy has three requirements: Did the customer utilize our business charge card, was the consumer a valued customer, and did the client place an order for 1,000 dollars or more? These circumstances can lead to one of four probable outcomes. Most tables, including this one, maybe made simpler, as was said in the section above (Pawlak & Sowinski, 1994). The following is clear from evaluating the circumstances and results:

- Rule 1 allows for 5% discounts because all three requirements are satisfied.
- A 5% discount is given if a favorite customer orders 1,000 dollars or more by Rule 2 but doesn't pay with our charge card (McCaffrey et al., 2015).
- It is possible to merge Rules 3 and 4 into one rule. Why? No matter how they pay with our credit card, preferred customers who do not place orders of 1,000 dollars or more receive only a 25-bonus voucher. Consequently, Rule 3 and Rule 4 make up one rule.
- Rules 5, 6, 7, and 8 can be merged into a single rule since the other qualifications are irrelevant if the person is not a favorite client and can only get a five-dollar bonus voucher. A dash is added whenever a condition seems unimportant, as seen in figure.

The table must resemble the one in Figure 4–12 if dashes have been included for rules that aren't even pertinent. Only four rules are left after combining and simplifying the results: Rule 1, Rule 2, Rule 3 (which combines the initial Rules 3 and 4), and Rule 4 (a collection of primary Rules 5–8). A complex set of criteria is frequently best described using decision tables. Analysts typically use decision tables because they are so convenient for the development process (Seo et al., 2021).

4.5.4. Decision Trees

A decision tree is a graphical representation of a decision table, including the conditions, steps, and rules included in the table. Decision trees are horizontal representations of the logic structure, with the roots at the left and the branches at the right. When demonstrating the system to upper management, decision trees and flowcharts are useful tools. Decision tables and decision trees produce the same results, although they do it differently. A graphic frequently serves as the most efficient form of communication (Rokach & Maimon, 2005). The criteria are located along the many branches of a decision tree, and the actions are located at the very right. It is common practice to read a decision tree from left to right. The instance comprises four terminating branches on the right end of the tree since there are two conditions and four sets of resultant actions in the example. You can use a decision table or tree to organize your options. A decision table might be helpful when dealing with multiple factors that interact with one another. In either case, a decision tree can serve as a helpful tool for describing a simple process (Kingsford & Salzberg, 2008).

4.6. PHYSICAL VERSUS LOGICAL MODELS

In addition to developing logical models for novel information systems, structured analysis tools can be used to build physical representations of existing systems. A working model of the system shows how its design intent is implemented. Following the logical model and including operational procedures and methods, the systems design phase developed a physical model of the new information system (Isakowitz et al., 1995).

4.6.1. Sequence of Models

One must look at the beginning of the systems analysis phase to know how physical and logical models are related. The physical activities were first analyzed before the logical model was developed to comprehend how the present system carried out its functions. Several systems analysts start by building a physical model of the current system, followed by a logical model. They can better comprehend the present system by taking that extra step (Jonsson et al., 1993).

4.6.2. Four-Model Approach

Numerous analysts employ a four-model technique, which entails developing not just a physical but also a logical, a physical, and an existent physical model of the system. The 4-model approach's main advantage is that it gives a clear picture of the current system because errors committed early in a system's development would impact subsequent stages of the SDLC and may generate dissatisfied clients and additional expenses (Schepers et al., 2008). Taking extra precautions to prevent such potentially expensive errors may be worthwhile. Another benefit is that a new data system's requirements are frequently comparable to those it replaces. This is particularly true when the proposal depends upon new computer technology instead of many new criteria. In such situations, converting the old system's logical model to the new one is simple (Meaney, 2005).

The additional time and expense needed to generate a physical and logical model of the existing system is the only drawback of the four-model approach. Due to the limited timelines of most projects, it may not be possible to generate the present system models. Clients and management also care less about documenting the old system because they would like to see progress on the newer one. The systems analyst needs to emphasize the value of thorough documentation and fight the urge to rush the development procedure at the risk of major difficulties down the road (Kunst et al., 2020).

ACTIVITY 4.1

Give a presentation on process description tools.

4.7. SUMMARY

A systems analyst creates graphical models throughout data and process modeling to demonstrate how the system converts data into meaningful information. The result of modeling data and processes is a logical model which will assist corporate operations and satisfy user requirements. Data and process modeling relies on three primary objects: a DFD, a data dictionary, and process descriptions.

DFDs graphically represent the circulation and transformation of data inside an information system. The DFD uses four symbols: the process symbol for data transformation; the data store symbol for data flow; the data at rest symbol for storage; and the external entity symbol for interactions with the outside world. The set of DFDs is made more digestible by applying various naming conventions, numbering schemes, organizational schemes, and annotation techniques.

The context diagram is at the summit of a pyramid-like structure, a set of DFDs. The breadth and relationships of the information system are depicted in the context diagram, but not its inner workings. An extended view of the core processes, data stores, and data flows of the data system is presented in Diagram 0 from the context diagram's process symbol, representing the entire information system. Lower-level DFDs display extra information about the information system through the leveling strategy of numbering and partitioning. Leveling keeps going until it reaches the functional primitive processes, which have been described in process descriptions and don't undergo further decomposition. To maintain uniformity and correctness, every diagram needs to be balanced. The primary documentation tool for structured analysis is the data dictionary. The data dictionary contains descriptions of all data items, information flow, data stores, entities, processes, and records. The analyst can more quickly evaluate the integrity and consistency of the data system and produce several relevant reports by centralizing the documentation in one place.

Utilizing decision tables, decision trees, and structured English, every functional primitive procedure is described. With the use of combinations of the fundamental building elements of the sequence, selection, and repetition, structured English specifies every process using a subset of Standard English. Decision trees and tables can also be used to document the logic. Structured analysis approaches can be used at one stage of systems analysis and the system's designing stage to develop a logical model. Several analysts employ a four-model method, which includes physical and logical models of the existing system and physical and logical models of the proposed new system.

REVIEW QUESTIONS

1. What is the purpose of data and process modeling?
2. How is data and process modeling used in software development?
3. How does data and process modeling improve the accuracy of a system?

4. What are the different types of data and process modeling techniques?
5. How can data and process modeling help to identify and reduce errors?
6. What tools and techniques are used to create data and process models?
7. What challenges can arise when creating data and process models?
8. What are the advantages and disadvantages of using data and process modeling?

MULTIPLE CHOICE QUESTIONS

1. What is the primary purpose of data modeling?

a. To create a visual representation of a database
b. To define business rules
c. To identify relationships between data elements
d. To monitor data usage
e. To reduce the complexity of data

2. What type of data model is used to represent a real-world concept or object?

a. Logical data model
b. Conceptual data model
c. Physical data model
d. Hierarchical data model
e. Network data model

3. What type of data model is used to create a physical implementation of the data?

a. Logical data model
b. Conceptual data model
c. Physical data model
d. Hierarchical data model
e. Network data model

4. What type of data model is used to represent relationships between data elements?

a. Logical data model
b. Conceptual data model
c. Physical data model
d. Hierarchical data model E. Network data model
e. Network data model

5. The data flow diagram (DFD) shows:

a. The flow of data
b. The processes

c. The areas where they are stored.
d. All of the above

Answers to Multiple Choice Questions

1. (a) 2. (b) 3. (c) 4. (e) 5. (d)

REFERENCES

1. Abedjan, Z., Schulze, P., & Naumann, F., (2014). DFD: Efficient functional dependency discovery. In: *Proceedings of the 23rd ACM International Conference on Conference on Information and Knowledge Management* (pp. 949–958).
2. Akundi, A., Smith, E., Tseng, T. L., & Rubio, I., (2018). INCOSE SE handbook v3. 2 and v4. 0 analysis of context diagrams set. In: *2018 Annual IEEE International Systems Conference (SysCon)* (pp. 1–5). IEEE.
3. Aldrich, J., Kostadinov, V., & Chambers, C., (2002). Alias annotations for program understanding. *ACM SIGPLAN Notices, 37*(11), 311–330.
4. Alvarado, F. L., (1999). Solving power flow problems with a Matlab implementation of the power system applications data dictionary. In: *Proceedings of the 32nd Annual Hawaii International Conference on Systems Sciences. 1999. HICSS-32; Abstracts and CD-ROM of Full Papers* (p. 7). IEEE.
5. Amamiya, M., Takesue, M., Hasegawa, R., & Mikami, H., (1987). DFM: The data flow machine highly parallel symbol manipulation. In: *Proceedings of the 1987 Fall Joint Computer Conference on Exploring Technology: Today and Tomorrow* (pp. 602–611).
6. Anderson, J. R., Qin, Y., Sohn, M. H., Stenger, V. A., & Carter, C. S., (2003). An information-processing model of the BOLD response in symbol manipulation tasks. *Psychonomic Bulletin & Review, 10*(2), 241–261.
7. Arnold, J. G., Bieger, K., White, M. J., Srinivasan, R., Dunbar, J. A., & Allen, P. M., (2018). Use of decision tables to simulate management in SWAT+. *Water, 10*(6), 713.
8. Astrahan, M. M., & Chamberlin, D. D., (1975). Implementation of a structured English query language. *Communications of the ACM, 18*(10), 580–588.
9. Baker, K., (1998). Structured English immersion. *Phi Delta Kappan, 80*(3), 199.
10. Bal, J., (1998). Process analysis tools for process improvement. *The TQM Magazine, 1*, 1–13.
11. Barsalou, L. W., (2019). Flexibility, structure, and linguistic vagary in concepts: Manifestations of a compositional system of perceptual symbols. In: *Theories of Memory* (pp. 29–101). Psychology Press.
12. Batini, C., Nardelli, E., & Tamassia, R., (1986). A layout algorithm for data flow diagrams. *IEEE Transactions on Software Engineering*, (4), 538–546.
13. Bleistein, S. J., Cox, K., & Verner, J., (2006). Validating strategic alignment of

organizational IT requirements using goal modeling and problem diagrams. *Journal of Systems and Software, 79*(3), 362–378.

14. Buck, J. T., & Lee, E. A., (1993). Scheduling dynamic dataflow graphs with bounded memory using the token flow model. In: *1993 IEEE International Conference on Acoustics, Speech, and Signal Processing* (Vol. 1, pp. 429–432). IEEE.
15. Butler, G., Grogono, P., Shinghal, R., & Tjandra, I., (1995). Retrieving information from data flow diagrams. In: *Proceedings of 2nd Working Conference on Reverse Engineering* (pp. 22–29). IEEE.
16. Byun, J. W., & Li, N., (2008). Purpose based access control for privacy protection in relational database systems. *The VLDB Journal, 17*(4), 603–619.
17. Carney, D., Çetintemel, U., Cherniack, M., Convey, C., Lee, S., Seidman, G., & Stonebraker, M., (2002). Monitoring streams—A new class of data management applications. In: *VLDB'02: Proceedings of the 28th International Conference on Very Large Databases* (pp. 215–226). Morgan Kaufmann.
18. Cattell, R., (2011). Scalable SQL and NoSQL data stores. *ACM SIGMOD Record, 39*(4), 12–27.
19. Chamberlin, D. D., & Boyce, R. F., (1974). SEQUEL: A structured English query language. In: *Proceedings of the 1974 ACM SIGFIDET (Now SIGMOD) Workshop on Data Description, Access and Control* (pp. 249–264).
20. Ciolfi, F. M., Fdili, A. S., & Mackay, W. E., (2018). Knotation: Exploring and documenting choreographic processes. In: *Proceedings of the 2018 CHI Conference on Human Factors in Computing Systems* (pp. 1–12).
21. Cooper, B. F., Sample, N., Franklin, M. J., Hjaltason, G. R., & Shadmon, M., (2001). A fast index for semi-structured data. In: *VLDB* (Vol. 1, pp. 341–350).
22. Cruzes, D. S., Jaatun, M. G., Bernsmed, K., & Tøndel, I. A., (2018). Challenges and experiences with applying Microsoft threat modeling in agile development projects. In: *2018 25th Australasian Software Engineering Conference (ASWEC)* (pp. 111–120). IEEE.
23. Dennis, J. B., (1974). First version of a data flow procedure language. In: *Programming Symposium* (pp. 362–376). Springer, Berlin, Heidelberg.
24. Echauz, J. R., & Vachtsevanos, G. J., (1995). Fuzzy grading system. *IEEE Transactions on Education, 38*(2), 158–165.
25. Ehrensberger, M., (1977). Data dictionary: More on the impossible dream. In: *Proceedings of the June 13–16, 1977, National Computer Conference* (pp. 9–11).
26. Ellis, J., Hetherington, R., Lovell, M., McConaghy, J., & Viczko, M., (2012). Draw me a picture, tell me a story: Evoking memory and supporting analysis through pre-interview drawing activities. *Alberta Journal of Educational Research, 58*(4), 488–508.
27. Fanti, G., Pihur, V., & Erlingsson, Ú., (2015). *Building a RAPPOR with the Unknown: Privacy-Preserving Learning of Associations and Data Dictionaries*. arXiv preprint arXiv:1503.01214.

28. Figl, K., Recker, J., & Mendling, J., (2013). A study on the effects of routing symbol design on process model comprehension. *Decision Support Systems, 54*(2), 1104–1118.

29. Flake, S., Müller, W., & Ruf, J., (2000). Structured English for model checking specification. In: *MBMV* (pp. 99–108).

30. Gopalan, P., Huang, C., Simitci, H., & Yekhanin, S., (2012). On the locality of codeword symbols. *IEEE Transactions on Information Theory, 58*(11), 6925–6934.

31. Gorla, N., Pu, H. C., & Rom, W. O., (1995). Evaluation of process tools in systems analysis. *Information and Software Technology, 37*(2), 119–126.

32. Grolinger, K., Higashino, W. A., Tiwari, A., & Capretz, M. A., (2013). Data management in cloud environments: NoSQL and NewSQL data stores. *Journal of Cloud Computing: Advances, Systems and Applications, 2*(1), 1–24.

33. Grulich-Henn, J., Wagner, V., Thon, A., Schober, E., Marg, W., Kapellen, T. M., & Holl, R. W., (2010). Entities and frequency of neonatal diabetes: Data from the diabetes documentation and quality management system (DPV). *Diabetic Medicine, 27*(6), 709–712.

34. Güngör, A., (2006). Evaluation of connection types in design for disassembly (DFD) using analytic network process. *Computers & Industrial Engineering, 50*(1–2), 35–54.

35. Guo, F., & Gershenson, J. K., (2004). A comparison of modular product design methods based on improvement and iteration. In: *International Design Engineering Technical Conferences and Computers and Information in Engineering Conference* (Vol. 46962, pp. 261–269).

36. Guthrie, J. T., Weber, S., & Kimmerly, N., (1993). Searching documents: Cognitive processes and deficits in understanding graphs, tables, and illustrations. *Contemporary Educational Psychology, 18*(2), 186–221.

37. Harel, G., & Kaput, J., (2002). The role of conceptual entities and their symbols in building advanced mathematical concepts. In: *Advanced Mathematical Thinking* (pp. 82–94). Springer, Dordrecht.

38. Hinton, G. E., (1990). Preface to the special issue on connectionist symbol processing. *Artificial Intelligence, 46*(1, 2), 1–4.

39. Huang, Z., Li, J., Dai, W., & Lin, R., (2019). Generalized multi-scale decision tables with multi-scale decision attributes. *International Journal of Approximate Reasoning, 115*, 194–208.

40. Huysmans, J., Dejaeger, K., Mues, C., Vanthienen, J., & Baesens, B., (2011). An empirical evaluation of the comprehensibility of decision table, tree and rule based predictive models. *Decision Support Systems, 51*(1), 141–154.

41. Ibrahim, R., (2010). *Formalization of the Data Flow Diagram Rules for Consistency Check.* arXiv preprint arXiv:1011.0278.

42. Isakowitz, T., Schocken, S., & Lucas, Jr. H. C., (1995). Toward a logical/physical theory of spreadsheet modeling. *ACM Transactions on Information Systems (TOIS),13*(1),

1–37.

43. Jeong, S., & Lee, J., (2015). Two dimensional inter-symbol interference compensation for holographic data storage. *Journal of The Institute of Electronics and Information Engineers, 52*(6), 10–14.
44. Jiang, T., Bu, C., Zhu, Y., & Wu, X., (2022). Combining embedding-based and symbol-based methods for entity alignment. *Pattern Recognition, 124*, 108433.
45. Jonsson, J., Norberg, T., Carlsson, L., Gustafsson, C., & Wold, S., (1993). Quantitative sequence-activity models (QSAM)—tools for sequence design. *Nucleic Acids Research, 21*(3), 733–739.
46. Kahn, B. K., & Lumsden, E. W., (1983). A user-oriented framework for data dictionary systems. *ACM SIGMIS Database: The DATABASE for Advances in Information Systems, 15*(1), 28–36.
47. Kettinger, W. J., Teng, J. T., & Guha, S., (1997). Business process change: A study of methodologies, techniques, and tools. *MIS Quarterly,* 55–80.
48. Kingsford, C., & Salzberg, S. L., (2008). What are decision trees? *Nature Biotechnology, 26*(9), 1011–1013.
49. Kohavi, R., (1995). The power of decision tables. In: *European Conference on Machine Learning* (pp. 174–189). Springer, Berlin, Heidelberg.
50. Koren, I., & Klamma, R., (2018). The exploitation of openAPI documentation for the generation of web frontends. In: *Companion Proceedings of the Web Conference 2018* (pp. 781–787).
51. Kunst, N., Wilson, E. C., Glynn, D., Alarid-Escudero, F., Baio, G., Brennan, A., & Heath, A., (2020). Computing the expected value of sample information efficiently: Practical guidance and recommendations for four model-based methods. *Value in Health, 23*(6), 734–742.
52. Kurgan, L. A., & Musilek, P., (2006). A survey of knowledge discovery and data mining process models. *The Knowledge Engineering Review, 21*(1), 1–24.
53. Kusters, R. J., & Wijers, G. M., (1993). On the practical use of CASE-tools: Results of a survey. In: *Proceedings of 6th International Workshop on Computer-Aided Software Engineering* (pp. 2–10). IEEE.
54. Lawson, R. M., & Richards, J., (2010). Modular design for high-rise buildings. *Proceedings of the Institution of Civil Engineers-Structures and Buildings, 163*(3), 151–164.
55. Lederer, A. L., & Mahaney, R. C., (1996). Using CASE tools in strategic IS planning. *Information Systems Management, 13*(4), 47–51.
56. Leoni, M. D., Munoz-Gama, J., Carmona, J., & Van, D. A. W. M., (2014). Decomposing alignment-based conformance checking of data-aware process models. In: *OTM Confederated International Conferences "On the Move to Meaningful Internet Systems"* (pp. 3–20). Springer, Berlin, Heidelberg.

57. Li, Q., & Chen, Y. L., (2009). Data flow diagram. In: *Modeling and Analysis of Enterprise and Information Systems* (pp. 85–97). Springer, Berlin, Heidelberg.
58. Lin, H. Y., & Tzeng, W. G., (2011). A secure erasure code-based cloud storage system with secure data forwarding. *IEEE Transactions on Parallel and Distributed Systems, 23*(6), 995–1003.
59. Liu, J., Song, H., & Kumar, B. V., (2003). Dual segmented Kalman filters-based symbol timing recovery for low-SNR partial response data storage channels. In: *GLOBECOM'03. IEEE Global Telecommunications Conference (IEEE Cat. No. 03CH37489)* (Vol. 7, pp. 4084–4090). IEEE.
60. Mariscal, G., Marban, O., & Fernandez, C., (2010). A survey of data mining and knowledge discovery process models and methodologies. *The Knowledge Engineering Review, 25*(2), 137–166.
61. Martin, P. W., (2008). Online access to court records-from documents to data, particulars to patterns. *Vill. L. Rev., 53*, 855.
62. McCaffrey, N., Agar, M., Harlum, J., Karnon, J., Currow, D., & Eckermann, S., (2015). Better informing decision making with multiple outcomes cost-effectiveness analysis under uncertainty in cost-disutility space. *PLoS One, 10*(3), e0115544.
63. Meaney, P. M., (2005). In: Paulsen, K. D., & Gilman, L. C., (eds.), *Alternative Breast Imaging: Four Model-Based Approaches* (Vol. 1, pp. 1–24). New York: Springer.
64. Miao, D. Q., Zhao, Y., Yao, Y. Y., Li, H. X., & Xu, F. F., (2009). Relative reducts in consistent and inconsistent decision tables of the Pawlak rough set model. *Information Sciences, 179*(24), 4140–4150.
65. Nilsson, N. J., (2007). The physical symbol system hypothesis: Status and prospects. *50 Years of Artificial Intelligence*, 9–17.
66. Osterweil, L. J., & Fosdick, L. D., (1976). DAVE—A validation error detection and documentation system for Fortran programs. *Software: Practice and Experience, 6*(4), 473–486.
67. Pawlak, Z., & Sowinski, R., (1994). Rough set approach to multi-attribute decision analysis. *European Journal of Operational Research, 72*(3), 443–459.
68. Pooch, U. W., (1974). Translation of decision tables. *ACM Computing Surveys (CSUR), 6*(2), 125–151.
69. Poranen, T., Mäkinen, E., & Nummenmaa, J., (2003). How to draw a sequence diagram. *SPLST, 3*, 17, 18.
70. Protsko, L. B., Sorenson, P. G., & Demblay, J. P., (1984). *Automatic Generation of Data Flow Diagrams from a Requirements Specification Language, 1,* 1–10.
71. Qian, Y., Liang, J., Li, D., Zhang, H., & Dang, C., (2008). Measures for evaluating the decision performance of a decision table in rough set theory. *Information Sciences, 178*(1), 181–202.
72. Rashid, S. M., McCusker, J. P., Pinheiro, P., Bax, M. P., Santos, H. O., Stingone, J. A., & McGuinness, D. L., (2020). The semantic data dictionary–an approach for

describing and annotating data. *Data Intelligence, 2*(4), 443–486.

73. Reps, T., Horwitz, S., & Sagiv, M., (1995). Precise interprocedural dataflow analysis via graph reachability. In: *Proceedings of the 22nd ACM SIGPLAN-SIGACT Symposium on Principles of Programming Languages* (pp. 49–61).
74. Roberts, D., (1994). Defining electronic records, documents and data. *Archives and Manuscripts, 22*(1), 14–26.
75. Rokach, L., & Maimon, O., (2005). Decision trees. In: *Data Mining and Knowledge Discovery Handbook* (pp. 165–192). Springer, Boston, MA.
76. Sagiv, M., Reps, T., & Horwitz, S., (1995). Precise interprocedural dataflow analysis with applications to constant propagation. In: *Colloquium on Trees in Algebra and Programming* (pp. 651–665). Springer, Berlin, Heidelberg.
77. Sakamoto, J. G., & Ball, F. W., (1982). Supporting business systems planning studies with the DB/DC data dictionary. *IBM Systems Journal, 21*(1), 54–80.
78. Salama, T., Salah, A., Moselhi, O., & Al-Hussein, M., (2017). Near optimum selection of module configuration for efficient modular construction. *Automation in Construction, 83*, 316–329.
79. Sansone, S. A., Gonzalez-Beltran, A., Rocca-Serra, P., Alter, G., Grethe, J. S., Xu, H., & Ohno-Machado, L., (2017). DATS, the data tag suite to enable discoverability of datasets. *Scientific Data, 4*(1), 1–8.
80. Schepers, J., Ceulemans, E., & Van, M. I., (2008). Selecting among multi-mode partitioning models of different complexities: A comparison of four model selection criteria. *Journal of Classification, 25*(1), 67–85.
81. Seifermann, S., Heinrich, R., Werle, D., & Reussner, R., (2022). Detecting violations of access control and information flow policies in data flow diagrams. *Journal of Systems and Software, 184*, 111138.
82. Seo, M., Furukawa, T. A., Veroniki, A. A., Pillinger, T., Tomlinson, A., Salanti, G., & Efthimiou, O., (2021). The kilim plot: A tool for visualizing network meta-analysis results for multiple outcomes. *Research Synthesis Methods, 12*(1), 86–95.
83. Shen, J., Nguyen, P., Wu, Y., Chen, Z., Chen, M. X., Jia, Y., & Rondon, P., (2019). *Lingvo: A Modular and Scalable Framework for Sequence-to-Sequence Modeling*. arXiv preprint arXiv:1902.08295.
84. Sparrow, J. M., Frost, N. A., Pantelides, E. P., & Laidlaw, D. A. H., (2000). Decimalization of the oxford clinical cataract classification and grading system. *Ophthalmic Epidemiology, 7*(1), 49–60.
85. Sullivan, L. H., (1989). Dataflow diagrams. *Just Enough Structured Analysis,* 146–195.
86. Takabayashi, M., Okamoto, A., Tomita, A., & Bunsen, M., (2011). Symbol error characteristics of hybrid-modulated holographic data storage by intensity and multi-phase modulation. *Japanese Journal of Applied Physics, 50*(9S1), 09ME05.
87. Tavakoli, M. S., Mariappan, J., & Huang, J., (2003). Design for assembly versus design for disassembly: A comparison of guidelines. In: *ASME International Mechanical*

Engineering Congress and Exposition (Vol. 37122, pp. 389–395).

88. Turcu, C., Prodan, R., Cerlinca, M., & Cerlinca, T., (2009). Object-oriented solutions for information storage on RFID tags. *Development and Implementation of RFID Technology, 1*, 1–17.
89. Turner, V., (1977). Process, system, and symbol: A new anthropological synthesis. *Daedalus,* 61–80.
90. Uhrowczik, P. P., (1973). Data dictionary/directories. *IBM Systems Journal, 12*(4), 332–350.
91. Vanthienen, J., & Wets, G., (1994). From decision tables to expert system shells. *Data & Knowledge Engineering, 13*(3), 265–282.
92. Wadge, W. W., & Ashcroft, E. A., (1985). *Lucid, the Dataflow Programming Language* (Vol. 303). London: Academic Press.
93. Wang, J., & Kumar, A., (2005). A framework for document-driven workflow systems. In: *International Conference on Business Process Management* (pp. 285–301). Springer, Berlin, Heidelberg.
94. Whittington, K., (2008). *The Cruciform Womb: Process, Symbol and Salvation in Bodleian Library MS. Ashmole, 1*, 1–5.
95. Wille, R., (1989). Lattices in data analysis: How to draw them with a computer. In: *Algorithms and Order* (pp. 33–58). Springer, Dordrecht.
96. Xu, J., Chen, E., & Chen, V., (2021). Energy-efficient data symbol detection via boosted learning for multi-actuator data storage systems. In: *2021 IEEE International Symposium on Circuits and Systems (ISCAS)* (pp. 1–5). IEEE.
97. Yampolskiy, M., Horvath, P., Koutsoukos, X. D., Xue, Y., & Sztipanovits, J., (2012). Systematic analysis of cyber-attacks on CPS-evaluating applicability of DFD-based approach. In: *2012 5th International Symposium on Resilient Control Systems* (pp. 55–62). IEEE.
98. Yang, B., & Mitchell, T., (2016). *Joint Extraction of Events and Entities Within a Document Context*. arXiv preprint arXiv:1609.03632.
99. Zhang, J., & Zhu, Y., (2015). A method based on graphic entity for visualizing complex map symbols on the web. *Cartography and Geographic Information Science, 42*(1), 44–53.
100. Zhu, J., Nie, Z., Wen, J. R., Zhang, B., & Ma, W. Y., (2006). Simultaneous record detection and attribute labeling in web data extraction. In: *Proceedings of the 12th ACM SIGKDD International Conference on Knowledge Discovery and Data Mining* (pp. 494–503).

CHAPTER 5

ARCHITECTURE DESIGN

UNIT INTRODUCTION

The architecture design, which details the hardware, software, and core network of the system, is a crucial part of the design process. Functional efficiency, safety, and social and political needs are the main criteria influencing architecture design. The architecture design and the software and hardware configuration are among the outcomes of the architecture design process. Most data systems currently use more than one computer (Wang & Dagli, 2012). For instance, an internet program on one computer browser can communicate with the web application (and perhaps other computers) through the internet. Any computer might have a Visual Basic application installed as part of a system that only communicates with other devices on a company's servers, such as a database system. Establishing the design approach, which outlines how the computer equipment will be divided among several processors and what technology, operating system (OS), and software applications will be utilized for each one, is a crucial element of the design process (Shaw & Clements, 2006).

Because developing the system's architecture can be challenging, many firms use the talents of seasoned, knowledgeable system architects (advisors or personnel) with expertise in the field. The important aspects of architectural design are considered in this chapter. It seems crucial to remember that doing it correctly requires much knowledge (Hofmeister et al., 2007). The unusable needs determined initially in the analysis stage are crucial to the design of the architecture. These criteria are reevaluated and improved into more specific needs that affect the system's architecture. In this chapter, we first define the most prevalent architecture, the client-server architecture, and then describe how developers think about architectural applications. The server-based and client-based architectures are briefly covered (Tang et al., 2009). We also talk about recent advancements in system design, such as virtualization and cloud services. The consequences for architecture design are then discussed as we look at how the unusable generic objectives from the evaluation stage are developed into more precise needs. We then look at the parameters for any hardware and software (such as a system database) required to facilitate the information system's development (Kruchten et al., 2006).

Learning Objective

After studying this unit, you will be able to:

- Construct a computer-based information system with proficiency.
- Identify and describe the different stages in the system development life cycle.
- Identify the factors that prompt users to change their requests.
- Identify and describe the various components of a feasibility study.
- Identify the key factors to consider when evaluating a candidate system.
- Plan and implement strategies for ensuring the success of a system.

Key Terms

- Architecture design
- Client server architectural design
- Virtualization
- Cloud computing
- Architectural components
- Client-server tiers

5.1. COMPONENTS OF AN ARCHITECTURE DESIGN

The goal of architecture design is to decide how the system's hardware components will be allocated to the software applications of the data system. To comprehend how the program can be broken down into separate sections, we first explore the program's main features in this part. Next, we quickly go through the main categories of hardware that the program can be installed. The client-server design is the most prevalent one; therefore, even if there are many ways the application programs can be organized on the hardware devices, we concentrate on it in this section (Perry & Wolf, 1992).

5.1.1. Architectural Components

The hardware and software make up the bulk architectural components of any system. The primary software elements of the system under development must be determined, and these elements must then be assigned to the several hardware components that the system will use. There are numerous ways to connect all these elements (Shaw et al., 1995).

Four fundamental characteristics can be used to categorize all software systems. Storage of data is the first. Whether it is a little file, like a list of chemicals that are not permitted to use at home for a prolonged period, or a sizable database that houses the human resources data of an organization, most data systems need the information to be saved and accessed (Thayer, 2002). These are the data objects that the ERDs list. The second role is shared data logic, which is the computation necessary to access data and frequently entails database searches in structured query language (SQL). The application logic—the logic described in the DFDs, use scenarios, and technical specifications are the third function. The users are informed, and their requests are accepted by the presentation logic, which is the fourth activity (the user interface (UI)). The fundamental components of any data system perform the following operations (Tibermacine et al., 2016):

i. Data storage;

ii. Data access logic;

iii. Application logic;

iv. Display logic.

Client computers, processors, and the network connecting them are a network's three main hardware parts. Client computers, which the user uses as input-output devices, are often a laptop or desktop computers but may also be mobile gadgets, cell phones, interfaces with specialized functions, and so on (Plasil & Visnovsky, 2002). Servers are often bigger computers with several users employed to keep software and data that anyone with user credentials can retrieve. The system that links the computers can be at any speed, from dial-up modems or slow cell phones to fast, always-on internet connections like cable box, DSL, or T1 circuits and extremely fast, very often Ethernet, T3, or ATM lines. It can also be a moderate packet-switching system (Kazman et al., 1996).

5.1.2. Client-Server Architectures

Client-server designs, which aim to equalize the operations between client computers and one or more server systems, are currently being used or adopted by most companies. The server oversees information storage and data access logic in these systems, while the client oversees display logic. Depending on the situation, the server, customer, or both may house the program logic (Figure 5.1). It is referred to as a thick or fat client if the client in Figure 5.1 included all or much of the program logic (Franks et al., 1995).

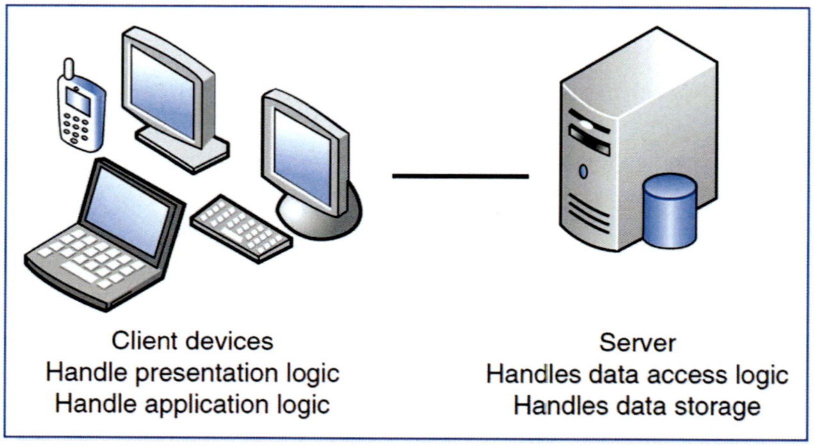

Figure 5.1. A client-server design that is two-tiered.

Source: Vincent P Wade, Creative Commons License.

Because of their cheaper overhead and simpler administration, thin clients—which only include a small fraction of the application programs are currently very popular. For instance, many Internet systems are created with the web server handling all the software architecture, all the shared data logic, and all the information storage. In contrast, the Web browser merely handles representation employing languages like JavaScript (Wood, 1995).

Four key advantages of client-server architectures should be noted. They are adjustable in the first place. Therefore, raising or lowering the servers' processing and storage capacities is simple. You can easily add a server if one gets too busy such that several servers are utilized to handle the application programs, shared data logic, or storage systems. You can improve in small amounts at a gradually increasing cost (Lewis, 1995).

Second, a wide variety of servers and clients can be supported by client-server systems. You can link computers with several OS to avoid being tied to a single supplier. Customers can select the kind of computer they desire (e.g., connecting Windows computers and Apple Macintoshes on the common network) (Bertocco et al., 1998).

A software system known as *Middleware* is used to translate between programs from various suppliers. Both the server and client computers are installed with *Middleware* software. The *Middleware,* which helps the server software, receives messages from the client program and can restructure them into a format that the software can understand (Sinha, 1992).

Thirdly, it is easy to distinguish between the functionality, application logic logically, and shared data in thin client-server designs that use internet protocols and construct each so that it is relatively independent. To indicate the appearance of the page on the screen, for instance, the presentation logic can be created in HTML or XML (Milosavljević & Tešendić, 2010).

Basic program statements connect several interface elements to application processing units that perform different functions. The application logic is unaffected by changes to these HTML or XML files that define the interface. The presentation logic and information, which are kept in databases and accessible by SQL queries, may be changed without modifying the application logic; this is also true (Adler, 1995).

In a client-server design, a server failure only affects the programs that depend on it. The applications can then be recovered after the failing server has been switched out and restored. Additionally, client-server designs have some severe drawbacks, with their intricacy ranking as the most significant. Client-side and server-side programs make up every program in client-server computers (Menascé & Gomaa, 2000). It is more challenging to write this program than the conventional all-in-one program used in server-based designs. It is also more challenging to update the entire system to the latest software version. When using client-server designs, you must upgrade all customers and servers and ensure that all machines have the upgrades installed (Hudli & Pidaparti, 1995).

5.1.3. Client-Server Tiers

The software application can be divided between the server and the client in various ways. A typical configuration is the one shown in Figure 5.2.

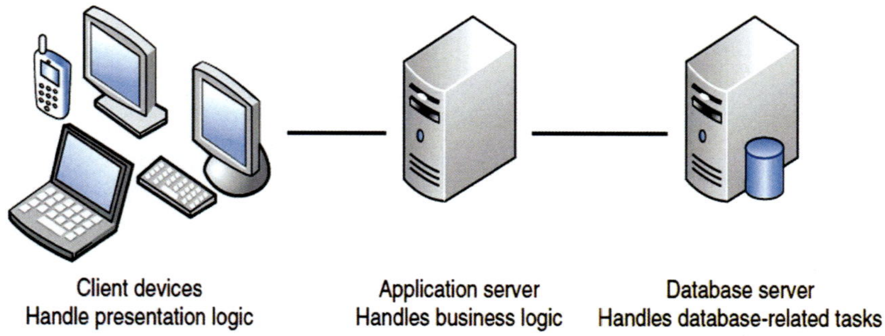

Figure 5.2. Client-server design that is three-tiered.

Source: Vincent P. Wade, Creative Commons License.

In this instance, the client oversees the program and representation while the server oversees the information. Because only two computer systems are used—clients and servers—this design is referred to as a two-tiered one. As seen in Figure 5.2, a three-tiered design employs three sets of computers. In this instance, the client computer's program oversees display processing, an application server oversees application programs, and a different database server oversees shared data logic and information storage (Gallaugher & Ramanathan, 1996).

The UI often has a common graphical UI and operates on a desktop Computer or workstation. One or more independent modules operating on a database server or work area may make up the application logic. The logic for data access and storage is finally housed in a relational DBMS operating on a database server (Thomas et al., 2009). An "n-tier architecture" is the name given to a general design where the central tier might be partitioned into tiers. The central tier of the application's workload is distributed over several levels of more sophisticated server systems using an n-tiered architecture. These architectural designs are frequently used in modern Internet e-commerce platforms (Ruffer et al., 1995).

Examine Figure 5.3 – a browser program of the Client's computer sends HTTP requests to the Web server(s) to see pages, and the Web server(s) react with HTML files, allowing the customer to see the goods for sale. Programs on the application server(s) are accessed when necessary to enable the customer to add products to a shopping cart, ascertain product cost and availability, calculate inventory costs, local taxes, and delivery charges, calculate purchase costs, approve payments, etc. (Chengalur-Smith & Duchessi, 2000). The application server(s) hold these components of core functionality or sophisticated processing, and all applications have access. For instance, the price-fixing business logic utilized by the e-commerce website may be applied to the cash register program that requires item price searches. Applications requiring specific business rules can employ customizable business logic (Subramanian & Lacity, 1997). The database server(s) oversee the data elements of the system. Since every one of the four factors is distinct, it is simple to distribute the various components over various servers and segregate the application programs between a server focused on the Web. A server focused on the enterprise (Schultheis & Bock, 1994).

An n-tiered client-server design is more adaptable than a two-tiered architecture (or a three-tiered with a two-tiered architecture) because it isolates the programming that takes place to balance the burden on the various servers effectively. Figure 5.3 shows three different server types, which gives us more power than if we employed a single server in a two-tiered system (Post & Kagan, 2005). If the web server is found to be overloaded, we can easily swap it out with a more physical server or add additional application servers to distribute the load. On the other hand, if we find that the database server isn't being utilized much, we might put information from some other program on it. When opposed to a two-tiered design, an n-tiered architecture has two main drawbacks (or a three-tiered one with a two-tiered one). The setting first increases the network's load. Figures 5.1–5.3 show that the n-tiered model necessitates greater interactions between the servers, increasing network activity and increasing the network (Borthick & Roth, 1994).

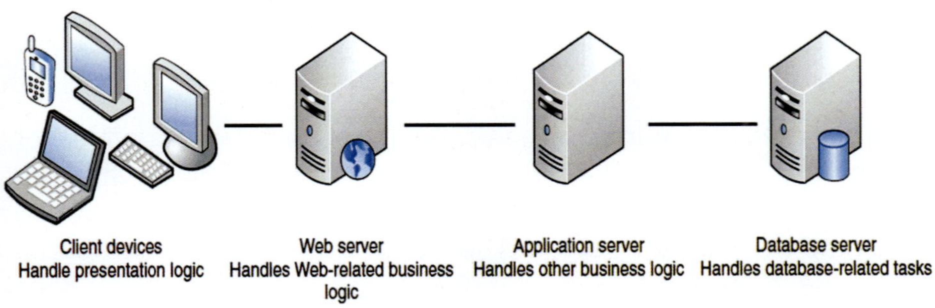

Figure 5.3. Client-server design that is n-tiered.

Source: Baeldung, Creative Commons License.

Second, software development and testing are substantially more challenging since more devices must successfully interact in n-tiered designs than in two-tiered structures (Aries et al., 2002).

5.1.4. Some Advance Architectures

Today, client-server architecture is the most common type of architecture. Two more architectures are employed in a few less widespread instances (Miller, 1997).

5.2. SERVER-BASED ARCHITECTURES

The original computing designs were server-based, with the server—typically a centralized monolithic computer—handling each of the four application activities. Users could communicate with the server computer using the customers, typically monitors. The customers recorded keystrokes, forwarded them to the server for functioning, and obeyed commands from the server regarding what ash to broadcast (Figure 5.4) (Filibeli et al., 2007).

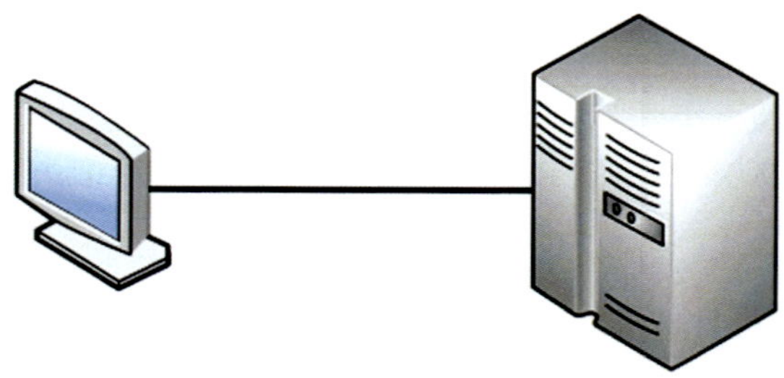

Figure 5.4. A server-based design.

Source: Arif Ridho Lubis, Creative Commons License.

This architecture is quite basic, but it frequently works effectively. The server develops and stores application software, and one computer houses all the information. Communication goes through the same centralized server. Therefore, there is only one control point. Due to the single computer of a system hosting all components, software development and management are made simpler OS and application programs (Gu et al., 2021). The earliest architecture employed in computer systems was server-based, but other options became available with the advancement of technology and software. Early server-based systems had the critical issue that the server performed all activity. Server computers were overburdened and incapable of efficiently handling increased user requests and the need for more applications. Response times slowed and IS management was forced to update the server computer at an escalating cost. Early on, moving to a bigger server computer was expensive and usually necessitated a behemoth. Only significant, pricey chunks of capacity growth were available (Sun et al., 2007).

The server-based architecture is still an option for modern architecture. Today's virtual desktop architecture frequently uses the server-based computing platform known as zero clients or ultrathin clients (VDI). A primary zero client computer is a compact box with an Ethernet connection, a mouse, a keyboard, and a monitor that links to a server remotely (Fujimaki et al., 2002). It is all hosted on the server, including the OS (an operating system) and any software the client uses. Both wireless and wired connections are available to the server. There are numerous advantages of zero-client computing.

In comparison with fat client installations, power consumption can be greatly reduced. With more businesses looking at green computing, this advantage is becoming more significant (Miano et al., 2019). The used equipment costs much less than Computers or thin network equipment. Malware cannot affect the client device since it lacks any software. The zero-client computing architecture offers an effective and safe method of distributing software to authorized customers. In VDI setups, the administration is simple, and numerous virtual PCs can run on server-class hardware, drastically decreasing the number of physical PCs that need to be purchased and maintained. Additionally, the server-based zero-client paradigm restricts the client computer's non-business usage, for example, no use of Facebook, no Farmville, etc. (Kim et al., 2018).

Did you Know?

Architectural design is a discipline that focuses on covering and meeting the needs and demands, to create living spaces, using certain tools and especially, creativity.

5.3. CLIENT-BASED ARCHITECTURES

In client-based designs, the server and clients are both computer servers connected to the same local area network. The display logic, application programming, and data service logic are all handled by the software applications of the client computer; the server only serves as information storage (Figure 5.5).

When there are few users or demands for data access, this basic architecture frequently performs admirably. All information on the server must be transferred to the customer for interpretation, which is the core issue with customer-based architecture. Assume, for instance, that the customer wants to present a report of all the employees who have life insurance via the organization (Fan et al., 2000). The customer conducts the inquiry to find every record that meets the information sought by the customer after receiving all the information from the server, where the personnel database is kept across the network. The shared data processing would be carried out on the server in the previous computing systems we have studied, and the search findings would be sent to the customer. The client system executes the logic of information access in the customer-based computing platform. As a result, processing cannot begin until the complete database has been sent to the client. As a result, the network and the computer power of the client may be overloaded (Abdmouleh et al., 2004).

Figure 5.5. A client-based design.

Source: Arif Ridho Lubis, Creative Commons License.

5.4. DEVELOPMENT IN ARCHITECTURAL CONFIGURATIONS

Numerous new architectural possibilities have emerged due to technology, programming, and networking developments. It is outside the purview of this book to discuss each of these choices in depth. We'll give a brief overview of virtualization and cloud services, two innovations now receiving significant attention (van der Hoek et al., 2001).

5.4.1. Virtualization

In the context of technology, this phrase describes establishing a virtual server or memory device. If you have divided the hard drive of a computer into further than independent hard disk, you could be acquainted with this idea. Even though your system only has one actual hard disk, you consider each segmented, "virtual" drive as if it was a separate physical storage system. As we talk about virtual servers, storage virtualization, network virtualization, and other forms of virtualization today, this phrase has developed into a term (Lombardi & Di Pietro, 2011).

Partitioning database hardware into smaller virtual machines is known as server virtualization. The actual server is divided into several virtual worlds using the software, often known as virtual or personal servers. The main drawback of earlier server-based systems, which relied on a single, costly, massive, inflexible computer, is now overcome (Bourguiba et al., 2013). Physical hardware equipment can now be utilized to host several virtual clients that co-exist on the same physical host but are separate from one another. Every virtual server has its computer program and can restart without affecting the other virtualized resources. A group of virtual servers requires less hardware than equivalent real servers, which lowers expenses. This design can reduce functional costs by maximizing the use of the physical server (Baroncelli et al., 2010).

Over 75% of mid-sized organizations plan to adopt virtualization technology extensively by 2012, according to the latest Gartner survey of mid-sized organizations. These firms claim to be actively looking for ways to reduce costs, boost efficiency, and improve reliability. They have discovered that server virtualization is a key factor in achieving these objectives (Luo, 2010). In storage virtualization, many network data stores are combined into what seems to be a single memory facility. Storage virtualization is used by a storage area network (SAN) to build a fast subnet of linked storage systems. Tasks like backing, archiving, and recovering are simpler and quicker in this context (García-Valls et al., 2014).

5.4.2. Cloud Computing

Organizations no longer need to own, operate, and govern their computing architecture. Anything from computing power to architecture, apps, business operations, and human interactions can be provided as a service whenever and wherever it is needed. This is the emergence of cloud technology (Wang et al., 2010). The infrastructure, networking, memory, applications, and connections that combine to supply various parts of computation as a service make up the "cloud" in cloud technology. Based on customer requests, cloud services comprise the distribution of programs, architecture, and data through the World Wide Web (either as individual elements or as a full framework) (Grossman, 2009). Personal, public, and community clouds are the three ways cloud technology can be used. With public clouds, little to no governance over the core technological architecture is exercised while services are delivered "as a service" over the Internet. While private clouds are implemented through a company network or a leased database server, they provide functions and activities "as a service." The strength of both public and personal clouds is combined in cloud infrastructure (Marston et al., 2011). Depending on their needs, tasks, and activities are assigned to personal or public clouds. Cloud computing is now in its infancy as a technology. The cloud technology concept has various benefits, according to its supporters. First, depending on usage, the available resources when using the cloud can be raised or lowered (Mirashe & Kalyankar, 2010).

The cloud can be upgraded during times of maximum demand and degraded during times of lower demand because of this property, known as flexibility. When more customers are added or the demands of the application change, cloud-based applications can be upgraded. Second, users of cloud services can easily acquire cloud resources. With the cloud service supplier, agreements are designed for a specific proportion of computation, memory, programs, processes, or other resources. These commodities can be surrendered once used if no longer needed (Sadiku et al., 2014).

Remember

Over 75 % of mid-sized organizations plan to adopt virtualization technology extensively by 2012, according to the latest Gartner survey of mid-sized organizations.

Third, standardized APIs are often included in cloud services (application program interfaces). This indicates that the companies have regulated how applications or data sources talk to one another. The customer can make connections between cloud services more quickly thanks to these capabilities. The architecture of cloud computing also makes it possible for users to be charged for services as they are consumed. Like how you use power in your residence, clients only pay for consumed resources when they use the cloud. From a cost perspective, cloud technology is quite appealing because of this capability (Wei & Blake, 2010).

Suppliers of cloud technology use hybridization as a crucial emerging factor. Meanwhile, cloud technology users aim to transfer IT programs, services, and technology using a charge per use. Businesses of all sizes are interested in and intrigued by cloud technology. The potential of virtualization is transformed into quantifiable economic value through the cloud-based computing architecture (Rajaraman, 2014). Even though the cloud computing approach has numerous advantages (including adaptability, cost savings, device autonomy, efficiency, and more), it remains in its adolescence, and businesses are still figuring out how to use it most effectively (Jaeger et al., 2008). One of the major cloud technology providers, Amazon, recently suffered a devastating breakdown that impacted numerous businesses that depend on cloud services to function in Amazon. To reduce the negative effects of a major collapse, businesses should be ready to properly design their cloud technology agreements and incorporate resilience into their programs (Lin et al., 2009).

5.5. OPERATING AN ARCHITECTURE DESIGN

The general architecture and the positioning of the hardware and software that will be employed are specified in the design process. We will provide an overview of the protocol here, but the design process is a very complicated subject frequently left to seasoned architects and advisors. Each one of the earlier stated computing systems has advantages and disadvantages. Whenever there are no other considerations beyond cost, customer architectures are typically employed today since most firms migrate to them for price and capacity reasons (Anderson et al., 1991).

Starting with the unusable criteria will help you create an architectural design. To choose the infrastructure that will be employed (server-based, client-based, or customer-based) and the application programs to be installed on every device, the first stage is to develop the unusable needs into more comprehensive needs (Engler et al., 1995). When using a custom design, one must choose between a two, three, or n-tier architecture. The software and hardware requirements are then created using the application architecture and unusable requirements. Operational needs, performance parameters, security protocols, and political and cultural criteria are the four main categories of unusual needs that can be significant when developing architecture. We briefly explain each before describing how it might influence the building design (Cunjiang et al., 2012).

5.5.1. Operational Requirements

The operational condition(s) within which the system should function, as well as any potential future changes, are specified by operating procedures. Typically, this includes the computer systems, software applications, and data management with which the system must communicate. However, the external environment may sometimes be included if it is crucial to the program, for instance, on a loud factory floor where no audio alerts can be heard. Four major functional requirement sectors are outlined in Figure 5.6, along with specific examples for each (Loques et al., 2004).

5.5.2. Requirements of Technical Environment

The kind of software and hardware the system will operate on is specified by the technical environment standards. These specifications often emphasize software such as Windows or Linux, database systems such as Oracle, and other software applications like Internet Explorer. Sometimes, hardware specifications may place significant restrictions on the system, like the need to run on a smartphone with a relatively small screen (Kolokotsa et al., 2002).

Type of Requirement	Definition	Examples
Technical Environment Requirements	Special hardware, software, and network requirements imposed by business requirements	• The system will work over the Web environment with Internet Explorer. • All office locations will have an always-on network connection to enable real-time database updates. • A version of the system will be provided for customers connecting over the Internet via a small-screen smartphone.
System Integration Requirements	The extent to which the system will operate with other systems	• The system must be able to import and export Excel spreadsheets. • The system will read and write to the main inventory database in the inventory system.
Portability Requirements	The extent to which the system will need to operate in other environments	• The system must be able to work with different operating systems (i.e., Linux; Windows 7). • The system may need to operate with handheld devices such as an iPad.
Maintainability Requirements	Expected business changes to which the system should be able to adapt	• The system will be able to support more than one manufacturing plant upon six months advance notice. • New versions of the system will be released every six months.

Figure 5.6. Operational based requirements.

Source: Ashok Ranchhod, Creative Commons License.

5.5.3. System Interpretational Requirements

Systems that function with other computer programs inside and outside the organization have system implementation needs. The connectors by which information will be transferred to other systems are often specified (Jin et al., 2014).

5.5.4. Portability Requirements

Information management is never static. Information systems that assist and operate on business requirements and functioning technologies must also adapt. The standards for adaptability specify how well the system should react as the technical functioning conditions change over time; for example, the system might run on Windows Vista and may have to run on Windows 7 and Linux in the future (Mooney, 1990). The term "portability requirements" also covers prospective adjustments to business needs that could result in adjustments to the technological environment. For instance, in response to consumer needs, many firms attempt to ensure their programs are suited for devices like the iPad (Chatras & Ozog, 2016).

5.5.5. Maintainability Requirements

The manageability requirements specify the changes in expected business needs. Some changes are predictable, while others are not. Consider a small business with only one production facility but plans to build a second one within the next five years. All computer systems, either for managing staff, budgets, or inventories, must be designed so that it is simple to follow each plant individually (Rajpal et al., 2006). The manageability criterion tries to foresee future requirements to make it simple to manage systems created today and when those requirements materialize. The maintenance cycle of the system, including the regularity of new iteration releases, may be defined by manageability criteria (Saltzer & Pogran, 1980).

5.5.6. Performance Requirements

Performance criteria heavily emphasize factors including responsibility, capacity, and dependability. The reliability of those standards is a crucial concern when analysts develop the productivity demands for the system. Each criterion must be quantifiable to enable benchmark comparisons. The only means to confirm the fulfillment of performance criteria is in this manner. In practice, many system developers build the criteria and then write an increasing application with a clear test for each of them simultaneously (Nygren et al., 2010). The development of inadequate performance standards like "The system must provide a reaction time quick enough to enable staff to execute their work efficiently" is avoided by paying conscious focus to system testing. Three important performance requirements categories are outlined in Figure 5.7, along with some illustrations (Fiandrino et al., 2020).

5.5.7. Speed Requirements

Speed requirements are precisely what they sound like: how quickly the system must function. This is the reaction time of a system, which comes first: How quickly would the system react to user requests? Even if this is not feasible, everyone must prefer that the system replies to user requests instantly and have short intervals (Zhang et al., 2020).

Such a system could be developed, yet it would be costly. Most consumers are aware that some system components respond more quickly than others. Typing, sliding, and dragging must instantly happen on the user's computer. In contrast, other actions that call for network communication can have longer reaction times (For example, a browser request) (Xu et al., 2020). Reaction times under seven seconds are often regarded as satisfactory when they include network communication. The second facet of speed requirements is how quickly transactions in one area of the system are represented in other areas. How quickly, for instance, would the items in order be indicated as being out-of-stock to other customers? Another person could order the identical item and discover afterward that it is currently out of stock if it is not revised immediately. Or how quickly is an order transmitted to the store to be picked up from stock and delivered after it is placed? A delay might not matter much in some situations (Reinhardt et al., 2020).

Type of Requirement	Definition	Examples
Speed Requirements	The time within which the system must perform its functions	• Response time must be 4 seconds or less for any transaction over the network. • The inventory database must be updated in real time. • Orders will be transmitted to the factory floor every 3 minutes.
Capacity Requirements	The total and peak number of users and the volume of data expected	• There will be a maximum of 2000 simultaneous users at peak use times. • A typical transaction will require the transmission of 300 K of data. • The system will store data on approximately 50,000 customers for a total of about 2 GB of data.
Availability and Reliability Requirements	The extent to which the system will be available to the users and the permissible failure rate due to errors	• The system should be available 24/7, with the exception of scheduled maintenance. • Scheduled maintenance shall not exceed one 6-hour period each month.

Figure 5.7. Performance-based requirements.

Source: Ashok Ranchhod, Creative Commons License.

5.5.8. Capacity Requirements

Capacity limitations try to foresee how many consumers the system will need to accommodate concurrently and overall. Determining the size of databases, the required computational power, and other factors depends on the capacity needs. The highest number of concurrent users is typically the most crucial criterion because it directly affects the processing capability of the computer(s) required to operate the system (Basney & Livny, 1999). Predicting the number of individuals for internal systems created to assist a firm's personnel is frequently simpler than predicting the number of users for systems intended to serve customers, mainly those accessible via the Internet. How many users at peak times will concurrently search weather information, according to weather.com's estimate? The team frequently offers a range of estimations because this is mostly an art as a science, with greater ranges used to indicate a less precise prediction (Zhang, 2010).

5.5.9. Security Requirements

Security is the capacity to guard against disturbance and accidental deletion in the data system, whether brought on by deliberate action (such as a hacking assault) or a chance occurrence (such as failure of the disk or tornado). The operations team oversees setting and maintaining security measures including routers, intrusion prevention systems, and regular backup and restoration procedures, and is mainly responsible for security. Although system developers oversee guaranteeing security within the information management itself, they must also ensure that the system's security results in sufficient safeguards to avert issues (Kumar & Goyal, 2019).

System designers must be aware of the security guidelines that apply to their companies. A variety of legal limitations govern some sectors. Consider the Sarbanes-Oxley Act, which is well-recognized for requiring publicly traded corporations to safeguard their banking systems against deception and misuse. Healthcare professionals, insurance providers, and health information controllers are subjected to the Health Insurance Portability and Accountability Act (HIPAA). In contrast, the financial sector is subjected to the regulations of the Graham-Leach-Bliley (GLB) Act.

Additionally, there are optional security protocols that businesses can choose to compare themselves, like those set forth by the International Standards Organization (ISO). Enterprises can meet the generally recognized information security standard ISO 17799 by having an approved external auditor review their security procedures. The Payment Card Industry Data Security Standards (PCIDSS), the leading credit card firms designed to guarantee the security of recorded client information, will be the merchants' primary concern (Dener, 2014).

In today's World Wide Web, security has become an issue. The biggest security risk in the past has originated from within the business. Organizational personnel has been responsible for the most computer fraud since the FBI started compiling statistics in the early 1980s and security companies started investigating computer fraud. In the early 2000s, external risks became a more serious issue. According to recent studies, local security concerns are bigger than external ones. With the compromise of secret documents, many firms are dealing with legal liability that puts hundreds of workers and clients at risk of identity crime (Iqbal et al., 2020).

Establishing security needs typically begins with an evaluation of the system and the significance of data. This makes it easier to identify vital systems to ensure that the operations personnel are conscious of the dangers. The security system is typically concerned with defining who has access to information, determining the requirement for encryption and certification, and ensuring that the program stops the propagation of infections.

Security standards increase the cost of the system. What should further money be allocated to system security? As a general thumb rule, calculate the estimated loss first, then calculate the likelihood that it will occur. The cost of security measures can be estimated by multiplying these figures. As a result, if a loss of $1,00,000,000 is anticipated with a 10% likelihood, then protection should cost $1,00,000,000 × 10% or up to $10,000,000 (Pal et al., 2020).

5.6. POLITICAL AND CULTURAL REQUIREMENTS

Country-specific cultural and political prerequisites must be met for the system to be employed there. Companies are extending their technologies to reach people worldwide in the current commercial climate. The effect of developing an application should not be understated, even though this can often make excellent financial sense. Considering the system's needs in terms of global culture and politics is an additional crucial component of the architecture's development (Swyngedouw, 2004).

5.6.1. Multilingual Requirements

Language is the foremost visible distinction between regionally specific programs and those created for a worldwide audience. The global application frequently has linguistic requirements; therefore, they must accommodate customers who communicate in other languages and use non-English characters when they write (for example, those with accents, Japanese, and Cyrillic). Even techniques only utilized in the U.S., for instance, may be employed in areas with sizable communities of immigrants who do not understand English. Having a competent translation of the information from the originating language into the target language is one of the trickiest parts of building international systems. It is crucial to utilize translators experienced in interpreting technical terms because words frequently have identical meanings but might quietly reflect different thoughts when translated.

Space on the screen is frequently another issue. The English-language text uses 20%–30% fewer characters than their equivalents in French or Spanish. More screen real estate must be devoted to text when designing worldwide systems rather than being done in the version of English-language. Certain systems are made to accommodate multiple languages at once so that users from various nations can use various languages at once; for example, the same system can accommodate multiple languages at once, a concurrent multilingual system.

Other systems require reinstallation before a particular language can be employed because they have independent components built in every language; each language is therefore offered by a unique version of the OS, limiting the number of languages that may be implemented at a time (i.e., a different linguistic system). Either strategy can work, but this feature needs to be built into the system before it is used.

5.6.2. Customization Requirements

The development team will have to consider customization needs for international applications: What proportion of the software will be primarily performed, and what proportion by a central organization? For instance, some businesses permit their affiliates in specific nations to alter the software by removing or including functionalities. As customization frequently makes it much more difficult for the development team to design and operate the software, this choice involves an exchange between control and flexibility. Additionally, it implies that training may vary depending on the division of the business, and customization issues may arise when staff members transfer between offices.

5.6.3. Unstated Norms

Unwritten standards that are not universally accepted exist in many nations. These presumptions must be stated explicitly by the program designer else they could generate confusion. In the U.S., the unwritten standard for entering dates is MM/DD/YY; in Canada and most European nations, the standard is DD/MM/YY. Identifying these implicit standards and making them clear when creating global systems is crucial so that consumers in various nations are not misled. The other aspect of system architecture that is occasionally forgotten is currencies; worldwide software systems must identify the currency in which data is being submitted and published.

ACTIVITY 5.1

What are the political and cultural requirement? List them.

5.6.4. Legal Requirements

Laws and governmental regulations set constitutional standards. System designers occasionally overlook constitutional requirements, but regrettably, they do not know that the law does not provide a defense. For instance, the Georgia Institute of Technology was found guilty of breaking French language laws by a French court (1997). A modest campus run by Georgia Tech in France hosted summer schedules for American students. Because classes are held in the English language, most of the content on the Web server of the campus was in English, which was against the law as French must predominate on all Web servers in France. By formally considering them, researchers can make sure that constitutional requirements are far less inclined to be overlooked.

5.7. SUMMARY

All software systems can be divided into four basic functions: data storage, data access logic (e.g., SQL), application logic (which is the logic that is documented in the DFDs, use cases, and functional requirements), and presentation logic (the user interface (UI)). Three fundamental computing architectures place these functions on different computers. In server-based architectures, the server performs all the functions. In client-based architectures, the client computers are responsible for presentation logic, application logic, and data access logic, with data stored on a file server. In client-server architectures, the client is responsible for the presentation logic, and the server is responsible for the data access logic and storage. In thin client-server architectures, the server performs the application logic, while in thick client-server architectures, the application logic is shared between the servers and clients. In a two-tiered client-server architecture, there are two groups of computers: one client and a set of servers. In a three-tiered client-server architecture, there are three groups of computers: a client, a set of application servers, and a set of database servers. Virtualization and cloud computing are two technological advances that are reshaping architectural options. Creating architecture designs begins with the nonfunctional requirements. Operational requirements specify the operating environment(s) in which the system must perform and how those may change over time (i.e., technical environment, system integration, portability, and maintainability). Performance requirements focus on performance issues such as system speed, capacity, availability, and reliability. Security requirements attempt to protect the information system from disruption and data loss (e.g., system value, access control, encryption, and authentication, and virus control). Cultural and political requirements are specific to the countries where the system will be used (e.g., multilingual, customization, unstated norms, and legal).

REVIEW QUESTIONS

1. What are the key elements of architectural design?
2. What is the process for designing a building from start to finish?
3. How does architectural design influence the functionality of a building?
4. How do climate and environment impact architecture design?
5. What are the most important considerations when selecting materials for architectural design?
6. What are the benefits of sustainable architecture design?
7. How has technology impacted the way architects design buildings?
8. What challenges do architects face when designing a building?
9. What are the advantages and disadvantages of different building materials?
10. How can architects create esthetically pleasing designs while remaining mindful of budget constraints?

MULTIPLE CHOICE QUESTIONS

1. What is the purpose of an architectural design?

a. To provide an outline of the software
b. To create a graphical representation of the software
c. To identify the components of the software
d. To design the interface of the software
e. All of the above

2. What is the best way to create a successful architectural design?

a. Use the latest tools and technologies
b. Take a systematic approach
c. Be creative and innovative
d. Make sure it's scalable
e. All of the above

3. What is meant by the term "modular architecture"?

a. It is the process of breaking down software into discrete components.
b. It is the process of combining multiple components into a single system.
c. It is the process of creating a framework for the software.
d. It is the process of creating a user interface for the software.
e. It is the process of creating a graphical representation of the software.

4. What are the benefits of using architectural design?

a. Improved scalability
b. Increased reliability
c. Reduced complexity
d. Improved maintainability
e. All of the above

5. Cloud computing is a kind of abstraction which is based on the notion of combining physical resources and represents them as .... resources to users.

a. Real
b. Cloud
c. Virtual
d. none of the mentioned

Answers to Multiple Choice Questions

1. (e) 2. (e) 3. (a) 4. (e) 5. (c)

REFERENCES

1. Abdmouleh, A., Spadoni, M., & Vernadat, F., (2004). Distributed client/server architecture for CIMOSA-based enterprise components. *Computers in Industry, 55*(3), 239–253.
2. Adler, R. M., (1995). Distributed coordination models for client/server computing. *Computer, 28*(4), 14–22.
3. Anderson, T. E., Levy, H. M., Bershad, B. N., & Lazowska, E. D., (1991). The interaction of architecture and operating system design. *ACM SIGPLAN Notices, 26*(4), 108–120.
4. Aries, J. A., Banerjee, S., Brittan, M. S., Dillon, E., Kowalik, J. S., & Lixvar, J. P., (2002). Capacity and performance analysis of distributed enterprise systems. *Communications of the ACM, 45*(6), 100–105.
5. Baroncelli, F., Martini, B., & Castoldi, P., (2010). Network virtualization for cloud computing. *Annals of Telecommunications-Annales des Télécommunications, 65*(11), 713–721.
6. Basney, J., & Livny, M., (1999). Improving goodput by co-scheduling CPU and network capacity. *The International Journal of High Performance Computing Applications, 13*(3), 220–230.
7. Bertocco, M., Ferraris, F., Offelli, C., & Parvis, M., (1998). A client-server architecture for distributed measurement systems. *IEEE Transactions on Instrumentation and Measurement, 47*(5), 1143–1148.
8. Borthick, A. F., & Roth, H. P., (1994). Understanding client/server computing. *Strategic Finance, 76*(2), 36.
9. Bourguiba, M., Haddadou, K., El Korbi, I., & Pujolle, G., (2013). Improving network I/O virtualization for cloud computing. *IEEE Transactions on Parallel and Distributed Systems, 25*(3), 673–681.
10. Chatras, B., & Ozog, F. F., (2016). Network functions virtualization: The portability challenge. *IEEE Network, 30*(4), 4–8.
11. Chengalur-Smith, I., & Duchessi, P., (2000). Client-server implementation: Some management pointers. *IEEE Transactions on Engineering Management, 47*(1), 127–145.
12. Cunjiang, Y., Huaxun, Z., & Lei, Z., (2012). Architecture design for smart grid. *Energy Procedia, 17*, 1524–1528.
13. Dener, M., (2014). Security analysis in wireless sensor networks. *International Journal of Distributed Sensor Networks, 10*(10), 303501.
14. Engler, D. R., Kaashoek, M. F., & O'Toole, Jr. J., (1995). Exokernel: An operating system architecture for application-level resource management. *ACM SIGOPS Operating Systems Review, 29*(5), 251–266.
15. Fan, M., Stallaert, J., & Whinston, A. B., (2000). The adoption and design methodologies

of component-based enterprise systems. *European Journal of Information Systems, 9*(1), 25–35.

16. Fiandrino, C., Zhang, C., Patras, P., Banchs, A., & Widmer, J., (2020). A machine-learning-based framework for optimizing the operation of future networks. *IEEE Communications Magazine, 58*(6), 20–25.
17. Filibeli, M. C., Ozkasap, O., & Civanlar, M. R., (2007). Embedded web server-based home appliance networks. *Journal of Network and Computer Applications, 30*(2), 499–514.
18. Franks, G., Hubbard, A., Majumdar, S., Neilson, J., Petriu, D., Rolia, J., & Woodside, M., (1995). A toolset for performance engineering and software design of client-server systems. *Performance Evaluation, 24*(1, 2), 117–136.
19. Fujimaki, A., Takai, Y., & Yoshikawa, N., (2002). High-end server based on complexity-reduced architecture for superconductor technology. *IEICE Transactions on Electronics, 85*(3), 612–616.
20. Gallaugher, J. M., & Ramanathan, S. C., (1996). Choosing a client/server architecture: A comparison of two-and three-tier systems. *Information Systems Management, 13*(2), 7–13.
21. García-Valls, M., Cucinotta, T., & Lu, C., (2014). Challenges in real-time virtualization and predictable cloud computing. *Journal of Systems Architecture, 60*(9), 726–740.
22. Grossman, R. L., (2009). The case for cloud computing. *IT Professional, 11*(2), 23–27.
23. Gu, R., Niu, C., Wu, F., Chen, G., Hu, C., Lyu, C., & Wu, Z., (2021). From server-based to client-based machine learning: A comprehensive survey. *ACM Computing Surveys (CSUR),54*(1), 1–36.
24. Hofmeister, C., Kruchten, P., Nord, R. L., Obbink, H., Ran, A., & America, P., (2007). A general model of software architecture design derived from five industrial approaches. *Journal of Systems and Software, 80*(1), 106–126.
25. Hudli, A. V., & Pidaparti, R. M. V., (1995). Distributed finite element structural analysis using the client–server model. *Communications in Numerical Methods in Engineering, 11*(3), 227–233.
26. Iqbal, W., Abbas, H., Daneshmand, M., Rauf, B., & Bangash, Y. A., (2020). An in-depth analysis of IoT security requirements, challenges, and their countermeasures via software-defined security. *IEEE Internet of Things Journal, 7*(10), 10250–10276.
27. Jaeger, P. T., Lin, J., & Grimes, J. M., (2008). Cloud computing and information policy: Computing in a policy cloud? *Journal of Information Technology & Politics, 5*(3), 269–283.
28. Jin, J., Gubbi, J., Marusic, S., & Palaniswami, M., (2014). An information framework for creating a smart city through internet of things. *IEEE Internet of Things Journal, 1*(2), 112–121.
29. Kazman, R., Abowd, G., Bass, L., & Clements, P., (1996). Scenario-based analysis of software architecture. *IEEE Software, 13*(6), 47–55.

30. Kim, H., Patel, P., Wang, S., & Rajkumar, R. R., (2018). A server-based approach for predictable GPU access with improved analysis. *Journal of Systems Architecture, 88*, 97–109.
31. Kolokotsa, D., Stavrakakis, G. S., Kalaitzakis, K., & Agoris, D., (2002). Genetic algorithms optimized fuzzy controller for the indoor environmental management in buildings implemented using PLC and local operating networks. *Engineering Applications of Artificial Intelligence, 15*(5), 417–428.
32. Kruchten, P., Obbink, H., & Stafford, J., (2006). The past, present, and future for software architecture. *IEEE Software, 23*(2), 22–30.
33. Kumar, R., & Goyal, R., (2019). On cloud security requirements, threats, vulnerabilities and countermeasures: A survey. *Computer Science Review, 33*, 1–48.
34. Lewis, T. G., (1995). Where is client/server software headed? *Computer, 28*(4), 49–55.
35. Lin, G., Fu, D., Zhu, J., & Dasmalchi, G., (2009). Cloud computing: IT as a service. *IT professional, 11*(2), 10–13.
36. Lombardi, F., & Di Pietro, R., (2011). Secure virtualization for cloud computing. *Journal of Network and Computer Applications, 34*(4), 1113–1122.
37. Loques, O., Sztajnberg, A., Curty, R., & Ansaloni, S., (2004). A contract-based approach to describe and deploy non-functional adaptations in software architectures. *Journal of the Brazilian Computer Society, 10*(1), 5–20.
38. Luo, Y., (2010). Network I/O virtualization for cloud computing. *IT Professional, 12*(5), 36–41.
39. Marston, S., Li, Z., Bandyopadhyay, S., Zhang, J., & Ghalsasi, A., (2011). Cloud computing—The business perspective. *Decision Support Systems, 51*(1), 176–189.
40. Menascé, D. A., & Gomaa, H., (2000). A method for design and performance modeling of client/server systems. *IEEE Transactions on Software Engineering, 26*(11), 1066–1085.
41. Miano, S., Doriguzzi-Corin, R., Risso, F., Siracusa, D., & Sommese, R., (2019). Introducing SmartNICs in server-based data plane processing: The DDoS mitigation use case. *IEEE Access, 7*, 107161–107170.
42. Miller, D. M., (1997). Enterprise client/server planning. *Information Systems Management, 14*(2), 41–47.
43. Milosavljević, B., & Tešendić, D., (2010). Software architecture of distributed client/server library circulation system. *The Electronic Library, 28*(2), 286–299.
44. Mirashe, S. P., & Kalyankar, N. V., (2010). *Cloud Computing*. arXiv preprint arXiv:1003.4074.
45. Mooney, J. D., (1990). Strategies for supporting application portability. *Computer, 23*(11), 59–70.
46. Nygren, E., Sitaraman, R. K., & Sun, J., (2010). The akamai network: A platform for high-performance internet applications. *ACM SIGOPS Operating Systems Review, 44*(3), 2–19.

47. Pal, S., Hitchens, M., Rabehaja, T., & Mukhopadhyay, S., (2020). Security requirements for the internet of things: A systematic approach. *Sensors, 20*(20), 5897.
48. Perry, D. E., & Wolf, A. L., (1992). Foundations for the study of software architecture. *ACM SIGSOFT Software Engineering Notes, 17*(4), 40–52.
49. Plasil, F., & Visnovsky, S., (2002). Behavior protocols for software components. *IEEE transactions on Software Engineering, 28*(11), 1056–1076.
50. Post, G. V., & Kagan, A., (2005). Systems development tools and the relationship to project design: Cost and budget implications. *Journal of International Technology and Information Management, 14*(1), 1.
51. Rajaraman, V., (2014). Cloud computing. *Resonance, 19*(3), 242–258.
52. Rajpal, P. S., Shishodia, K. S., & Sekhon, G. S., (2006). An artificial neural network for modeling reliability, availability and maintainability of a repairable system. *Reliability Engineering & System Safety, 91*(7), 809–819.
53. Reinhardt, L. B., Pisinger, D., Sigurd, M. M., & Ahmt, J., (2020). Speed optimizations for liner networks with business constraints. *European Journal of Operational Research, 285*(3), 1127–1140.
54. Ruffer, S. M., Yen, D., & Lee, S., (1995). Client/server computing technology: A framework for feasibility analysis and implementation. *International Journal of Information Management, 15*(2), 135–150.
55. Sadiku, M. N., Musa, S. M., & Momoh, O. D., (2014). Cloud computing: Opportunities and challenges. *IEEE Potentials, 33*(1), 34–36.
56. Saltzer, J. H., & Pogran, K. T., (1980). A star-shaped ring network with high maintainability. *Computer Networks (1976),4*(5), 239–244.
57. Schultheis, R. A., & Bock, D. B., (1994). Benefits and barriers to client/server computing. *Journal of Systems Management, 45*(2), 12.
58. Shaw, M., & Clements, P., (2006). The golden age of software architecture. *IEEE Software, 23*(2), 31–39.
59. Shaw, M., DeLine, R., Klein, D. V., Ross, T. L., Young, D. M., & Zelesnik, G., (1995). Abstractions for software architecture and tools to support them. *IEEE Transactions on Software Engineering, 21*(4), 314–335.
60. Sinha, A., (1992). Client-server computing. *Communications of the ACM, 35*(7), 77–98.
61. Subramanian, A., & Lacity, M. C., (1997). Managing client/server implementations: Today's technology, yesterday's lessons. *Journal of Information Technology, 12*(3), 169–186.
62. Sun, X. H., Byna, S., & Chen, Y., (2007). Server-based data push architecture for multi-processor environments. *Journal of Computer Science and Technology, 22*(5), 641–652.
63. Swyngedouw, E., (2004). Globalization or 'glocalization'? Networks, territories and rescaling. *Cambridge Review of International Affairs, 17*(1), 25–48.

64. Tang, A., Han, J., & Vasa, R., (2009). Software architecture design reasoning: A case for improved methodology support. *IEEE Software, 26*(2), 43.

65. Thayer, R. H., (2002). Software system engineering: A tutorial. *Computer, 35*(4), 68–73.

66. Thomas, M. A., Redmond, R. T., & Weistroffer, H. R., (2009). Moving to the cloud: Transitioning from client-server to service architecture. *Journal of Service Science (JSS),2*(1), 1–10.

67. Tibermacine, C., Sadou, S., That, M. T. T., & Dony, C., (2016). Software architecture constraint reuse-by-composition. *Future Generation Computer Systems, 61*, 37–53.

68. Van, D. H. A., Mikic-Rakic, M., Roshandel, R., & Medvidovic, N., (2001). Taming architectural evolution. *ACM SIGSOFT Software Engineering Notes, 26*(5), 1–10.

69. Wang, L., Von, L. G., Younge, A., He, X., Kunze, M., Tao, J., & Fu, C., (2010). Cloud computing: A perspective study. *New Generation Computing, 28*(2), 137–146.

70. Wang, R., & Dagli, C. H., (2012). Computational system architecture development using a holistic modeling approach. *Procedia Computer Science, 12*, 13–20.

71. Wei, Y., & Blake, M. B., (2010). Service-oriented computing and cloud computing: Challenges and opportunities. *IEEE Internet Computing, 14*(6), 72–75.

72. Wood, A., (1995). Predicting client/server availability. *Computer, 28*(4), 41–48.

73. Xu, X., Tan, M., Corcoran, B., Wu, J., Nguyen, T. G., Boes, A., & Moss, D. J., (2020). Photonic perceptron based on a Kerr microcomb for high-speed, scalable, optical neural networks. *Laser & Photonics Reviews, 14*(10), 2000070.

74. Zhang, D., Liu, D., Wu, X., & Nesset, D., (2020). Progress of ITU-T higher speed passive optical network (50G-PON) standardization. *Journal of Optical Communications and Networking, 12*(10), D99–D108.

75. Zhang, Y., (2010). Network structure and capacity requirement: The case of China. *Transportation Research Part E: Logistics and Transportation Review, 46*(2), 189–197.

CHAPTER 6

USER INTERFACE DESIGN

UNIT INTRODUCTION

A user interface (UI) design is just a system component that facilitates communication between the system and its end users. It incorporates the display that indicates navigation around the system, and screens, including forms, used to collect data and results generated by the system (whether on paper, on the Web, or via some other media) (Oppermann, 2002). This chapter focuses on building the factor and standards and introduces the fundamental ideas and procedures involved in UIs. Interface design refers to the method of establishing how a system would interface with elements that are external to it (e.g., customers, suppliers, and other systems). Inside this chapter, our primary focus is on creating UIs; however, it is essential to keep in mind that there are additional systems interfaces that allow one system to communicate and share information with another system. A system's interface design typically takes place by integrating many systems. These are developed in-depth through the process of programmed design and information storage design. These are stated in broad's terms as a component of the physical flow diagrams (DFDs) as well as the non-functional requirements (operating needs) (Carroll et al., 1988).

The UI layout establishes how users will communicate with the system and the characteristics of outputs and inputs that a system would receive and create, respectively. Three primary components make up the UI. The first component is the *navigational mechanism*, often known as the interface through which the user communicates with the system and instructs it on how to operate (e.g., buttons, menus) (Morris, 1994). The second element is the *system's input process,* which serves as the means through which the computer collects data (e.g., forms for adding new customers). The third component is the *output process*, which refers to how the system communicates with the user with information or other computers (e.g., reports, Web pages). Although these are all theoretically different, they are all intricately connected (Bowman et al., 2001). Most computer displays also have output and input devices and navigational mechanisms, which are standard across all computer screens. Because of this, the navigation, input, and output design are closely related. The field of Research known as human-computer interaction (HCI) is focused on finding ways to enhance how people use technology by programming software that is more approachable and responsive to users' requirements. Some companies employ professional HCI designers. These designers are experts in applying design methods to produce graphical interfaces, including Web interfaces (Sridevi, 2014).

At the beginning of this chapter, some basic concepts of the design of UIs are presented. Second, it outlines the steps involved in designing UIs. After that, it summarizes the nautical, inputting, and output elements employed inside the design of interfaces. The design of Internet interfaces, including graphical user interfaces (GUIs) that make use of panels, menus, symbols, as well as a mouse, is the primary topic of discussion throughout this chapter (e.g., Windows, Macintosh) (Bollini, 2017). The graphical user interface (GUI) is likely to be the most prevalent interface you will use, with the potential for exception certifications and references even though text-based interactions are still extensively used for mainframe computers and UNIX systems (Welie et al., 2001).

Learning Objective

After studying this unit, you will be able to:

- Understand the principles of user interface design;
- Understand the user interface design process;
- Functions of navigation design;
- Functions of input design.

Key Terms

- User interface design
- Navigation design
- Interface structure
- Input design
- User experience

6.1. PRINCIPLES FOR USER INTERFACE (UI) DESIGN

Graphical user design is a skill in several aspects. The interface should be visually beautiful and easy to use, with the minimum effort required from users to complete their tasks. The system never serves as a goal unto itself; instead, it serves as a tool for the organization to carry out its operations (Bhaskar et al., 2011).

We have discovered that efficiently utilizing space is the biggest challenge seasoned designers face. In other words, there is additional information to give that there is space (Najjar, 1998). Analysts should strike a balance between the necessity for clarity and a pleasing esthetic and the requirement to deliver the information over several pages and screens, reducing simplicity. We go through some basic interface design ideas in this part that apply to input and navigation design, including output design (Table 6.1) (Blair & Zender, 2008).

Table 6.1. User Interface Design Principles

Principle	Description
Layout	The interface must consist of several screen regions routinely utilized for various tasks, such as a top region for instructions, including navigation, a middle region for data input or output, and a bottom region for status information.
Content awareness	The location they are in the network and the data being shown must always be known to users.
Aesthetics	By carefully choosing colors, and white space, including typefaces, interfaces must be usable and esthetically pleasing to users. The amount of white space required to create the interface visually appealing must frequently be balanced against the loss of space necessary to accommodate crucial data on the screen.
User experience	Although the simplicity of use and the simplicity of learning frequently influence the same design choices, there is occasionally a trade-off between the two. Frequent usage will favor the simplicity of use, but novice or infrequent software users will favor the simplicity of learning.
Consistency	Consistent interface design allows users to foresee what will happen when they perform a task. It is among the most crucial components for esthetics, usability, and simplicity of learning.
Minimize user effort	The user interface must be straightforward. Most designers envision consumers performing work after no more than three mouse clicks from the start menu.

6.1.1. Layout

The first rule of user interface (UI) design covers the screen, application, or reporting layout. The term "layout" describes how distinct portions of a display or document are arranged for various functions and how those regions are regularly used across the user experience (UX) (Lok & Feiner, 2001). Most software made for personal computers uses a standard window or Macintosh screen layout. The display is divided into three primary sections using this method: The user's options for navigating the system are displayed in the top section, their work is shown in the middle, which is the most significant area, and their activity is tracked inside the bottom region (Kusiak & Heragu, 1987).

Many times, different layout regions are employed, especially on the internet. A display having five navigation sections is depicted in Figure 6.1. Every area is set up to offer a particular function, including navigation inside a different system region. The typical web browser navigation and command controls that modify the contents of the overall network are in the top section (Bruno & Cutting, 1988). The left edge's navigation bar switches between divisions and all the stuff to its right. There are more options to move between parts of two additional section navigation bars at the top and the bottom of the page. The material in the center of the screen displays the outcomes (i.e., articles regarding software evaluations) and offers additional page navigation for such reviews (Liggett, 2000).

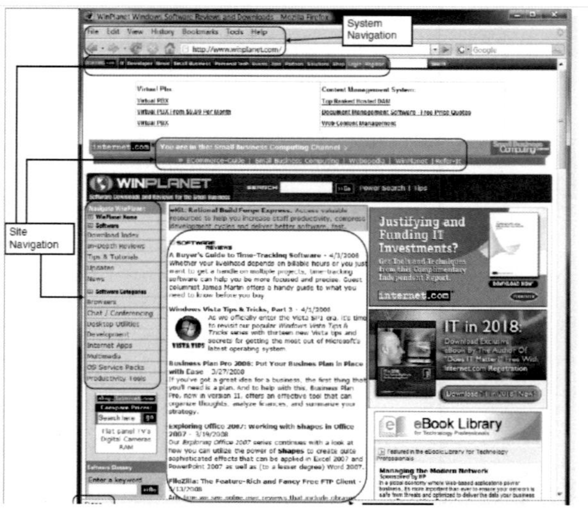

Figure 6.1. Multiple navigation areas on a website.

Source: Kinsta, Creative Commons License.

For navigation, several layout regions are used. This also holds for outputs and inputs. Upon reports and documents, information assets are frequently separated into subfields, each of which is utilized for specific information. These spaces are typically rectangular; however, occasionally, strange forms are necessary due to space limitations (Soukup, 1981). The margins along the display's edges must be uniform. The reports or forms of many sections are made to store various types of data. For example, on such an order sheet (or order report), a section for customer data (such as the name and address), a section for data about just the order in general (such as time and payment data), and a section again for order specifics may all be utilized (e.g., how many units of which items at what price each). Every section is independent, preventing data crossing between them (Phan et al., 2005).

To reduce the time users spend moving from one section to the next, the content inside them must have a natural, logical flow. Accordingly, relevant information must be arranged so that it can be utilized in this sequence (for example, address lines accompanied by city, state/province, and afterward ZIP code/postal code) (Ousterhout et al., 1985). Individuals living in Western countries (such as Europe and North America tend to read from top to bottom as well as left to right. The order might also be sequential, from broad to specialized, or used most often to least commonly (Hoiem et al., 2007). In any case, the analyst must clearly grasp what organization makes one of the most logical for how the forms or statements would be utilized first before sections are placed on such forms or reports. The movement between portions, horizontally or vertically, must also be constant. For the forms used to input data (whether on paper or a screen) and the reporting used to convey it, these areas should ideally keep the same size, shape, and location (Balakrishnan & Cheng, 1998).

6.1.2. Content Awareness

The capacity of an interface that makes accessibility of data it contains with the lowest number of users that referred to it as content awareness (Krauss et al., 2008). It is crucial for forms or documents used rapidly or sporadically to give as much information and awareness as feasible across all interface components, including navigation, input, and output (e.g., a Web site). The interface is subject to information awareness (Rose et al., 1993). Every interface must include titles (on the screen frame, for example). Menus should display the user's current location and, if feasible, their route to get there. For instance, in Figure 6.1, the top line of the middle site navigation bar indicates that the visitor is currently on the winplanet.com website's Small Business Computing Channel page. The space inside forms and reports is subject to content awareness (Van Driel et al., 1998). To lessen the probability that users would be confused about the material in any area, all regions must be distinct and properly defined (including titles if space enables). Users may then easily find the section of a form and report which is most likely to provide the data they want. The site navigation links just on the left side of Figure 6.2 are an example of where lines, colors, or headers sometimes show the regions; in other instances, the areas are just suggested (e.g., the page links in the center of Figure 6.1) (Chi & Ceci, 1987).

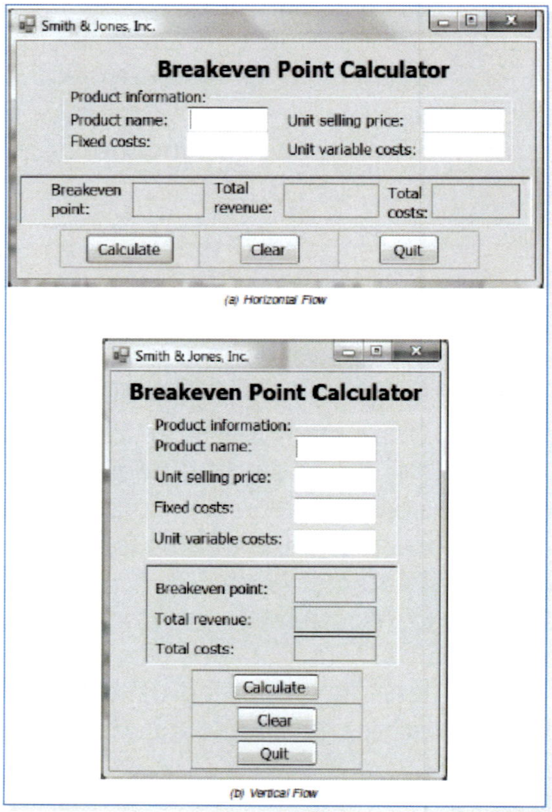

Figure 6.2. Flow between sections at the interface.

Source: Angus R. Simpson, Creative Commons License.

The field inside each region must also be aware of its respective content. The distinct pieces of data which are input or produced are called fields. The field names must be concise and precise, mainly on the interface—two frequently incompatible goals. No doubt should exist regarding the Format of data included in fields, whether for input or display (Baxter & Lederman, 1999). For instance, if you live in the United States (October 5, 2012) or Canada, a date of 10/5/12 has distinct meanings (May 10, 2012). Any fields with doubt or conflicting interpretations must include clear justifications. The data included in such a form and report is subject to content understanding (Loewenberg et al., 2008). To make the information available to age clear, every form of every report must include a production date (i.e., the day it was printed or even the date the information was finished). Similarly, all software, including printed forms, must include version numbers so that customers, analyzers, and programmers can recognize out-of-date information. There is a distinct, natural order to the address fields inside the address section (Magnusson et al., 1999). Field labels are kept as brief as feasible (top left), but where more data is required to avoid misunderstanding (bottom left), they are kept longer.) (Stein & Nelson, 2003).

6.1.3. User Experience (UX)

Developing the interface with users' degree of computer experience is considered "user experience (UX)." Both persons with and without expertise will be using a computer network. Thus, the UI needs to be made for both. Most often, the simplicity of learning—how fast and easy they can pick up using the system—is what novice users are most interested in (Hassenzahl & Tractinsky, 2006). Users are often more interested in the simplicity of use—how fast they can use the system to achieve a task after figuring out how to utilize it. These two goals frequently overlap and influence the same design choices, although occasionally, there are trade-offs. For instance, novices frequently like menus that display all possible system operations since they facilitate learning. On the other hand, experts occasionally favor a few menus arranged around the most frequently used features (Law et al., 2009).

Most users for systems that will be used often by numerous individuals are more likely to be the experts (e.g., order entry systems). These systems must focus more on the simplicity of use than on ease of understanding, even if interfaces must attempt to strike a balance between the two (Karapanos et al., 2009). Users must be able to easily access frequently used functionalities with a minimal number of keystrokes or menu selections (Allam & Dahlan, 2013). For the duration of numerous other systems (like decision-support systems), most users would only occasionally utilize them. In this situation, learning convenience may be given more weight than usability. Even if the simplicity of operation and ease of understanding frequently go along, they occasionally don't. According to research, experienced and beginner users can have distinct needs and behavioral tendencies (Law et al., 2008). For instance, professionals resort to a status bar whenever they need information, whereas beginners hardly ever look at the bottom portion of a screen, which displays information and updates. Except for systems intended to be utilized infrequently and where many newcomers or occasional customers are anticipated, most systems must be built to accommodate frequent users (e.g., the Web). Likewise, systems with capability that is just seldom utilized must

Did you Know?

User interface (UI) design focuses on anticipating what users might need to do and ensuring that the interface has elements that are easy to access, understand, and use to facilitate those actions.

have a very user-friendly interface or provide clear instructions on how to use it (Law & Van Schaik, 2010).

It may be difficult for interface designers to balance providing rapid access to frequently used and very well features and guiding users through new and lesser-known functionalities. Doing so frequently calls for esthetic solutions. For instance, the "show me" features in Microsoft Office solve this issue by displaying the menus and buttons for actions. Until new users require them, these functions are hidden within the background (or even knowledgeable users when they use an unacquainted part of the system) (Laugwitz et al., 2008).

6.1.4. Consistency

Because it allows users to anticipate outcomes, consistency within the design is perhaps the most crucial component of making a system easy to use. Aside from the components that are exclusive to those sections, users may interact, including one component of the system but then understand how to engage with the others whenever interfaces are uniform (Sowers, 1965). Typically, reliability relates to an interface of a single computer system, ensuring that every component functions uniformly.

But preferably, the system must also be compatible with other computer networks inside the company and any commercial software employed (e.g., Windows) (Thomson, 1990). For instance, Web-like interfaces could lessen the amount of user learning necessary because many users were familiar only with the Web. The process for a new system is significantly lowered since the user may utilize Web information in this way (Mackworth, 1977).

There are many various levels of consistency. The consistency of the navigational controls communicates how system activities must be carried out. It is easy to see how changes will be made throughout the system when that icon or command is used to alter each item. Additionally important is terminology consistency (Hart & Mas, 1989), which relates and uses the same terminology for components on forms and reports, such as avoiding using the terms "*customer*" as well as "*client*" interchangeably.

Whereas one study indicates that being overly consistent might lead to issues, we also think it's critical to maintain uniformity in the report and form design (O'Neill, 2020). Users occasionally utilize the erroneous report and form but either enter inaccurate data or misread its contents when reports and forms are substantially similar, save for minor title variations. The design implication is to keep the results and forms comparable while giving them some distinguishing features (such as color or headline size) that let users recognize the differences right away (Lowe, 1987).

6.2. USER INTERFACE (UI) DESIGN PROCESS

Iterative interface design 5 is a five-stage approach; analysts sometimes skip steps instead of going from stage 1 to step 5 in order (Figure 6.3) (Granlund et al., 2001). Creating use setups that represent users' typical activity patterns for the interface could facilitate users performing these setups rapidly and efficiently; analysts first evaluate the DFDs and then use cases created in the analysis stage and speak with users. The analyst creates the interface structure diagram (ISD), which outlines the fundamental structure of both interfaces (Sridevi, 2014). This diagram (or series of diagrams) depicts each of the system's interfaces, such as screens, applications, and reports, as well as their connections (Wilson & Rosenberg, 1988).

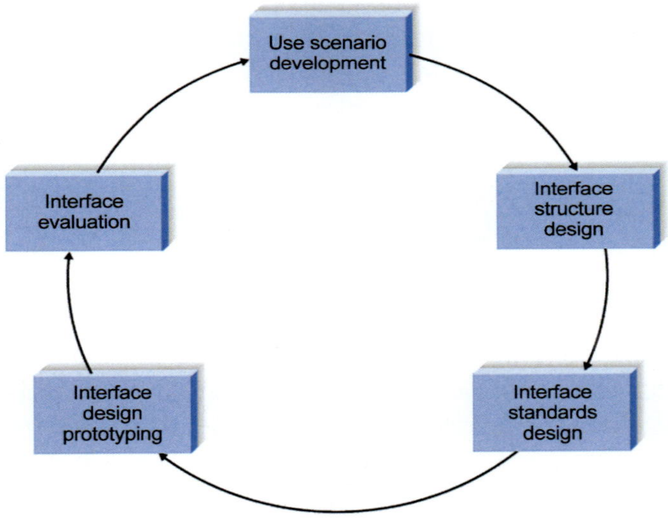

Source: Gerrit van der Veer, Creative Commons License.

Figure 6.3. Process for creating user interfaces.

Third, the analysts create interface standards, the fundamental design components that serve as the framework for network equipment. Fourth, the analysts develop an interaction prototype model for every system's distinct interfaces, including forms (containing printed-up paper forms), reporting, and navigational controls (Salman et al., 2012). The various interfaces are then evaluated to see if they are adequate and how they might be made better. Additions are nearly always found during interface assessments; therefore, the interaction design method is cycled through until no further improvements are found (Savage, 1996). Most analysts work very closely with users throughout the interface design phase, giving them several opportunities to examine the interface as it develops instead of waiting for a final, comprehensive interface evaluation. If modifications are discovered relatively soon, it is preferable for everyone involved (researchers and users). For instance, it is preferable to detect modifications before most of the screens that utilize the guidelines have been developed if such interface design and standards need to be improved (Kamaruzaman et al., 2016).

6.2.1. Use Scenario Development

A usage scenario is a breakdown of users' actions to complete a task at work. One frequent route through a usage instance is a use scenario. Remember that there might be various methods for the reaction to the event to be finished with use cases with data flow diagrams (DFDs).

Consider the level 1 DFD-modeled Search, with Browse Tunes, use case with Chapter 4's Figure 4–12 as an illustration. This diagram demonstrates how process 1.2 (process search requests) differs from procedure 1.3 (process tune selection). Since they are independent processes under process 1, we model and then write the two options individually (search and browse tunes) (Volkery et al., 2008).

The system's whole function, or potential routes through to the use case, is what the DFD was created to model. Use CASE scenarios, however, are only one route through to the use CASE. In one use CASE, for instance, a user will listen to various songs, just like someone in a physical music shop, to find intriguing music. They will look for a song, hear a sample, possibly add it to their shopping basket, look through more, etc. (De Girolamo & Porto, 2012). The consumer will eventually wish to buy the download(s) and may do so after eliminating certain items from the shopping basket.

Another use CASE is a user who wants to purchase a particular song. Like someone racing into such a store, making a rush for only one item they want, paying right away, and walking out of the store, they will walk straight to the song, price it, and buy it right away. This user would then gain entry to the tune relevant data in the system's search window, check the cost data that appears, and either immediately purchase the download or exit. They run the risk of losing the sale if something slows them down. We must ensure that such an interface's path to the DFD for this use CASE is quick and easy, with a minimum number of menus and mouse clicks (Mahmoud et al., 2009).

Simple narrative descriptions of use CASEs are provided and are connected to the DFD. The two usage situations are depicted in Figure 6.4. When employing use situations for UIs, it's important to remember that you shouldn't include all potential use situations in some use CASEs, as it would amount to doing the DFD over again. The intention is to outline the few use CASEs that arise most frequently so that the interface may be created to enable those frequent uses to be carried out quickly and efficiently (Reed et al., 2013).

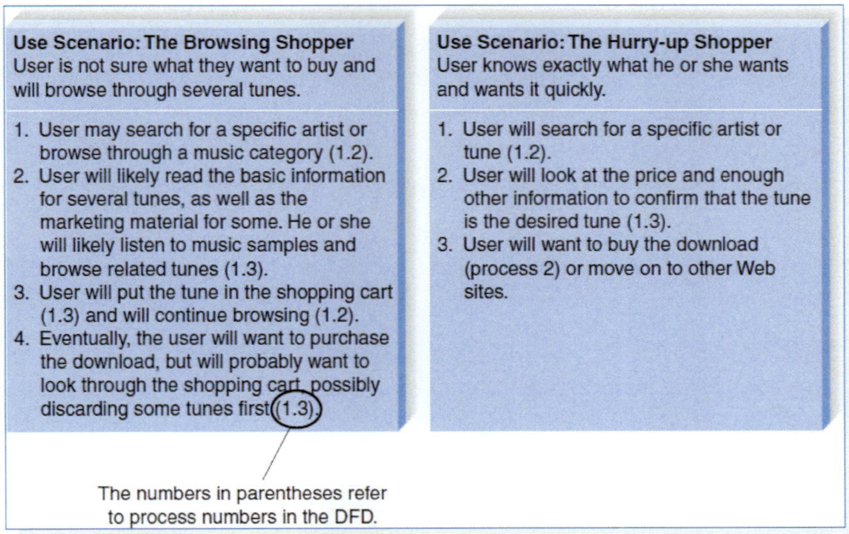

Figure 6.4. The search and browse tunes use CASE has two use scenarios.

Source: csis.pace.edu, Creative Commons License.

6.2.2. Interface Structure Design

The interface design and construction outline the interface's fundamental elements and how they interact to give users function. The relationship between each screen, application, and report utilized by the system is displayed using an ISD and the way the user navigates between them. Many networks have ISDs, one for each significant system component (Demkowicz et al., 2012).

It employs boxes and lines to depict structure; an ISD and a DFD are relatively comparable. Contrary to DFDs, there are no widely accepted guidelines or criteria for their creation. According to one method, every interface component (such as a screen, forms, or reports) on an ISD is represented as a box and given a different number (at the top) and a different name (in the middle). Usually, but not always, the numbers are organized tree-like. Furthermore, unlike with the DFDs, the numbers often suggest linkages between such a menu and a submenu rather than each screen belonging to *"parents"* higher within the tree. The lines represent the capacity to move between menus (Gan, 2009).

Every *ISD* box also displays (at the bottom) the *DFD procedure* that the interface supports (Figure 6.5). At times, there could be more than an interface for a particular process (as in Figure 6.5 when interfaces 1.1 through 1.3 transition process 1.1.1). Still, there may also be one interface for every activity in other circumstances (e.g., interfaces 3.1 through 3.3 support processes 1.1.3.1 through 1.1.3.3) (Liang et al., 2020). Lines connecting each interface demonstrate how users may move from one interface to another. The interfaces often create a hierarchy or even a tree. Still, occasionally, as seen by the linkage from Form *J* to Form *B*, an interaction may be linked to another within the hierarchy (e.g., the capability to update client information, such as speech, while incoming a new order) (Lu & Qin, 2016).

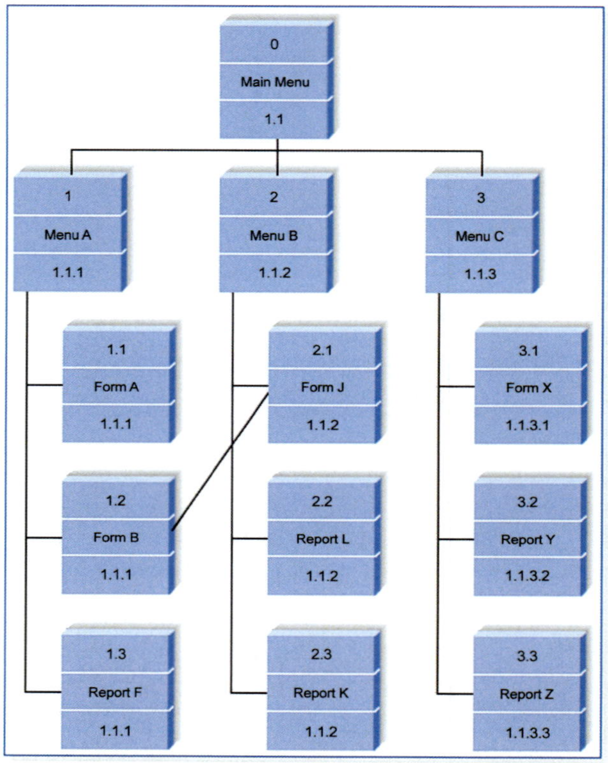

Figure 6.5. Interface structure diagram example.

Source: Thongchai Kaewkiriya, Creative Commons License.

The interface's fundamental arrangement mirrors business operations as specified within-process model. Starting with the DFD, the analyst creates the system's basic command flow as it progresses through each process. Like how a DFD has numerous high-level operations, an information system often has several significant components, every of which is separate. Just on level 0 DFD, there is typical—but not always—one ISD for every process (Gao et al., 2019).

Afterward, the analyst looks at the use CASEs to evaluate how effectively the ISD serves them. The usage scenarios frequently reveal ISD passageways that are more difficult than necessary. After that, the analyst redesigns the ISD to make the interface that supports the usage scenarios easier. Sometimes involves making significant changes to a menu design; other times, it just introduces shortcuts (Banovic et al., 2012).

6.2.3. Interface Standards Design

The interface guidelines are the fundamental design components shared by all the system's displays and forms, including reports. Various system components could be distinct sets implemented accordingly based on the application (e.g., one for Web screens, one for paper reports, and one for input forms). Data input operators may utilize a portion of the system like other data input apps of that business. Yet, a Web interface that is used to show information from this system might follow a conventional Web format (Thovtrup & Nielsen, 1991). These same standards serve as the yardstick that helps ensure the interactions are consistent throughout the system even though every individual interface may not even consist of all the components in the standards (for example, a report screen might very well not have an "*edit*" capability). Likewise, they might even contain more characteristics than those inside the standards (Reed et al., 1999).

Remember

User interface (UI) design focuses on anticipating what users might need to do and ensuring that the interface has elements that are easy to access, understand, and use to facilitate those actions.

6.3. NAVIGATION DESIGN

The user may input instructions to explore the system and carry out operations to enter and evaluate the information it includes in the interface's navigational component. The navigational element also informs the user via messages if their activities were successful or unsuccessful. Making the navigation system as user-friendly as feasible is its primary objective. A practical navigational element is something that the user hardly ever notices. Because it just performs as expected, the user does not give it any attention (Djonov, 2007).

6.3.1. Basic Principles

Understanding how to utilize the navigational controls to get a computer system to perform what you require is among the most challenging aspects of utilizing one (Diehl et al., 1978). Analysts must assume that users have not read the Handbook, have not gone to training, and do not have access to external support immediately. All controls must be easy to use, understandable, and situated just on the screen logically. The controls must preferably anticipate whatever the user will perform and reduce the amount of work required. For instance, many installation tools are made such that a user only needs to keep clicking "*Next*" to complete a conventional installation (Pollard & Bijker, 2021).

6.3.1.1. Prevent Mistakes

The fundamental design tenet for navigational controls is keeping the user from committing mistakes. Time is lost, and frustration results from an error. Even worse, a string of errors may lead the user to give up on the system. Mistakes could be minimized by carefully identifying orders and activities and restricting alternatives. The user may become confused when there are too many options, especially ones that are similar and difficult to express in the limited area on the screen. Consider adding a second level of menus or a set of alternatives for basic instructions when there are several comparable choices on a menu (Cox & Robinson, 2017).

Never show a command that is not operatable. For instance, most Windows programs *"gray out"* inoperative instructions; these commands are visible on pulldown menus in very light type but cannot be chosen. This demonstrates their availability and the fact that they will not be applicable in the given situation (Grout, 2006). All menu items are also kept in the exact location. It's crucial to get the user's consent before performing any crucial actions that are difficult or impossible to undo (like removing a file, for example) (and make sure the selection was not made by mistake). This is often accomplished by asking the user to reply to a message box that details the action they have requested and asking them to confirm that it is accurate (Antonelli & Stadnicka, 2019).

6.3.1.2. Simplify Recovery from Mistakes

Users would make errors no matter what the design engineer does. The system needs to make it as simple as possible to fix these mistakes (Brewer, 2012). An "Undo" button which makes errors simple to correct, should be included in the system; yet, creating the software for this kind of button may be highly challenging (Lu, 2004).

6.3.1.3. Use Consistent Grammar Order

The choice of grammatical order is among the most crucial ones. For most instructions, the user must specify an object (such as a file, record, or word) and the operation to be carried out on that item (e.g., copy, delete). The interface may ask users to select the object before performing the behavior (an object-action sequence) or to select the action before selecting the item (an action-object order). Most Windows programs employ object-action grammar (e.g., think about copying a block of text in your word processor) (Akhtar, 1999).

At both the level of individual data elements and the general menu, the grammatical arrangement should be identical throughout the system. Although experts disagree on whether the technique is best, many systems are still built using the object-action order since it is the most often used one (Bates et al., 1982).

6.3.2. Types of Navigation Controls

The keypad and a pointing device, including a mouse, trackpad, and touchpad, are examples of conventional hardware that may be used to manage the UI. Voice recognition technology has emerged recently, although it is not yet widely used. User commands can be defined by software using one of three fundamental methods: languages, menus, or manipulation of objects (Dailey, 2004).

6.3.2.1. Languages

A command language allows users to submit instructions uniquely explicitly designed for computer systems (e.g., UNIX and SQL both use command languages). Because users can mix language features in ways developers had not intended, command languages could occasionally provide more flexibility than other methods (Staiger, 1997). However, instead of allowing users to choose from a clearly defined, constrained set of options, they place a higher load on them by requiring them to learn the syntax and write instructions. Systems nowadays only sometimes employ command languages unless there are so many possible command combinations that it would be impracticable to attempt to construct every such combination into such a menu (e.g., SQL queries for databases) (Nygaard & Dahl, 1978). Language processing interfaces aim to comprehend the user's native tongue (e.g., English, French, and Spanish). Such UIs try to understand the user's meaning, and frequently they provide the user with a selection of possible interpretations to pick from. Today, many *"help"* systems allow users to ask open-ended inquiries to receive assistance (Fishman, 2017).

6.3.2.2. Menus

The menu is currently the most used sort of navigation mechanism. The user is shown a set of options on a menu, which may be picked individually.

Because user views are an orderly but constrained collection of options, menus are more straightforward to understand than languages. It just requires a little effort to click on such an item using a pointing device or hit a key corresponding to the menu option (such as a function key). Menus are typically favored over languages (Mitchell & Shneiderman, 1989). Because consumers cannot see the submenus below a menu bar until they click on it, menu designs must be carefully considered. Instead of making thin and deep menus, it is preferable to make them broad and shallow (every menu comprising several things and every item including just one or two levels of menus) (Sears & Shneiderman, 1994). (i.e., each menu comprises only a few items, but each item is essential to three or more layers of menus). A broad and shallow menu gives the user the most data at once, allowing them to view many possibilities and only a few clicks of the mouse or keyboard to complete an activity. Users must search for things concealed beneath menu options in a narrow, deep menu, and additional clicks or keystrokes are needed to complete an activity (Callahan et al., 1988).

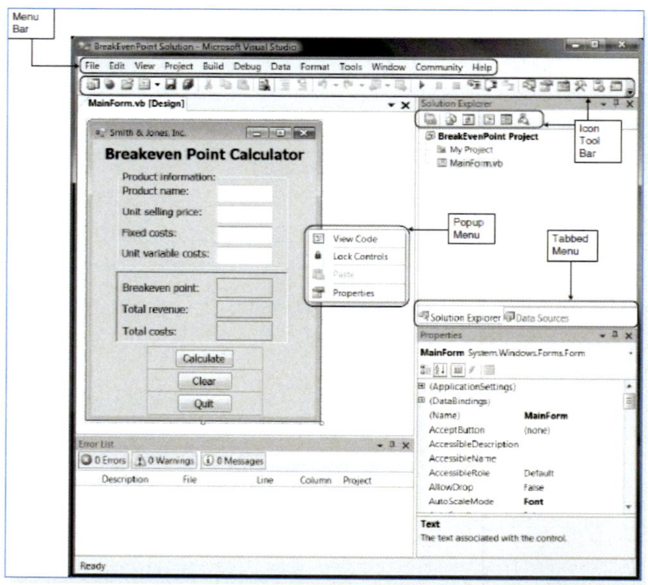

Figure 6.6. Common types of menus – Part A.

Source: Brainkart, Creative Commons License.

According to Research, in a perfect world, a menu must include no and over eight variables and would only need two mouse clicks and keystrokes to accomplish an operation (or three from the main menu that starts a system). However, analysts may have to deviate from this rule while designing complicated systems. In this instance, menu items are frequently arranged in groups and divided by horizontal lines (Figure 6.6). *Hotkeys* are frequently available for menu items, allowing knowledgeable users to swiftly execute a task with keystrokes instead of selecting it from the menu (e.g., Control-F in Word appeals the Find knowledge, whereas Alt-F opens the File menu) (Bederson, 2000).

Similar things should be grouped on menus, so the user can quickly and easily determine what every menu offers. Instead of grouping items on the menu by communication actions (e.g., New, Keep updating, Format), often these designers advise grouping menu options by interface items (e.g., Consumers, Sales Order, Inventory) so that every activity about one item are all in each menu, all activities for another item are in a special menu, so on. However, this is entirely reliant on the interface. As shown in figure, Microsoft Visuals arranges menu options on the same menus by interface items (such as File, Projects, and Windows) and so by interface activities (such as Editing, Display, or Build). Menu bars, drop-down menus, pop-up menus, tabbed menus, toolbars, and picture maps, are a few of the more popular forms of menus (*see* Figures 6.6 and 6.7). (Dachselt & Hübner, 2007).

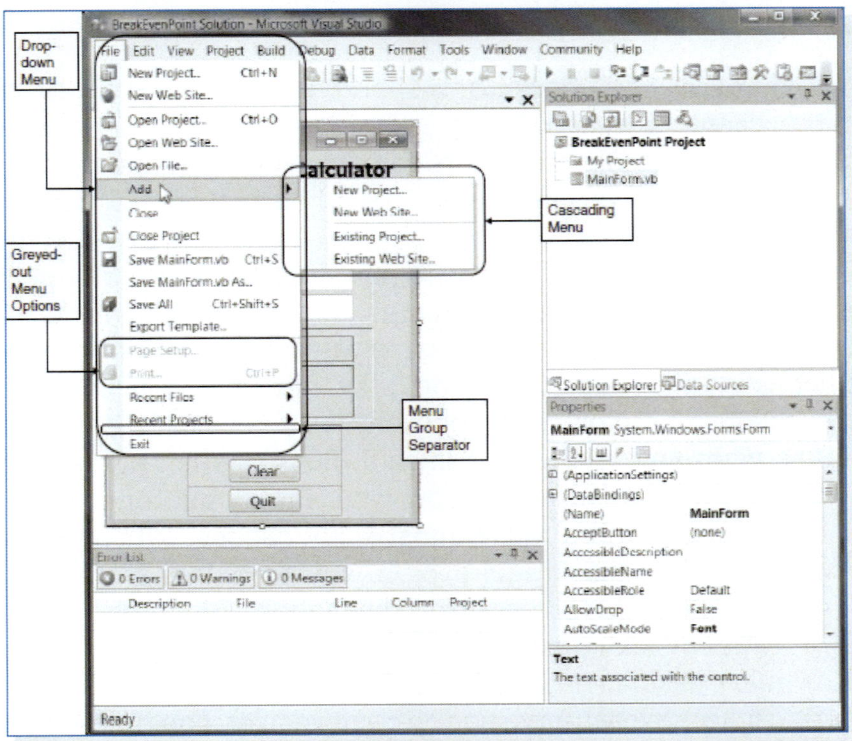

Figure 6.7. Common menu formats – Part B.

Source: Brainkart, Creative Commons License.

6.3.2.3. Direct Manipulation

The user interacts with interface items directly to input commands when using direct manipulation. Users may, for instance, drag the edges of an object in Microsoft PowerPoint to adjust its size, or they could drag the titles of files in Windows to move them from one location to another. Direct manipulation might be straightforward, but it has two drawbacks (Hutchins et al., 1985). First, people used to menu- or language-based interfaces may not always anticipate it. Second, not every command is clear-cut (for instance, how do you copy files in Windows rather than move them?) (Shneiderman & Maes, 1997).

6.3.3. Messages

The system replies to a customer and updates them on the progress of the engagement through messages. Errors, verification messages, acknowledgment messages, delayed messages, and assistance messages are just a few examples of various messages. Messages must be thorough, concise, and clear objectives that might occasionally clash. Except when they contain the users' jargon and abbreviations, all communications must be perfectly correct and devoid of jargon and abbreviations. Negatives should be avoided since they might be confusing (instead of asking if you would like to continue, ask if you want to stop). Avoid comedy as well; it rapidly loses its appeal once the same message is repeated several times (Woollacott, 2005).

Messages should not only be shown for a short period before disappearing; they must need the client to acknowledge these (by clicking, for instance). Messages informing the user of delays are an exception; these messages must vanish once the wait is over. Messages are often text, but occasionally they can include common symbols. Windows 7, for instance, shows a rotating circle whenever the machine is busy. While all messages must be thoughtfully written, error messages and assistance messages demand extra consideration. Messages (particularly error messages) must always describe the issue in courteous, succinct language (e.g., what the user did poorly). They should describe remedial action as simply and concisely as feasible to ensure that the user understands what must be done (Howard, 2014). When a user enters a complex error, the error message must show what they input, offer potential user answers, and speculate on the fault's most likely causes. While in doubt, give the user more data than they require or a way to obtain more data. A message number must be included in error messages. Although message numbers are still not meant for consumers, the fact that they exist makes it easier for people at help desks, including customer service lines, to spot issues and assist users because several messages utilize similar content (Malhotra et al., 2012).

6.4. INPUT DESIGN

Data entry into the computers is made more accessible by input methods, whether it is highly organized information, including order data (including such item numbers, quantities, and costs), or unstructured data (e.g., comments). Developing input entails creating the displays about which users entered data in addition to any types on which they write and type it (e.g., timecards, expense claims) (Jansson & Hjalmarsson, 2005).

6.4.1. Basic Principles

The objective of input design is to make it simple and convenient for the system to collect reliable information. The guiding principles regarding input design consider the type of inputs (batching or online) and how to make their gathering as simple as possible (Heirung & Mesbah, 2019).

6.4.1.1. Use Online and Batch Processing Appropriately

There are two general approaches for entering data into a computer network: online computing and batch processing. Every input item (e.g., a client order, a sales order) is input into the system separately using online processing (also known as processing transactions), generally at the same moments as the events or transaction generating the input (Aumi & Mhaskar, 2012). For instance, whether you loan a book from a library, buy something at the shop, or make an airline booking, the computer system that facilitates each operation employs online computing to record the event in the proper database as soon as possible(s). Online processes are typically employed when valuable facts regarding the business activity are required. For instance, when you secure an airline ticket, the chair is no longer usable for another person. Thus the data should be recorded promptly (Aumi et al., 2013).

ACTIVITY 6.1

According to you what are the principles of user interface design.

Batch processing involves gathering all the inputs acquired for more than a period and simultaneously entering them into the systems. Certain business operations create data in batches by default. Many hourly payrolls, for instance, are batch processing since timecards are acquired in bunches and analyzed all at once. Batch production is also employed in transaction processing which does not need real-time data (Peng et al., 2016). Most retailers, for instance, communicate sales data to district headquarters such that replacement part inventory may be bought. To notify the district's offices as soon as a sale is made, this data might be provided live time because it is recorded in the shop. If businesses do not require real-time data updated each second, they will gather sales information during the day and send it in batches to the district office each evening (Nomikos & MacGregor, 1994). This batching streamlines data transmission and frequently lowers communications expenses. However, it does imply that inventories are only correct after the week after the batches have been completed and are not correct in live time (Zhao et al., 2011).

6.5. SUMMARY

User interface (UI) design is designing and creating user-friendly interfaces for computer applications, websites, and mobile devices. It involves the design of both the UI and the user experience (UX). UI design focuses on the visual elements and interactions of the interface, such as buttons, menus, icons, and other graphical elements. UX design focuses on the interface's usability, such as the navigation, flow, and overall UX. UI design is an essential part of the software development process. It helps the developer create a functional and esthetically pleasing interface. Good UI design is based on an understanding of user needs and goals. It should be designed with the user, keeping usability and accessibility in mind. The UI design process involves Research, analysis, prototyping, testing, and implementation. The designer must understand the user's needs and goals during the research phase. They must also understand the technology being used to create the interface. During the analysis phase, the designer must create a visual representation of the UI. The designer must also create a navigation structure and determine the elements necessary for the interface. During the prototyping phase, the designer must create a UI prototype. This prototype can be tested to ensure it meets the user's requirements. During the testing phase, the designer must evaluate the interface's usability and make any necessary changes. Finally, during the implementation phase, the designer must create the final version of the UI. UI design is a complex and vital process that requires understanding user needs, technology, and design principles. It is essential for creating compelling and user-friendly interfaces that provide a positive UX.

REVIEW QUESTIONS

1. What are the fundamental principles of user interface design?
2. What techniques can be used to create compelling user interfaces?
3. What are the benefits of user interface design?
4. What challenges do designers face when creating user interfaces?
5. How does user interface design affect user experience?
6. What tools are available to help with user interface design?
7. How can user interface design be optimized for different devices?
8. How do user interface design trends impact the overall user experience?
9. What are some best practices for designing efficient user interfaces?
10. What are the common mistakes designers make when creating user interfaces?

MULTIPLE CHOICE QUESTIONS

1. What is the main focus of user interface design?

a. Creating a visually appealing design

b. Ensuring the user has an intuitive experience
c. Optimizing the speed of the interface
d. Maximizing the data storage capacity
e. Reducing the number of users clicks

2. **What is the primary goal of user interface design?**
a. Developing an efficient user interface
b. Improving user experience
c. Increasing user engagement
d. Reducing operating costs
e. Maximizing profits

3. **What is the essential element of user interface design?**
a. Navigation
b. Usability
c. Visuals
d. Interactivity
e. Functionality

4. **What type of design should be used when designing a user interface?**
a. Minimalistic
b. Responsive
c. Flat
d. Material
e. Parallax

5. **What is the primary goal of user interface design?**
a. Creating a visually appealing design
b. Ensuring the user has an intuitive experience
c. Optimizing the speed of the interface
d. Maximizing the data storage capacity
e. Making the user's task easier

Answers to Multiple Choice Questions

1. (b) 2. (b) 3. (b) 4. (b) 5. (b)

REFERENCES

1. Akhtar, N., (1999). Acquiring basic word order: Evidence for data-driven learning of syntactic structure. *Journal of Child Language, 26*(2), 339–356.
2. Allam, A. H., & Dahlan, H. M., (2013). User experience: Challenges and opportunities. *Journal of Information Systems Research and Innovation, 3*(1), 28–36.

3. Antonelli, D., & Stadnicka, D., (2019). Predicting and preventing mistakes in human-robot collaborative assembly. *IFAC-PapersOnLine, 52*(13), 743–748.
4. Aumi, S., & Mhaskar, P., (2012). Integrating data-based modeling and nonlinear control tools for batch process control. *AIChE Journal, 58*(7), 2105–2119.
5. Aumi, S., Corbett, B., Clarke-Pringle, T., & Mhaskar, P., (2013). Data-driven model predictive quality control of batch processes. *AIChE Journal, 59*(8), 2852–2861.
6. Balakrishnan, J., & Cheng, C. H., (1998). Dynamic layout algorithms: A state-of-the-art survey. *Omega, 26*(4), 507–521.
7. Banovic, N., Grossman, T., Matejka, J., & Fitzmaurice, G., (2012). Waken: Reverse engineering usage information and interface structure from software videos. In: *Proceedings of the 25th Annual ACM Symposium on User Interface Software and Technology* (pp. 83–92).
8. Bates, E., McNew, S., MacWhinney, B., Devescovi, A., & Smith, S., (1982). Functional constraints on sentence processing: A cross-linguistic study. *Cognition, 11*(3), 245–299.
9. Baxter, J. A., & Lederman, N. G., (1999). Assessment and measurement of pedagogical content knowledge. In: *Examining Pedagogical Content Knowledge* (pp. 147–161). Springer, Dordrecht.
10. Bederson, B. B., (2000). Fisheye menus. In: *Proceedings of the 13th Annual ACM Symposium on User Interface Software and Technology* (pp. 217–225).
11. Bhaskar, N. U., Naidu, P. P., Babu, S. R. R. C., & Govindarajulu, P., (2011). General principles of user interface design and websites. *International Journal of Software Engineering (IJSE),2*(3), 45–60.
12. Blair-Early, A., & Zender, M., (2008). User interface design principles for interaction design. *Design Issues, 24*(3), 85–107.
13. Bollini, L., (2017). Beautiful interfaces. From user experience to user interface design. *The Design Journal, 20*(sup1), S89–S101.
14. Bowman, D. A., Kruijff, E., LaViola, J. J., & Poupyrev, I., (2001). An introduction to 3-D user interface design. *Presence, 10*(1), 96–108.
15. Brewer, E., (2012). CAP twelve years later: How the "rules" have changed. *Computer, 45*(2), 23–29.
16. Bruno, N., & Cutting, J. E., (1988). Minimodularity and the perception of layout. *Journal of Experimental Psychology: General, 117*(2), 161.
17. Callahan, J., Hopkins, D., Weiser, M., & Shneiderman, B., (1988). An empirical comparison of pie vs. linear menus. In: *Proceedings of the SIGCHI Conference on Human Factors in Computing Systems* (pp. 95–100).
18. Carroll, J. M., Mack, R. L., & Kellogg, W. A., (1988). Interface metaphors and user interface design. In: *Handbook of Human-Computer Interaction* (pp. 67–85). North-Holland.
19. Chi, M. T., & Ceci, S. J., (1987). Content knowledge: Its role, representation, and restructuring in memory development. *Advances in Child Development and Behavior,*

20, 91–142.

20. Cox, III. J. F., & Robinson, E. G., (2017). Applying Goldratt's thinking processes to prevent mistakes. *Human Systems Management, 36*(4), 315–340.
21. Dachselt, R., & Hübner, A., (2007). Three-dimensional menus: A survey and taxonomy. *Computers & Graphics, 31*(1), 53–65.
22. Dailey, L., (2004). Navigational web atmospherics: Explaining the influence of restrictive navigation cues. *Journal of Business Research, 57*(7), 795–803.
23. De Girolamo, A. M., & Porto, A. L., (2012). Land use scenario development as a tool for watershed management within the Rio Mannu basin. *Land Use Policy, 29*(3), 691–701.
24. Demkowicz, M. J., Misra, A., & Caro, A., (2012). The role of interface structure in controlling high helium concentrations. *Current Opinion in Solid State and Materials Science, 16*(3), 101–108.
25. Diehl, P., Fluck, E., & Kosfeld, R., (1978). *Basic Principles and Progress* (Vol. 5, pp. 110–129). Springer-Verlag, Berlin/Heidelberg/New York.
26. Djonov, E., (2007). Website hierarchy and the interaction between content organization, webpage and navigation design: A systemic functional hypermedia discourse analysis perspective. *Information Design Journal, 15*(2), 144–162.
27. Fishman, J. A., (2017). *National Languages and Languages of Wider Communication in the Developing Nations 1* (pp. 27–56). Routledge.
28. Gan, Y. X., (2009). Effect of interface structure on mechanical properties of advanced composite materials. *International Journal of Molecular Sciences, 10*(12), 5115–5134.
29. Gao, B., Gao, P., Lu, S., Lv, J., Wang, Y., & Ma, Y., (2019). Interface structure prediction via CALYPSO method. *Science Bulletin, 64*(5), 301–309.
30. Granlund, Å., Lafrenière, D., & Carr, D. A., (2001). A pattern-supported approach to the user interface design process. In: *Proceedings of HCI International 2001 9th International Conference on Human-Computer Interaction* (pp. 282–286).
31. Grout, J. R., (2006). Mistake proofing: Changing designs to reduce error. *BMJ Quality & Safety, 15*(suppl 1), i44–i49.
32. Hart, S., & Mas-Colell, A., (1989). Potential, value, and consistency. *Econometrica: Journal of the Econometric Society,* 589–614.
33. Hassenzahl, M., & Tractinsky, N., (2006). User experience-a research agenda. *Behavior & Information Technology, 25*(2), 91–97.
34. Heirung, T. A. N., & Mesbah, A., (2019). Input design for active fault diagnosis. *Annual Reviews in Control, 47*, 35–50.
35. Hoiem, D., Efros, A. A., & Hebert, M., (2007). Recovering surface layout from an image. *International Journal of Computer Vision, 75*(1), 151–172.
36. Howard-Jones, P. A., (2014). Neuroscience and education: Myths and messages. *Nature Reviews Neuroscience, 15*(12), 817–824.

37. Hutchins, E. L., Hollan, J. D., & Norman, D. A., (1985). Direct manipulation interfaces. *Human–Computer Interaction, 1*(4), 311–338.

38. Jansson, H., & Hjalmarsson, H., (2005). Input design via LMIs admitting frequency-wise model specifications in confidence regions. *IEEE transactions on Automatic Control, 50*(10), 1534–1549.

39. Kamaruzaman, M. F., Rani, N. M., Nor, H. M., & Azahari, M. H. H., (2016). Developing user interface design application for children with autism. *Procedia-Social and Behavioral Sciences, 217*, 887–894.

40. Karapanos, E., Zimmerman, J., Forlizzi, J., & Martens, J. B., (2009). User experience over time: An initial framework. In: *Proceedings of the SIGCHI Conference on Human Factors in Computing Systems* (pp. 729–738).

41. Krauss, S., Brunner, M., Kunter, M., Baumert, J., Blum, W., Neubrand, M., & Jordan, A., (2008). Pedagogical content knowledge and content knowledge of secondary mathematics teachers. *Journal of Educational Psychology, 100*(3), 716.

42. Kusiak, A., & Heragu, S. S., (1987). The facility layout problem. *European Journal of Operational Research, 29*(3), 229–251.

43. Laugwitz, B., Held, T., & Schrepp, M., (2008). Construction and evaluation of a user experience questionnaire. In: *Symposium of the Austrian HCI and Usability Engineering Group* (pp. 63–76). Springer, Berlin, Heidelberg.

44. Law, E. L. C., & Van, S. P., (2010). Modelling user experience–an agenda for research and practice. *Interacting with Computers, 22*(5), 313–322.

45. Law, E. L. C., Roto, V., Hassenzahl, M., Vermeeren, A. P., & Kort, J., (2009). Understanding, scoping and defining user experience: A survey approach. In: *Proceedings of the SIGCHI Conference on Human Factors in Computing Systems* (pp. 719–728).

46. Law, E., Roto, V., Vermeeren, A. P., Kort, J., & Hassenzahl, M., (2008). Towards a shared definition of user experience. In: *CHI'08 Extended Abstracts on Human Factors in Computing Systems* (pp. 2395–2398).

47. Liang, L., Zhang, W., Zhao, F., Denis, D. K., Zaman, F. U., Hou, L., & Yuan, C., (2020). Surface/interface structure degradation of Ni-rich layered oxide cathodes toward lithium-ion batteries: Fundamental mechanisms and remedying strategies. *Advanced Materials Interfaces, 7*(3), 1901749.

48. Liggett, R. S., (2000). Automated facilities layout: Past, present and future. *Automation in Construction, 9*(2), 197–215.

49. Loewenberg, B. D., Thames, M. H., & Phelps, G., (2008). Content knowledge for teaching: What makes it special? *Journal of Teacher Education, 59*(5), 389–407.

50. Lok, S., & Feiner, S., (2001). A survey of automated layout techniques for information presentations. *Proceedings of SmartGraphics, 2001*, 61–68.

51. Lowe, D. G., (1987). The viewpoint consistency constraint. *International Journal of Computer Vision, 1*(1), 57–72.

52. Lu, S. L., (2004). Speeding up processing with approximation circuits. *Computer, 37*(3), 67–73.
53. Lu, W. J., & Qin, R. S., (2016). Influence of κ-carbide interface structure on the formability of lightweight steels. *Materials & Design, 104*, 211–216.
54. Mackworth, A. K., (1977). Consistency in networks of relations. *Artificial Intelligence, 8*(1), 99–118.
55. Magnusson, S., Krajcik, J., & Borko, H., (1999). Nature, sources, and development of pedagogical content knowledge for science teaching. In: *Examining Pedagogical Content Knowledge* (pp. 95–132). Springer, Dordrecht.
56. Mahmoud, M., Liu, Y., Hartmann, H., Stewart, S., Wagener, T., Semmens, D., &Winter, L., (2009). A formal framework for scenario development in support of environmental decision-making. *Environmental Modelling & Software, 24*(7), 798–808.
57. Malhotra, A., Malhotra, C. K., & See, A., (2012). How to get your messages retweeted. *MIT Sloan Management Review, 53*(2), 61–66.
58. Mitchell, J., & Shneiderman, B., (1989). Dynamic versus static menus: An exploratory comparison. *ACM SigCHI Bulletin, 20*(4), 33–37.
59. Morris, J. M., (1994). User interface design for older adults. *Interacting with Computers, 6*(4), 373–393.
60. Najjar, L. J., (1998). Principles of educational multimedia user interface design. *Human Factors, 40*(2), 311–323.
61. Nomikos, P., & MacGregor, J. F., (1994). Monitoring batch processes using multiway principal component analysis. *AIChE Journal, 40*(8), 1361–1375.
62. Nygaard, K., & Dahl, O. J., (1978). The development of the SIMULA languages. In: *History of Programming Languages* (pp. 439–480).
63. O'Neill, O., (2020). Consistency in action. In: *Immanuel Kant: Groundwork of the Metaphysic of Morals in Focus* (pp. 154–181). Routledge.
64. Oppermann, R., (2002). User-interface design. In: *Handbook on Information Technologies for Education and Training* (pp. 233–248). Springer, Berlin, Heidelberg.
65. Ousterhout, J. K., Hamachi, G. T., Mayo, R. N., Scott, W. S., & Taylor, G. S., (1985). The magic VLSI layout system. *IEEE Design & Test of Computers, 2*(1), 19–30.
66. Peng, K., Zhang, K., You, B., Dong, J., & Wang, Z., (2016). A quality-based nonlinear fault diagnosis framework focusing on industrial multimode batch processes. *IEEE Transactions on Industrial Electronics, 63*(4), 2615–2624.
67. Phan, D., Xiao, L., Yeh, R., & Hanrahan, P., (2005). Flow map layout. In: *IEEE Symposium on Information Visualization, 2005; INFOVIS 2005.* (pp. 219–224). IEEE.
68. Pollard, A. J., & Bijker, E. M., (2021). A guide to vaccinology: From basic principles to new developments. *Nature Reviews Immunology, 21*(2), 83–100.
69. Reed, M. S., Kenter, J., Bonn, A., Broad, K., Burt, T. P., Fazey, I. R., & Ravera, F., (2013). Participatory scenario development for environmental management: A

methodological framework illustrated with experience from the UK uplands. *Journal of Environmental Management, 128*, 345–362.

70. Reed, P., Holdaway, K., Isensee, S., Buie, E., Fox, J., Williams, J., & Lund, A., (1999). User interface guidelines and standards: Progress, issues, and prospects. *Interacting with Computers, 12*(2), 119–142.
71. Rose, D. E., Mander, R., Oren, T., Ponceleon, D. B., Salomon, G., & Wong, Y. Y., (1993). Content awareness in a file system interface: Implementing the "pile" metaphor for organizing information. In: *Proceedings of the 16th Annual International ACM SIGIR Conference on Research and Development in Information Retrieval* (pp. 260–269).
72. Salman, Y. B., Cheng, H. I., & Patterson, P. E., (2012). Icon and user interface design for emergency medical information systems: A case study. *International Journal of Medical Informatics, 81*(1), 29–35.
73. Savage, P., (1996). User interface evaluation in an iterative design process: A comparison of three techniques. In: *Conference Companion on Human Factors in Computing Systems* (pp. 307–308).
74. Sears, A., & Shneiderman, B., (1994). Split menus: Effectively using selection frequency to organize menus. *ACM Transactions on Computer-Human Interaction (TOCHI),1*(1), 27–51.
75. Shneiderman, B., & Maes, P., (1997). Direct manipulation vs. interface agents. *interactions, 4*(6), 42–61.
76. Soukup, J., (1981). Circuit layout. *Proceedings of the IEEE, 69*(10), 1281–1304.
77. Sowers, G. F., (1965). Consistency. *Methods of Soil Analysis: Part 1 Physical and Mineralogical Properties, Including Statistics of Measurement and Sampling, 9*, 391–399.
78. Sridevi, S., (2014). User interface design. *International Journal of Computer Science and Information Technology Research, 2*(2), 415–426.
79. Staiger, L., (1997). ω-languages. In: *Handbook of Formal Languages* (pp. 339–387). Springer, Berlin, Heidelberg.
80. Stein, M. K., & Nelson, B. S., (2003). Leadership content knowledge. *Educational Evaluation and Policy Analysis, 25*(4), 423–448.
81. Thomson, W., (1990). The consistency principle. In: *Game Theory and Applications* (pp. 187–215). Academic Press.
82. Thovtrup, H., & Nielsen, J., (1991). Assessing the usability of a user interface standard. In: *Proceedings of the SIGCHI Conference on Human Factors in Computing Systems* (pp. 335–341).
83. Van, D. J. H., Verloop, N., & De Vos, W., (1998). Developing science teachers' pedagogical content knowledge. *Journal of Research in Science Teaching: The Official Journal of the National Association for Research in Science Teaching, 35*(6), 673–695.

84. Volkery, A., Ribeiro, T., Henrichs, T., & Hoogeveen, Y., (2008). Your vision or my model? Lessons from participatory land use scenario development on a European scale. *Systemic Practice and Action Research, 21*(6), 459–477.
85. Welie, M. V., Veer, G. C., & Eliëns, A., (2001). Patterns as tools for user interface design. In: *Tools for Working with Guidelines* (pp. 313–324). Springer, London.
86. Wilson, J., & Rosenberg, D., (1988). Rapid prototyping for user interface design. In: *Handbook of Human-Computer Interaction* (pp. 859–875). North-Holland.
87. Woollacott, J., (2005). Messages and meanings. In: *Culture, Society and the Media* (pp. 96–118). Routledge.
88. Zhao, C., Mo, S., Gao, F., Lu, N., & Yao, Y., (2011). Statistical analysis and online monitoring for handling multiphase batch processes with varying durations. *Journal of Process Control, 21*(6), 817–829.

CHAPTER 7

MANAGING SYSTEMS IMPLEMENTATION

UNIT INTRODUCTION

Managing system implementation entails system changeover, data conversion, training, documentation, testing, application development, and post-implementation evaluation of outcomes. The complete plan of the system serves as a guide for building the proposed system throughout its implementation (Saarinen & Vepsäläinen, 1993). The first stage of system implementation involves programmers and systems analysts teaming up to generate the necessary code and software modules (Ruzevicius et al., 2004). Before the system conversion, data must be modified, well documented, and tested, and users must be modified. Following the launch of the advanced system, a proper assessment of the outcomes is evaluated and included in an official report to the administration (Wardhani et al., 2009).

Learning Objective

After studying this unit, you will be able to know that:

- Understand the concepts and processes involved in system implementations;
- Develop an understanding of the principles and practices of software quality assurance;

- Gain knowledge and skills in the field of software engineering, including the design, development, and testing of software;
- Learn how to create structured charts using appropriate tools and techniques.

Key Terms

- Project management
- Software engineering
- Structure charts
- Cohesion
- Coupling

7.1. SOFTWARE QUALITY ASSURANCE

Companies place a lot of emphasis on the quality of their goods and services in today's highly competitive business environment. Every aspect of a successful firm must be improved, including its data management. High-quality IT skills require top management's guidance, support, and engagement (Buckley & Poston, 1984). Regardless of how is meticulously a system planned and executed, issues might still arise. Although thorough testing might catch flaws during execution, fixing errors made during the early stages of development is significantly less expensive. The chief purpose of quality control is to recognize issues quickly and prevent them. Inaccurate specifications, problematic designs, incorrect coding, ineffective testing, and all inadequate documentation can contribute to poor quality. Software system designers should use software engineering and globally accepted quality standards to improve the final output (Lee, 2014).

7.2. SOFTWARE ENGINEERING

Software engineering is known as the implementation of engineering concepts to the development of sophisticated and durable applications. Technology, process, and people are combined here. Software engineering is more than just development. It includes five technical domains: specifications, design, building, maintenance, testing, and evolution. And is supported by non-technical tasks: process improvement, project management, effort, and cost estimation (Boehm, 1976).

As a software engineering innovator, the Software Engineering Institute of Carnegie Mellon University webpage offers quality guidelines and recommended practices for programmers and systems analysts (Biolchini et al., 2005).

The main goal of SEI is to develop more effective, efficient, and affordable ways. SEI develops the capability maturity model (CMM) to achieve that goal. It is a significant set of standards for application development and has been successfully implemented by many businesses around the globe (Boehm, 1984).

The purpose of a model is to speed up software development, save expenses, and enhance software quality. Figure 7.1displays five software CMM maturity levels. Other CMMs have been introduced since the original CMM software was published and revised. The

Did you Know?

A management system is a framework that enables companies to achieve their operational and business objectives through continuous improvement.

SEI's new approach is capability maturity model integration (CMMI). It joins system and software design into a single context. The CMMI employs five maturity levels to measure an organization's performance. Level 1 is unpredictable, poorly managed, and responsive to level 5, where process improvement is the expected outcome (Boehm, 2006).

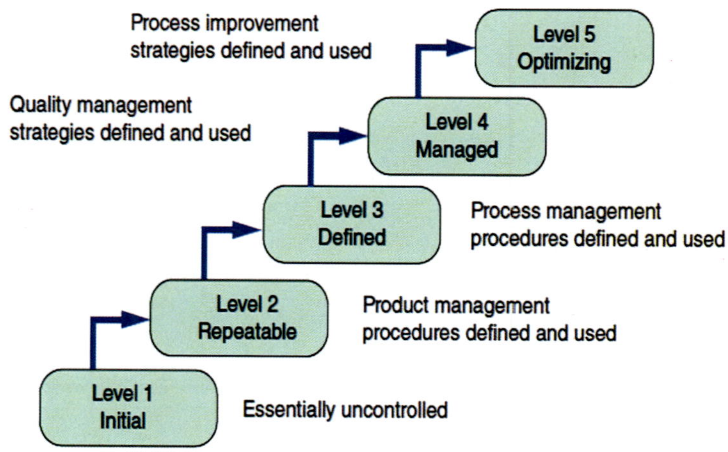

Figure 7.1. From Level 1 (initial), which is essentially unregulated development, to Level 5 (optimizing), when process improvement methods are created and applied, the CMM has five maturity levels.

Source: Bill Curtis, Creative Commons License.

7.2.1. The International Organization for Standardization (ISO)

What similarities do software, water, and automobiles have? They all follow regulations the ISO (International Standardization Organization) sets, like numerous other goods and services. Globally known symbols, like those in Figure 7.2, are just one example that follows ISO standards. Another is the numbering scheme of ISBN, which uses to identify this textbook. Additionally, ISO aims to provide a universally accepted definition of good managerial practices that businesses may use consistently to deliver high-quality services and goods, including software (Heires, 2008).

Due to the significance of software to an organization's performance, many companies are seeking reassurance that software systems, whether bought or built internally, will adhere to strict quality standards. ISO upgraded a series of regulations termed ISO 9000-3:2014 in 2014. It establishes a structure for quality control in software development and management (Nah et al., 2017). ISO standards comply with guaranteeing the finished products.

When purchasing software from a source, a company might apply ISO guidelines while developing software internally or request ISO requirements. According to ISO, a particular development strategy is necessary, outlining a bit-by-bit procedure for converting operator needs into a final product. ISO guidelines can be specific. A software supplier, for instance, must record all testing and keep track of test findings as required by ISO. The issues must be fixed after identifying them, and any relevant modules must be re-evaluated. All test equipment's hardware and software characteristics must also be recorded and incorporated into the testing records (Bialous & Yach, 2001).

Figure 7.2. Internationally recognized symbols included in the ISO.

7.3. OVERVIEW OF APPLICATION DEVELOPMENT

Codes and algorithmic modules are built that serves as an information system's building block. This process is known as application development. Previously it has been discussed that three common developmental approaches are O-O (object-oriented) analysis, agile methodologies, and structured analysis. The goal is to translate it into algorithmic modules and code that will function correctly regardless of the approach. Because setting up a system usually requires a lot of work, developers frequently employ project management approaches to regulate timelines and budgets (Korzun et al., 2011).

7.3.1. Application Development Tasks

If conventional structure or O-O approaches are used during a system's design, then the design transformation to a usable application can begin (Mazorchuck et al., 2018). The initial phases of the project development start with an agile software development approach that includes project design, setting the stage, assembling the team, and preparing to communicate with the customers (Ardito et al., 2020).

7.3.1.1. Traditional Methods

When developing a new system, careful planning is required. Once the overall strategy is ready, each module must be well-planned, written, coded, and tested. The program code is broken into small, manageable units to form modules. After the development of modules, testing, and documentation is necessary for the entire system, as shown in Figure 7.3, more testing is carried out (Lazcka et al., 2007).

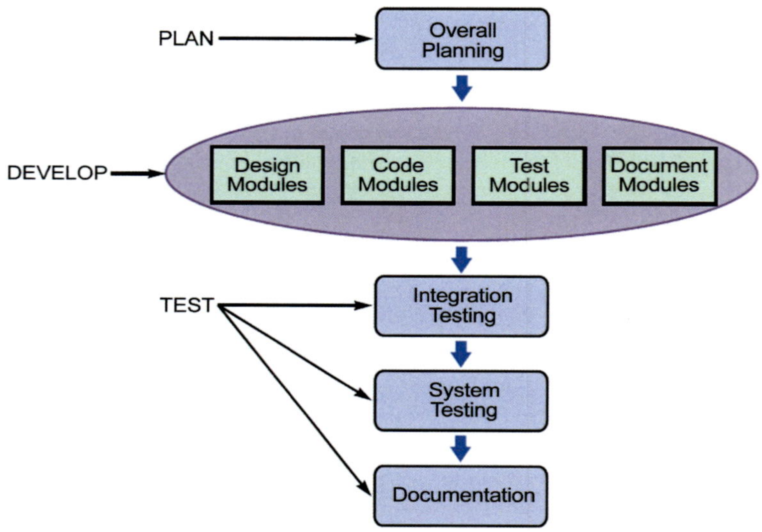

Figure 7.3. The primary steps in creating a typical application.

Source: Koombea, Creative Commons License.

When using structured or O-O approaches to develop program modules, the first step is to analyze the documentation requirements from earlier SDLC phases and produce a set of program designs. A reference report is a source of knowledge previously established in the product development process and is regularly updated (Cook & Leviton, 1980). The primary focus of the documentation is the system design specification, which contains user comments, information dictionary entries, report designs, screen designs, reference papers, and diagrams. The job of an analyst would be much simpler if the design process and systems analysis utilized

CASE software. Testing and coding start at this time. IT managers generally appoint systems analysts to collaborate with programmers as a workgroup, even though programmers do the actual coding (Maul, 2017).

7.3.1.2. Agile Methods

If an agile strategy is chosen, the IT staff, customers, or users will collaborate and communicate closely. The goal is to develop the system through testing, coding, designing, and an iterative approach to planning. In agile projects, various incremental and iterative models, such as extreme programming (XP), are used, as depicted in Figure 7.4 (Cohen et al., 2004).

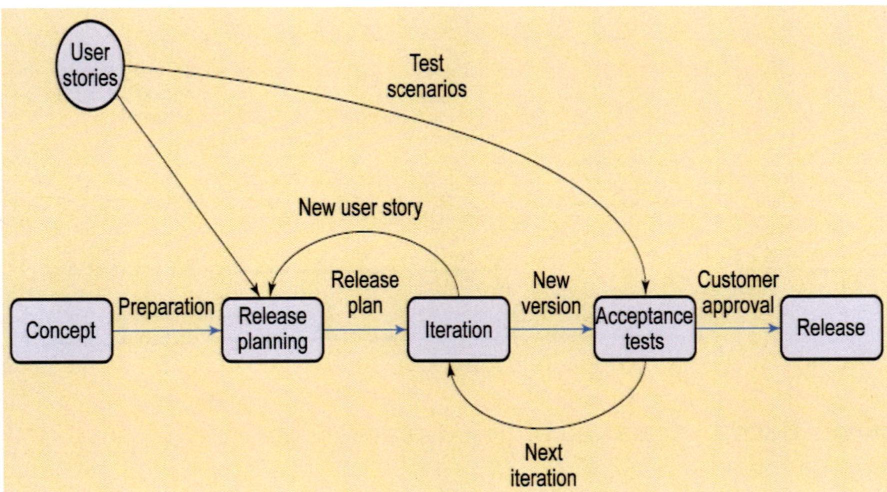

Figure 7.4. A simplified model of extreme programming (XP) projects. Take notice of the focus on testing and iteration.

Source: Geeks for Geeks, Creative Commons License.

7.3.1.3. Flowcharts

Flowcharts are excellent for displaying a designed module and can be utilized to illustrate the program's logic. A flowchart utilizes a variety of symbols joined by arrows to represent graphical interactions and show logical rules. Programmers can divide complex systems into smaller parts that are easier to understand using flowcharts (Scanlan, 1989).

7.3.2. Project Management

Any project, no matter how small or large, could have hundreds of thousands of modules, irrespective of whether it uses O-O design, structured analysis, or agile methodologies. Consequently, managing product development can be rather challenging. Project management is very crucial at this point. Management and users anticipate the introduction of the new scheme; therefore, it's very critical to plan genuinely, fulfill project aims, keep expenses in check, and guarantee eminence. To accomplish these objectives, the project manager or analyst should utilize project management techniques and tools to regulate and monitor the development work (Levitt, 2011).

The process of application development is discussed in the section follows. The discussion starts with structured application development and tools, then moves on to agile development and O-O approaches(Figure 7.5) (Henrie & Sousa, 2005).

Figure 7.5. A decision-making example is an advertising and promoting policy.

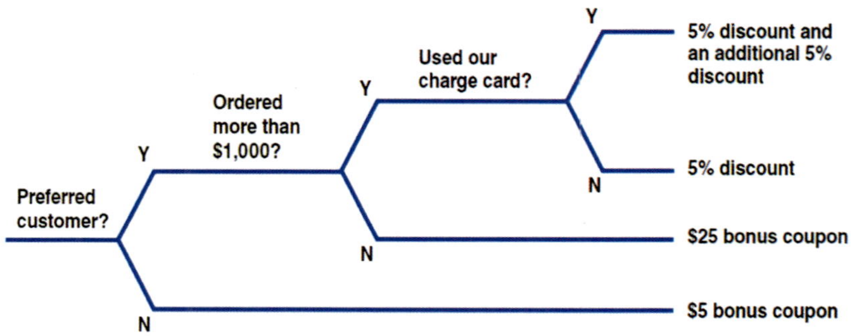

Source: Bandar Khalaf Alharthey, Creative Commons License.

7.4. STRUCTURED APPLICATION DEVELOPMENT

A top-down technique is typically used in structured application development, moving from a broad idea to a specific structure. The process of "partitioning" is where a systems analyst divides the system into modules and subsystems after documenting the system's needs. This method, often known as "modular design," is similar to creating a flattened set of DFDs. Diverse programming teams can work on distinct developmental areas by delegating modules to them. The project management tool is utilized to inspect progress on the individual module, estimate the whole progress time, measure the number of essential technical and human capital, and identify the project's major milestones. Building a solid, well-integrated architecture requires caution and regular feedback from IT management and programmers because all the modules must work properly together. The analysts must also guarantee that each idea has been carefully considered and can lead (Gellersen & Gaedke, 1999).

7.4.1. Structure Charts

Program modules and their relationships are displayed on a structured chart. Rectangles are used to represent the software module, and arrows and other symbols are used to indicate additional information. Control modules are typically at higher levels, and command and subordinate modules are at lower levels. In a structure chart, various conditions or actions are symbolized to represent control couples, data couples, loops, and conditions (Benedusi et al., 1992).

Remember

The process of defining how the information system should be built (i.e., physical system design), ensuring that the information system is operational an disused to ensure that the information system meets the quality standard (i.e., quality assurance) is called system implementation.

7.4.1.1. Module

A rectangle symbolizes a module, as illustrated in Figure 7.6. Module 1.3 is a library module, as seen in the figure, which indicates the two vertical straight lines at the corners of a box. A library module can be called from multiple points in the diagram and is composed of reusable code (Trexler et al., 2000).

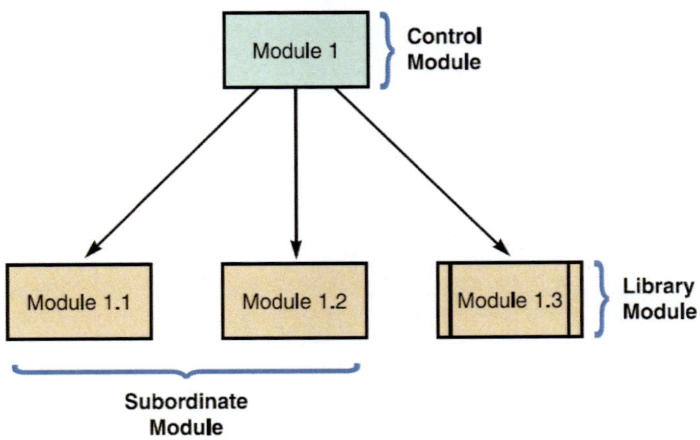

Figure 7.6. A module from a structure diagram.

Source: Geeks for Geeks, Creative Commons License.

The symbol for a data pair is an arrowhead with an empty circle. Data passed from one module to another is displayed in a data pair. The MCD (Maintain Customer Data) module and the LCN (Look-Up Customer Name) module exchange information in the sample data pair that can be seen in Figure 7.7 (Anderson, 1988).

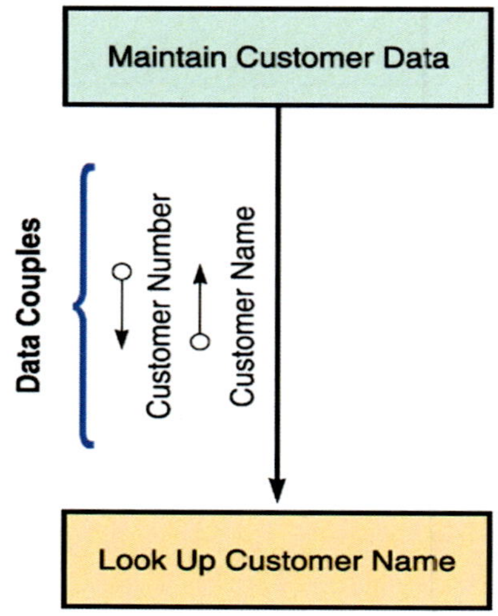

Figure 7.7. An illustration of a data couple in a structure chart.

Source: Geeks for Geeks, Creative Commons License.

7.4.1.2. Control Couple

An arrowhead with a filled ring serves to represent a control couple. A note from one module—often referred to as a status flag—is sent to another and displayed by a control couple (Williamson et al., 2016). According to the specimen in Figure 7.8, the UCF (Update Customer File) module directs a flag for an overdue justification to the MCD (Maintain Customer Data) module. One module utilizes an indicator to alert another module to the exact condition or a course of action (Hinnen et al., 2008).

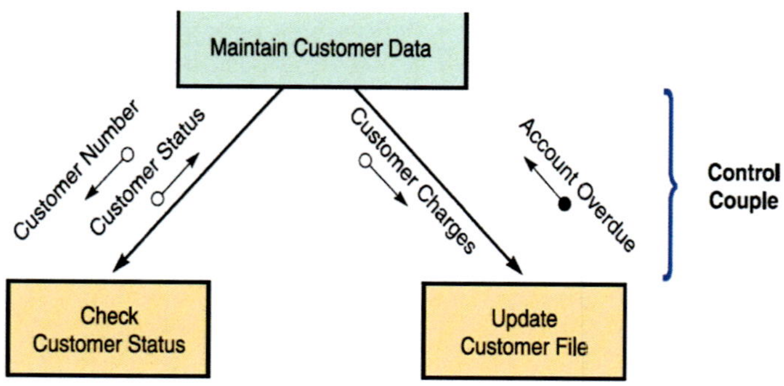

Figure 7.8. An example of a structure chart control couple.

Source: Geeks for Geeks, Creative Commons License.

7.4.1.3. Condition

A condition represented by a line ends at the diamond. A condition line determines that a control module that chooses subordinate modules would be triggered based on a specific condition. In Figure 7.9, a control module sorting inventory parts, triggers any subordinate modules from those three with a condition line (Burq & Gérard, 1997).

7.4.1.4. Loop

In Figure 7.10, a curved arrow represents a loop, indicating the repetition of one or more modules. In this example "Calculate GPA" and "Get Student Grades" modules are repetitive (Benjamin et al., 2019).

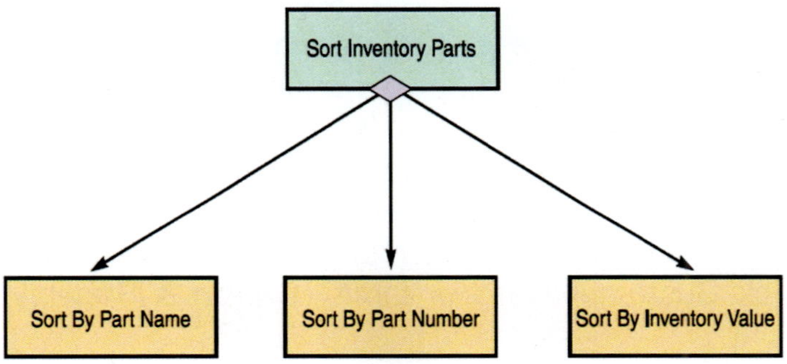

Figure 7.9. The diagram shows a control module that triggers three subordinate modules.

Source: Geeks for Geeks, Creative Commons License.

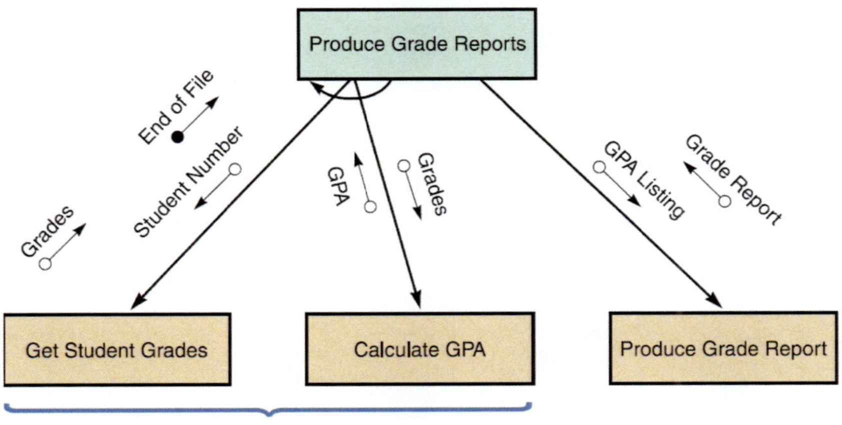

Figure 7.10. Two modules are recurring in the diagram of a structure chart with a loop.

Source: Geeks for Geeks, Creative Commons License.

7.4.2. Cohesion and Coupling

Cohesion and coupling are crucial tests for assessing a complete product plan (Dhama, 1995). The need for highly coherent and loosely coupled modules is explained in the following sections. If not, then the structural changes are difficult to make, increasing the cost of system maintenance (Candela et al., 2016).

7.4.2.1. Cohesion

It evaluates the range and processing properties of a module. A module with a significant desirable level of cohesion performs a sole task or function. A coherent module is considerably simple to code and can be reutilized because of its focus on a single job. For instance, a module named "Verify Customer Number" has a better overall structure than "Calculate and Print Remarks." If a word serves as the name of a module, then many tasks are required (Friedkin, 2004). A module will require more sophisticated codes and is more challenging to develop and maintain if it needs to execute numerous jobs. Divide a module into distinct units with a defined purpose to strengthen its cohesion. One way to improve cohesion is to split "the Check Customer Number and Credit Limit module" in Figure 7.11 into two separate modules, "Check Customer Credit" and "Check Customer Number Limit."(Carron & Brawley, 2000).

7.4.2.2. Coupling

The level of interdependence between modules is described. Independent modules that are weakly connected are preferred the most. Since the logic inside one module doesn't change the logic in another, loosely connected modules are simpler to modify and maintain (Weinberg, 1974).

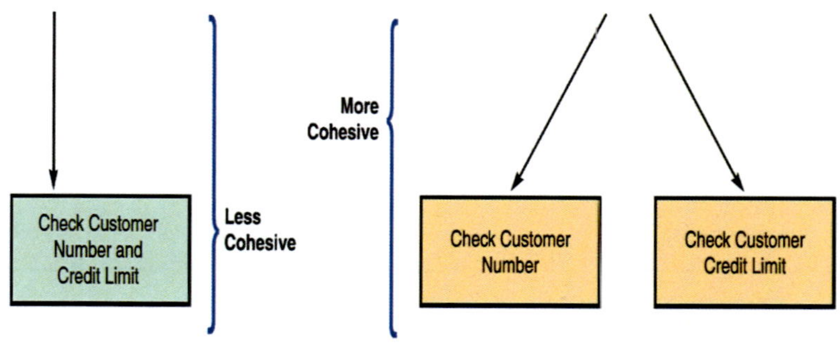

Figure 7.11. Two illustrations of cohesiveness: Observe how the two modules on the right are more coherent than the single module on the left.

Source: Erwin Rauch, Creative Commons License.

A programmer can complete the work in one place if a loosely connected module needs to be updated. When modules are closely coupled, the internal logic of one module is connected to another. For instance, Module A might refer to internally presenting a variable in Module B. In that situation, a logical mistake in Module B will affect Module A's processing. Because of this, it is considered a bad design to send a status flag from a control module as a message. To prevent a chain of logical errors in the control module, it is preferable to execute subordinate modules' processing duties independently with feasibility (Siemsen et al., 2000).

The closely coupled example in Figure 7.12 on the left demonstrates how the subordinated module "Estimate Current Charges" depends on the flag's status that is passed up from the control module "Update Customer Balance." The modules should ideally be independent and connected lightly. Because Apply Discount, a subordinate module, manages discount processing independently in the example on the right, there is no need for a status flag. Any logical mistakes are restricted to the module of Apply Discount (Bock et al., 2009).

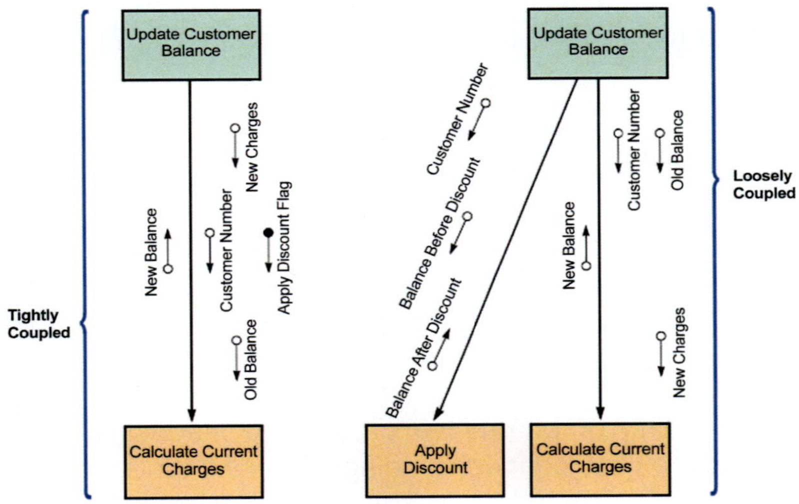

Figure 7.12. An illustration of a structure chart with tightly and loosely coupled elements.

Source: Erwin Rauch, Creative Commons License.

7.4.3. Drawing a Structure Chart

If the system design employs an organized analysis approach, the structure charts will be built on the DFDs throughout the process and data modeling production (Zhang et al., 2022). Typically, a structure chart is created in four steps DFDs are examined to determine the procedures and techniques, the software modules, and the command-and-control hierarchy. Couplings and loops have been added as symbols, and the structure chart is in line with the system description (Burkhard & Lee, 1986).

7.4.3.1. Step 1: Review the DFDs

Revision of each DFD for completeness and accuracy comes first, particularly if adjustments were made in the following systems analysis phase (Tropman, 1989). If representations of the items are developed, these should be reviewed to identify the objects, the functions that each object must do, and the relationships among the objects. Similarly, to a functional primitive, a method needs code to carry out the required operations (Bishop, 1986).

7.4.3.2. Step 2: Identify Modules and Relationships

Program modules are produced when function data structures or object methods are transformed into a logical model. To achieve functional data structures when utilizing DFDs, one advance from the classification-based diagrams to the smaller ones while identifying control and subordinate modules. If more cohesion is required, processes can be divided into more control modules that each carry out a single task (Langfelder & Horvath, 2007).

ACTIVITY 7.1

Give a detailed presentation on software engineering.

7.4.3.3. Step 3: Add Couples, Loops, and Conditions

The structure chart is then expanded to include couples, loops, and conditions. When DFDs are in operation, the data flow and the information dictionary can identify which data items are transferred from one component to another (Drukker et al., 1999). Regulator couples are also introduced when a module transmits a regulator parameter, such as an indicator, to another module, in addition to data couples. Loops and condition lines are also introduced to denote recurring or alternative processing stages. The classes, objects, and object connection diagrams can be examined if an object model is created to ensure that the interaction between objects is completely understood (Semnani et al., 2003).

7.4.3.4. Step 4: Analyze the Structure Chart and the Data Dictionary

Now that the structure chart is ready, it can be thoroughly examined. Each procedure, data element, and subject approach should be double-checked to ensure that the chart appropriately reflects all prior information and is rationally solid (Mayer et al., 2020). Strong cohesion and loose coupling should be present among all components. Frequently, the chart needs to be drawn in multiple iterations. The chart can be analyzed using CASE tools to help pinpoint problematic areas (DeMarco, 1979).

7.5. SUMMARY

Applications must be developed, tested, installed, and evaluated before the new system is evaluated during the implementation phase. Analysts choose the general design strategy for the application while it is being developed, and they collaborate with programmers to finish the design, programming, testing, and documentation. When implementing new ideas, quality control is crucial. The International Organization for Standardization's (ISO) quality standards and software engineering is widely used by companies. Tools variations depend on the system development strategy. For example, data flow diagrams (DFDs) with structure charts are crucial to organized development. Loops, conditions, data couples, control couples, and software modules represent the symbols on a structure chart. Use of CASE, class, series, and transition state diagrams are among the UML diagrams used in O-O approaches. Iterative and incremental modeling is a hallmark of agile methodologies.

To assist them in converting the logic of the system into correctly working program modules, developers can also employ more general tools. Some tools include institutional diagrams, flowcharts, pseudocode, mathematical reasoning, and judgmental trees. When using an agile methodology, the client makes operator sections that specify features requirement and priority stages. Following numerous iterations and meticulous customer testing, a new system is released to utilize agile methodology.

A module's scope and processing properties are measured by cohesion. A module at the upper level of cohesion performs a particular required function. Coupling gages, the dependencies, and interactions between modules. Modules should be loosely connected because they work independently. Although they are equally applicable to O-O programming, cohesion, and coupling ideas are employed in structure development.

Typically, a structure chart is created in four steps. The processes and procedures were examined using DFDs and object models. The software modules were identified along with control-subordinate relationships. Couples and loops were added using symbols, and it was checked to see if the structure chart agreed with the system documentation.

REVIEW QUESTIONS

1. What are the challenges of managing systems implementation?
2. What strategies can be utilized to ensure successful implementation?
3. What strategies can help minimize disruption to existing systems during implementation?
4. How can a project manager ensure that the stakeholders are fully engaged in the process?
5. How can feedback from stakeholders be effectively incorporated into the implementation plan?
6. What are the key elements of a successful change management plan?

7. How can conflicts between stakeholders be effectively managed during implementation?
8. What are the benefits of involving outside experts in the systems implementation process?
9. How can the risks associated with systems implementation be effectively managed?
10. What steps can be taken to ensure the timely and successful completion of the project?

MULTIPLE CHOICE QUESTIONS

1. What is the main goal of managing systems implementation?
   a. To minimize the cost of implementation
   b. To improve system performance
   c. To ensure the system meets user requirements
   d. To reduce system risk

2. What is the primary role of the systems implementation manager?
   a. To develop the system
   b. To oversee the implementation process
   c. To provide user training
   d. To maintain the system

3. What are the three main phases of systems implementation?
   a. Design, development, and deployment
   b. Design, testing, and deployment
   c. Planning, development, and training
   d. Planning, testing, and deployment

4. What is one way to reduce the risk of system failure during implementation?
   a. Utilizing a detailed project plan
   b. Testing the system thoroughly
   c. Ensuring user training is comprehensive
   d. All of the above

5. What is a critical success factor for successful systems implementation?
   a. Having a clear timeline
   b. Ensuring user satisfaction
   c. Identifying potential risks
   d. All of the above

Answers to Multiple Choice Questions

1. (b) 2. (d) 3. (d) 4. (d) 5. (d)

REFERENCES

1. Anderson, J. R., (1988). The expert module. *Foundations of Intelligent Tutoring Systems*,21–53.
2. Ardito, L., Coppola, R., Malnati, G., & Torchiano, M., (2020). Effectiveness of Kotlin vs. Java in android app development tasks. *Information and Software Technology, 127*, 106374.
3. Benedusi, P., Cimitile, A., & De Carlini, U., (1992). Reverse engineering processes, design document production, and structure charts. *Journal of Systems and Software, 19*(3), 225–245.
4. Benjamin, E. J., Muntner, P., Alonso, A., Bittencourt, M. S., Callaway, C. W., Carson, A. P., & American Heart Association Council on Epidemiology and Prevention Statistics Committee and Stroke Statistics Subcommittee, (2019). Heart disease and stroke statistics—2019 update: A report from the American Heart Association. *Circulation, 139*(10), e56-e528.
5. Bialous, S. A., & Yach, D., (2001). Whose standard is it, anyway? How the tobacco industry determines the international organization for standardization (ISO) standards for tobacco and tobacco products. *Tobacco Control, 10*(2), 96–104.
6. Biolchini, J., Mian, P. G., Natali, A. C. C., & Travassos, G. H., (2005). Systematic review in software engineering. *System Engineering and Computer Science Department COPPE/UFRJ, Technical Report ES, 679*(05), 45.
7. Bishop, J. M., (1986). A complete notation for Ada charts. *ACM SIGAda Ada Letters, 6*(6), 49–53.
8. Bock, J. J., Gundersen, J., Lee, A. T., Richards, P. L., & Wollack, E., (2009). Optical coupling. In: *Journal of Physics: Conference Series* (Vol. 155, No. 1, p. 012005). IOP Publishing.
9. Boehm, B. W., (1976). Software engineering. *IEEE Trans. Computers, 25*(12), 1226–1241.
10. Boehm, B. W., (1984). Software engineering economics. *IEEE Transactions on Software Engineering*, (1), 4–21.
11. Boehm, B., (2006). A view of 20th and 21st century software engineering. In: *Proceedings of the 28th International Conference on Software Engineering* (pp. 12–29).
12. Buckley, F. J., & Poston, R., (1984). Software quality assurance. *IEEE Transactions on Software Engineering*, (1), 36–41.
13. Burkhard, B., & Lee, M., (1986). Drawing Ada structure charts. *ACM SIGAda Ada Letters, 6*(3), 71–80.
14. Burq, N., & Gérard, P., (1997). Condition nécessaire et suffisante pour la contrôlabilité exacte des ondes. *Comptes Rendus de l'Académie des Sciences-Series I-Mathematics, 325*(7), 749–752.
15. Candela, I., Bavota, G., Russo, B., & Oliveto, R., (2016). Using cohesion and

coupling for software remodularization: Is it enough? *ACM Transactions on Software Engineering and Methodology (TOSEM),25*(3), 1–28.

16. Carron, A. V., & Brawley, L. R., (2000). Cohesion: Conceptual and measurement issues. *Small Group Research, 31*(1), 89–106.
17. Cohen, D., Lindvall, M., & Costa, P., (2004). An introduction to agile methods. *Adv. Comput., 62*(03), 1–66.
18. Cook, T. D., & Leviton, L. C., (1980). Reviewing the literature: A comparison of traditional methods with meta-analysis 1. *Journal of Personality, 48*(4), 449–472.
19. DeMarco, T., (1979). Structure analysis and system specification. In: *Pioneers and Their Contributions to Software Engineering* (pp. 255–288). Springer, Berlin, Heidelberg.
20. Dhama, H., (1995). Quantitative models of cohesion and coupling in software. *Journal of Systems and Software, 29*(1), 65–74.
21. Drukker, N., Gross, D. J., & Ooguri, H., (1999). Wilson loops and minimal surfaces. *Physical Review D, 60*(12), 125006.
22. Friedkin, N. E., (2004). Social cohesion. *Annual Review of Sociology,* 409–425.
23. Gellersen, H. W., & Gaedke, M., (1999). Object-oriented web application development. *IEEE Internet Computing, 3*(1), 60–68.
24. Heires, M., (2008). The international organization for standardization (ISO). *New Political Economy, 13*(3), 357–367.
25. Henrie, M., & Sousa-Poza, A., (2005). Project management: A cultural literary review. *Project Management Journal, 36*(2), 5–14.
26. Hinnen, C., Ranchor, A. V., Sanderman, R., Snijders, T. A., Hagedoorn, M., & Coyne, J. C., (2008). Course of distress in breast cancer patients, their partners, and matched control couples. *Annals of Behavioral Medicine, 36*(2), 141–148.
27. Korzun, D. G., Balandin, S. I., Luukkala, V., Liuha, P., & Gurtov, A. V., (2011). Overview of smart-M3 principles for application development. In: *Proc. Congress on Information Systems and Technologies (IS&IT'11), Conf. Artificial Intelligence and Systems (AIS'11)* (Vol. 4, pp. 64–71).
28. Langfelder, P., & Horvath, S., (2007). Eigengene networks for studying the relationships between co-expression modules. *BMC Systems Biology, 1*(1), 1–17.
29. Lazcka, O., Del Campo, F. J., & Munoz, F. X., (2007). Pathogen detection: A perspective of traditional methods and biosensors. *Biosensors and Bioelectronics, 22*(7), 1205–1217.
30. Lee, M. C., (2014). Software quality factors and software quality metrics to enhance software quality assurance. *British Journal of Applied Science & Technology, 4*(21), 3069–3095.
31. Levitt, R. E., (2011). Towards project management 2.0. *Engineering Project Organization Journal, 1*(3), 197–210.
32. Maul, A., (2017). Rethinking traditional methods of survey validation. *Measurement: Interdisciplinary Research and Perspectives, 15*(2), 51–69.

33. Mayer, C. S., Williams, N., & Huser, V., (2020). Analysis of data dictionary formats of HIV clinical trials. *Plos One, 15*(10), e0240047.
34. Mazorchuck, M., Dobriak, V., & Chumachenko, D., (2018). Web-application development for tasks of prediction in medical domain. In: *2018 IEEE 13th International Scientific and Technical Conference on Computer Sciences and Information Technologies (CSIT)* (Vol. 1, pp. 5–8). IEEE.
35. Nah, E. H., Cho, S., Kim, S., Cho, H. I., Stingu, C. S., Eschrich, K., & Friedberg, R. C., (2017). International organization for standardization (ISO) 15189. *Annals of Laboratory Medicine, 37*(5), 365–370.
36. Ruzevicius, Adomaitiene, & Sirvidaite. (2004). Motivation and efficiency of quality management systems implementation: A study of Lithuanian organizations. *Total Quality Management & Business Excellence, 15*(2), 173–189.
37. Saarinen, T., & Vepsäläinen, A., (1993). Managing the risks of information systems implementation. *European Journal of Information Systems, 2*(4), 283–295.
38. Scanlan, D. A., (1989). Structured flowcharts outperform pseudocode: An experimental comparison. *IEEE Software, 6*(5), 28–36.
39. Semnani, D., Latifi, M., Hamzeh, S., & Jeddi, A. A. A., (2003). A new aspect of geometrical and physical principles applicable to the estimation of textile structures: An ideal model for the plain-knitted loop. *Journal of the Textile Institute, 94*(3, 4), 202–211.
40. Siemsen, P., Livingston, R. C., & Diederich, F., (2000). Acetylenic coupling: A powerful tool in molecular construction. *Angewandte Chemie International Edition, 39*(15), 2632–2657.
41. Slomkowski, S., Penczek, S., & Duda, A., (2014). Polylactides—An overview. *Polymers for Advanced Technologies, 25*(5), 436–447.
42. Trexler, M., Bányai, L., & Patthy, L., (2000). The LCCL module. *European Journal of Biochemistry, 267*(18), 5751–5757.
43. Tropman, J. E., (1989). The organizational circle: A new approach to drawing an organizational chart. *Administration in Social Work, 13*(1), 35–44.
44. Wardhani, V., Utarini, A., Van, D. J. P., Post, D., & Groothoff, J. W., (2009). Determinants of quality management systems implementation in hospitals. *Health Policy, 89*(3), 239–251.
45. Weinberg, B. H., (1974). Bibliographic coupling: A review. *Information Storage and Retrieval, 10*(5, 6), 189–196.
46. Williamson, H. C., Altman, N., Hsueh, J., & Bradbury, T. N., (2016). Effects of relationship education on couple communication and satisfaction: A randomized controlled trial with low-income couples. *Journal of Consulting and Clinical Psychology, 84*(2), 156.
47. Zhang, Y., Zhang, A., Gao, M., & Liang, Y., (2022). Research on three-dimensional electronic navigation chart hybrid spatial index structure based on quadtree and R-tree. *ISPRS International Journal of Geo-Information, 11*(5), 319.

CHAPTER 8

MANAGING SYSTEMS SUPPORT AND SECURITY

UNIT INTRODUCTION

When a system is first put into operation, a new phase known as "systems support as well as security" kicks off and remains in effect until the technology has reached the end of its productive life. Throughout the development phase, the goal has been to provide an information management system that is not always effective but also user-friendly and reasonably priced. After the technology has been delivered, the information technology (IT) group's primary focus shifts to maintenance and support activities. Customer expectations, operation of the system, as well as security needs are the three immediate problems that need to be managed while providing support and protection for computer systems (Le & Hoang, 2016).

An inside consultant in the role of a computer programmer who offers direction, assistance, including training to the organization. Customers of successful systems typically require the most excellent support since they want to become familiar with the characteristics, test out all the possibilities, and learn how well the system could assist them in carrying out their responsibilities (Almorsy & Grundy, 2014). Half of the work done by an IT staff in most companies goes toward maintaining already-installed software and hardware. This chapter will begin with a study of the many aspects of system support, such as user training, including help desks. We will talk about the four primary maintenance types: corrective, adaptable, perfective, and preventative maintenance. In addition, how the IT department handles maintenance staff, configuration, maintenance issues, and the utilization of performance concerns using maintenance tools are investigated. Analyzes are conducted on the safety system on every one of the following six levels: security management, network monitoring, security testing, file security, personal security, and procedure security. The significance of problems with data recovery and backup problems is also considered. The distinguishing characteristics of an obsolete system are detailed in this chapter. In conclusion, a discussion is had about some potential difficulties and possibilities that system designers may face in years to come (Viana et al., 2022).

Learning Objective

After studying this unit, you will be able to:

- Understand the concepts and practices of systems support and security, including identifying and mitigating potential threats and ensuring the smooth operation of a system.
- Identify and describe user support's various functions and responsibilities, including troubleshooting, problem resolution, and user education.
- Understand the importance of regular maintenance tasks and their role in maintaining the performance and security of a system, including identifying and implementing necessary updates and upgrades.
- Understand the key components of system performance management, including monitoring, troubleshooting, and performance optimization techniques.

Key Terms

- System support management
- User support
- Help desks
- Outsourcing issues
- Maintenances management

8.1. USER SUPPORT

Businesses provide various user support services, such as user involvement and technical support providing technical support and guidance (Brajnik et al., 1996).

8.1.1. User Training

As previously detailed, the first training is carried out whenever a new system is implemented. New hires must also receive training on the organization's information systems. The IT staff could register for a new training module if significant modifications are made to the current system or when the latest version is issued. Based on the change, the bundle could include formal training, a customized website, a modification to the owner's manual, or an addition to the guidebook. Similarly to basic training, system changes need user education. The primary goal is to demonstrate to customers how the technology may assist them in carrying out their duties (Gupta et al., 2010).

8.1.2. Help Desks

Users want ongoing assistance and direction as systems and information structures get more complicated. Many IT organizations establish help desks to increase user empowerment and data accessibility. A contact center, also known as a service counter, is the main center operated by IT specialists who give users the assistance they require to complete their tasks (Halverson et al., 2004). The three primary goals of a help desk are to: (i) make consumers more efficient by educating them on how to fulfill their information requirements; (ii) resolve operational or technical problems; and (iii) educate individuals on how to utilize systems resources more efficiently. Users often go to a helpline first if they need support or data. A contact center does not perform conventional IT support and maintenance tasks. Help desks, on the other hand, increase efficiency and enhance how well a firm uses its data resources (González et al., 2005).

Because they contact customers across many departments, helping desk staff need interpersonal solid, technological, and business knowledge. All questions, assistance requests, and exercise habits should be meticulously recorded by a help desk (Kriegsman & Barletta, 1993). The data can assist in creating a technical support base of knowledge by identifying patterns and prevalent issues. Utilizing remotely controlled software that enables IT, professionals to take over a user's desktop and give support, including troubleshooting, a help desk may increase its efficiency. Among many more, popular remotely controlled software applications include GoToMyPC by Citrix (shown in Figure 8.1), LogMeIn Pro by LogMeIn, and PC Now by WebEx (Heckman & Guskey, 1998).

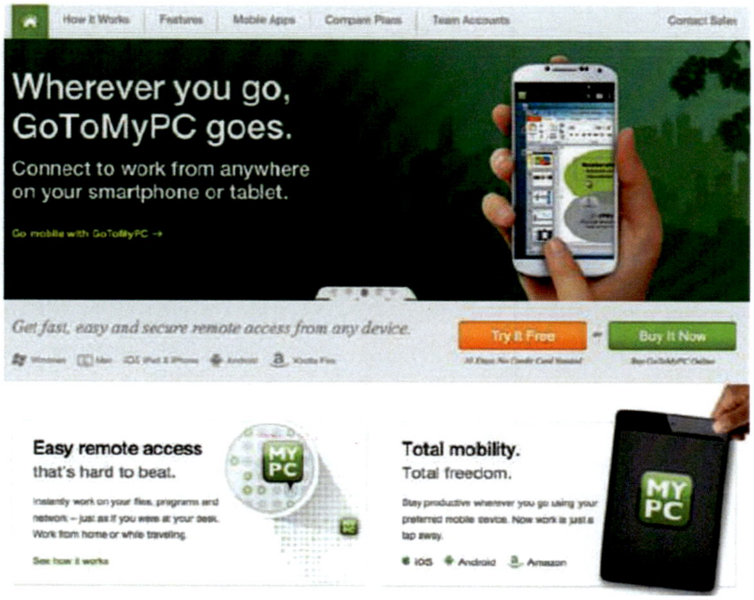

Figure 8.1. Users can access their PCs from anywhere, even with their cellphones or tablets, thanks to remote access software like the one GoToMyPC shows here.

Source: GoTo Support, Creative Commons License.

The help desk employees depicted in Figure 8.2 might need to carry out the following duties during a typical day:

- Describe how to make a database query and report showing the user-specific business data;
- Identify and fix password or network access issues;
- Showcase a sophisticated system or software package capability;
- Aid a user in recovering corrupted data;
- Provide advice for improved operation;
- Describe a software feature that is not documented;
- Demonstrate web conferencing to a user (Al-Hawari & Barham, 2021);
- Describe how to reach the corporate website or intranet;
- Help a user create a primary database to keep track of the time spent on different tasks;
- Provide information about software updates and licensing;
- Describe the system requirements and the price of new software and hardware;
- Offer a system strategy that integrates information from diverse sources to address a business issue (Poi, 2002);
- Installing or reconfiguring equipment, including scanning,

printing, network interface cards, wireless connections, optical drives, backups devices, and multimedia applications, will provide hardware assistance;

- Tell customers how to preserve data integrity and consistency across a desktop, a laptop, and a portable device or smartphone;
- Using remote control software, troubleshoot software problems (Armstrong, 1992).

Figure 8.2. System users can get assistance from a help desk, also known as a service desk.

Source: Freepik, Creative Commons License.

The help desk is a crucial communication channel among customers and IT employees and is the primary point of contact for all IT maintenance tasks. Users can report system issues, seek repairs, or create new system threats at the helpline. Like external vendors, a contact center could use various automated assistance methods, such as email replies, on-demand faxing, an online body of knowledge, frequently asked queries (FAQs), discussion forums, and bulletin boards, including automatic voicemail messages. For customers who shop online, a lot of businesses now provide live chat (Gutierrez et al., 2003).

8.1.3. Outsourcing Issues

Numerous businesses outsource different facets of app development, as was covered in Chapter 7. This tendency also involves contracting out help desks and IT assistance. Outsourcing offers benefits and drawbacks, much like any business decision. Cost-cutting is typically the key driver of outsourcing. In addition to reducing costs, offshore contact centers may free up critical human capital for product design (Altinkemer et al., 1994).

However, businesses have discovered that even if technical support quality declines, consumers will probably notice and may start doing their business elsewhere. Phone long waits, the effectiveness of the support staff, and online assistance resources might all be crucial elements (Sako, 2005). The fundamental issue is whether a business can make the needed savings without jeopardizing its standing and clientele. Risks may be reduced only if the company actively manages and monitors support consistency and quality (Krishna et al., 2004).

Did you Know?

Systems support and security provides a vital protection and maintenance for the system.

8.2. MAINTENANCE TASKS

The period of native support and security is crucial to TCO (total cost of ownership) since continuing maintenance costs might affect the system's economic lifespan. A typical trend of maintenance and operation costs across a system's service life is depicted in Figure 8.3. Expenses for consumables, equipment rentals, and program leases are included in operational costs. Figure 8.3 illustrates fixed operations expenditures in the lower region, while maintenance costs are displayed in the upper section (Dunlap, 1984). Throughout the system's operating life, the cost of maintenance changes dramatically and supports expenses for maintenance tasks. Modifying programs, processes, or documents to guarantee the proper performance of a system, adjusting the system to meet changing needs, and improving the system's performance are all examples of maintenance operations. Correction, adaptability, perfective, and preventive maintenance take care of such demands (Ko et al., 2006).

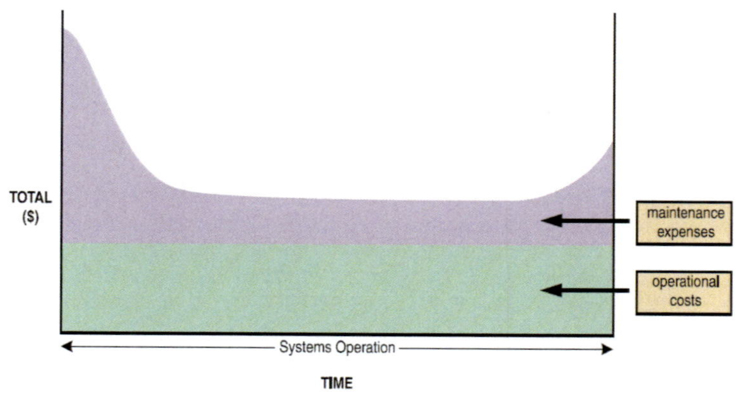

Figure 8.3. Operational and maintenance costs are included in the total price of running an information system. While maintenance expenses (purple) fluctuate over time, operating expenditures (green) are generally stable.

Source: Olaf Maier, Creative Commons License.

The samples in Figure 8.4 illustrate four different maintenance tasks, but there is a slight overlap. Errors are fixed through maintenance tasks, whereas the ability to adapt provides new functionality and additions, perfective maintenance boosts productivity, and predictive maintenance lowers the likelihood of a system failure occurring in the future. Some experts say care refers to problem-solving corrective maintenance (Aissani et al., 2009). Therefore, it is beneficial to approach the maintenance notion more generally and recognize many duties. Maintenance costs are often significant whenever a system is first put into service because repairing should be used to identify, investigate, and fix faults. Prices usually stay low as the system stabilizes and requires minimal adaptive maintenance. Ultimately, in a dynamic corporate environment, combined adaptive and perfective maintenance operations rise (Curtis et al., 1979).

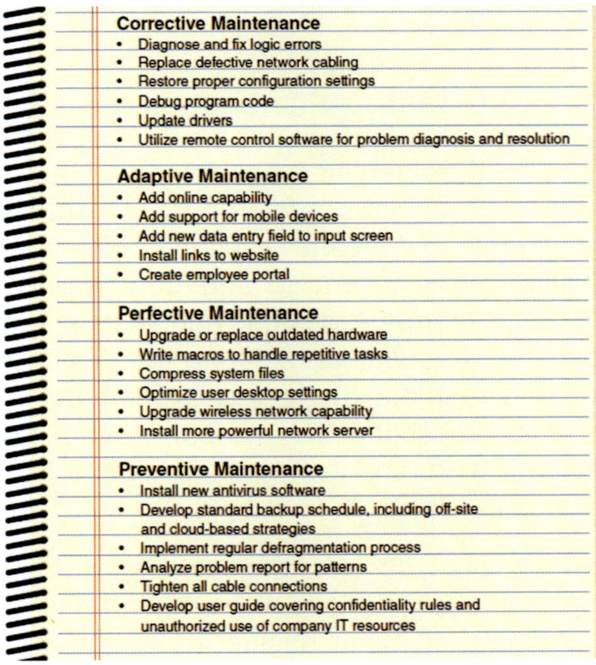

Figure 8.4. Errors and issues are fixed by corrective maintenance.

Source: UpKeep, Creative Commons License.

Adaptive and corrective maintenance costs soar as both systems near the end of their useful life, whereas corrective and preventive maintenance costs typically fall as it becomes evident that the organization intends to replace the equipment. The usual trends for every one of the four types of maintenance operations throughout a system's life are depicted in Figure 8.5 (Toriizuka, 2001).

	Immediately After Implementation	Early Operational Life	Middle Operational Life	Later Operational Life
Corrective Maintenance	High	Low	Low	High
Adaptive Maintenance (Minor Enhancements)	None	Medium	Medium	Medium
Adaptive Maintenance (Major Enhancements)	None	None	Medium to High	Medium to High
Perfective Maintenance	Low	Low to Medium	Medium	Low
Preventive Maintenance	Low	Medium	Medium	Low

Figure 8.5. The kind of maintenance and the age of the system are factors in information systems maintenance.

Source: UpKeep, Creative Commons License.

8.2.1. Corrective Maintenance

Corrective maintenance identifies and fixes problems in a system that is in use. All repair jobs need rigorous examination before making modifications to prevent creating new issues. The ideal maintenance strategy is a concise summary of the SDLC itself, wherein inquiry, assessment, design, and testing are carried out before adopting any solution, considering the distinctions between such a testing environment and an environmental situation. Any maintenance tasks impacting the system should first be carried out in the testing environment before moving to the live system (Sheut & Krajewski, 1994).

Depending on the type and intensity of the fault, IT support personnel will react to it in various ways. Most firms have standard operating procedures for minor mistakes like an inaccurate report headline or an improperly formatted data item. In such a typical process, a client submits a system request, which the administrator or the system design review committee evaluates, prioritizes, and schedules. The maintenance people develop, test, and file, as well as enforce a solution if such a request is granted (Wang et al., 2014).

For systems inquiries, many companies employ a typical web form. Smaller businesses may use a simple email message for such a procedure. A user sends a system's demand with accompanying documentation for more significant circumstances, such as incorrect report totals or conflicting data (Stenström et al., 2016). These requests are prioritized, and a maintenance crew fixes the issue immediately. A technical fault is the direst scenario. When an emergency arises, the maintenance crew skips the preliminary processes and seeks to resolve the problem directly. This medium frequently calls for a patch, a specifically created software component that offers short-term fixes so that activities may continue. In the meantime, a customer or employee of the IT sector creates demand for a written system and adds it to the repair record. The maintenance staff identifies the root cause, investigates the issue, and develops a long-term remedy once the system is up and running again. The IT responses team creates comprehensive documentation, extensively analyzes the system, and refreshes the testing data files. No matter how the objectives are determined, a conventional ranking system can be helpful. A three-level structure for the possible impact of IT support, for instance, is shown in Figure 8.6 (Kajko, 2005).

PRIORITY	IMPACT	TIME FRAME
Level 1	Significant impact on IT operations, security, or business activity that requires immediate attention.	Implement patch as soon as possible.
Level 2	Some impact on IT operations, security, or business activity. Requires prompt attention, but operations can continue.	Patch as necessary and begin implementation prior to next release.
Level 3	Little or no impact on current IT operations, security, or business activity	Implement in the next release.

Figure 8.6. This three-level framework for IT support ranking considers the response's potential impact and urgency.

Source: Geeks for Geeks, Creative Commons License.

8.2.2. Adaptive Maintenance

An operating system (OS) is improved via the capability to adapt, which also makes the system simpler to operate. A new function or capacity constitutes an improvement. A service or product, a shift in manufacturing techniques, or support for just a modern web operation are just a few examples of how the requirement for the capability to adapt typically results from changes in the industry. Minor ability to adapt follows a similar process to regular corrective maintenance (Unckless & Lazzaro, 2016). The systems evaluation committee assesses and ranks the system requests that users submit. The improvement is then evaluated, created, tested, and put into practice by maintenance staff. Even though the two forms of maintenance have similar methods, adaptive maintenance calls for more effort from the IT staff than simple maintenance tasks (Fioravanti & Nesi, 2001).

Because of how similar the design process is for large and small SDLC projects, they are comparable. Because improvements should fit within the present structure's limitations, adapting might be more challenging than creating new systems (Abeygunawardane et al., 2013).

Remember

The three main elements of system security: confidentiality, integrity, and availability.

8.3. MAINTENANCE MANAGEMENT

Efficient leadership, quality control, including budget control are necessary for maintenance tasks. Companies employ a variety of tactics, including a maintenance staff, maintenance, and management program, configurations process management, and a service release strategy, to meet these objectives. Firms also track system updates and examine the system's life cycle using baselines, including version control. The subsections describe these ideas (Ben-Daya et al., 2009).

8.3.1. The Maintenance Team

A network administrator, one or more system engineers, and developers make up a maintenance staff. The system administrator must be knowledgeable in technology and have experience installing hardware and software platforms. Excellent IT knowledge, analytical ability skills, effective communication, and general awareness of company processes are requirements for influential analysts (Deeter & Ramsey, 2003).

8.3.1.1. System Administrator

A system administrator manages network and computer systems. A network manager needs to be able to grasp and handle complicated problems quickly, in addition to operating under stress and with others. The management, configuration, and safety of one or even more systems, are the critical responsibilities of a system administrator in most businesses. The network manager is now in charge of routine maintenance and is typically permitted to take preventative measures to avert an urgent problem, including a server breakdown, network outage, security issue, or equipment failures. One essential task is network administration. *LISA* (Large Installations System Administration), the *USENIX* particular interest organization for system administrators, is among the most prominent professional organizations that foster cooperation and assistance. It is seen in Figures 8.6 (Barrett et al., 2004).

8.3.1.2. Systems Analysts

When allocated to maintenance staff, systems analysts act as competent investigators who quickly identify the cause of a problem through analysis. Synthesis is just the study of the pieces to comprehend the total system (Green, 1989). At the same time, the research examines the whole to learn about individual components. An analyst needs to be highly technical and have a firm understanding of business operations. Additionally, analysts should have good communication skills and be enthusiastic, innovative, and open to learning new things (Schenk et al., 1998).

8.3.1.3. Programmers

A developer may be required to undertake various responsibilities in a small business, but programming work is frequently more specialized in more prominent organizations. A systems programmer specializes in OS programs and services, a databases developer focuses on developing and maintaining massive data systems, and an applications developer works on creating and maintaining new devices. In several IT organizations, roles requiring both programming and systems analysis abilities are referred to as programmer analyst (Lahtinen et al., 2005).

8.3.1.4. Organizational Issues

IT supervisors frequently divide systems analysts and developers into two groups: one group develops new systems, whereas the other oversees maintenance. Some businesses adopt a more flexible strategy and appoint IT personnel to specific initiatives as they arise. The personnel designing the system take on responsibility for sustaining it by merging support with development tasks. Extra training or expenditure is not necessarily so because a team is already familiar with the job; therefore, individuals are likely to feel responsible immediately. Unfortunately, many experts believe that creating new systems is more intriguing and innovative than maintaining existing ones. Additionally, it may be difficult for an analyst to debug and assist somebody else's work that may have been inadequately structured and documented (Lorenzi & Riley, 2003).

People are shifted between assignments in specific organizations with distinct maintenance and new platform groups. The company is more adaptable, and workers may change roles to suit shifting business demands as analysts acquire new abilities. For example, system designers engaged in maintenance initiatives understand the significance of creating formation comprises. Similarly, analysts designing new systems have a deeper understanding of the design trade-offs required to achieve business goals. The rotation has the drawback of increasing overhead costs due to the time wasted when employees switch jobs. Systems analysts have little chance to specialize in any one profession when they always alternate between maintenance and new development tasks (Weinzimmer et al., 1998).

Because their supervisors think examining current infrastructure and documents is a beneficial experience, newly recruited and recently appointed IT staff employees are frequently given maintenance tasks. In addition, the mini-SDLC employed in several adaptive maintenance initiatives is a beneficial practice for such full-scale SDLC. Therefore, as system routine maintenance may be more challenging for a novice systems analyst than system design, it may be wise to put a new hire on a design team where veteran analysts can offer instruction and direction (Kaplan, 1997).

8.4. SYSTEM PERFORMANCE MANAGEMENT

While most businesses relied on a computer system to process information in the past, managing a system, including determining its effectiveness, was relatively straightforward. Complex networks and customer systems, including cloud services environments, are being used by businesses to fulfill operational demands. A framework dependent on other customers, servers, networking, and information spread around the firm is frequently accessed by a user at such a client workstation. The system's capabilities and performance are determined by integrating all those components, not by a single computer. IT managers usually manage complicated systems using automated technology and CASE techniques. The IT department should handle system errors and disruptions, gage system burden and efficiency, and foresee future requirements to guarantee that business processes are supported effectively. These themes are covered in subsections (Lægreid et al., 2006).

8.4.1. Fault Management

Every system would encounter issues, including hardware problems, software flaws, and user errors, including power outages, regardless of how it's being constructed. A network manager must identify and fix operational issues as soon as they arise. This process—often referred to as fault management—involves checking for warning signals of malfunction, keeping track of any system failures, identifying the issue, and taking corrective action. Analysis of symptoms and cause-and-effect relationships can be challenging for increasingly complicated systems. It's critical to assess performance relationships and correlations along with solving the present issue (Paradis & Han, 2007). The Activities Monitoring program, for instance, runs on Apple's Mac OS X and displays all running apps' CPU, memory, power, and disk, including network activity in live time. On Windows, some apps are comparable, including the Resource Monitor. Software for managing faults can shorten reaction times, uncover root causes, and minimize service interruptions. While system administrators should address errors and disruptions when they occur, the best course of action is to foresee issues by focusing on system burden and performance (Yu et al., 2007).

ACTIVITY 8.1

Explain the importance of maintenance tasks.

8.4.2. Performance and Workload Measurement

Slow performance within e-business might be just as damaging as no response. Consumer happiness, user efficiency, and company outcomes are all impacted by network delays, including application bottlenecks. Because networking delays happen more frequently and therefore are challenging to forecast, detect, and avoid, many IT managers think they inflict more harm than genuine stoppages. Consumers anticipate a dependable, quick answer every single day of the week. Companies utilize performance measurement software to support such a level of service (Eggemeier et al., 2020).

Many businesses utilize benchmark testing, which employs a series of established tests to gage the capacity and performance of systems, to monitor the performance of a system. In addition to benchmarking testing, performance measurements, often known as metrics, may track internet data volume and the number of transactions executed in a specific time frame. Refresh rate, capacity, throughput, and turnaround are just a few networking performance indicators (Rose et al., 2002).

8.5. SUMMARY

This chapter focuses on the importance of managing the support and security of systems in an organization. It begins by discussing the importance of system support, which includes ensuring that systems are functioning correctly and addressing any issues. It also covers the importance of security in systems, which includes protecting systems from unauthorized access, data breaches, and other cyber threats.

The chapter also covers the different system support and security types, including preventive, detective, and corrective measures. Preventive measures include implementing security policies, procedures, and controls to prevent potential threats. Detective measures include monitoring systems for signs of security breaches and taking action when necessary. Corrective measures include taking action to resolve issues and restoring systems to normal operation.

REVIEW QUESTIONS

1. What security systems are discussed in "Managing Systems Support and Security"?
2. How does the book address the challenges of maintaining system security?
3. What strategies does the book recommend for managing system support and security?
4. What are the fundamental principles of effective security management discussed in the chapter?
5. How can this book help IT professionals develop a successful security management plan?

MULTIPLE CHOICE QUESTIONS

1. What is the most critical factor in managing systems support and security?

a. Security policies

b. System updates

c. Firewall protection

d. Access control

2. What is the most effective way to protect a system from unauthorized access?

a. Implementing user authentication

b. Installing antivirus software

c. Establishing a password policy

d. Restricting physical access

3. What is the primary purpose of installing a firewall?

a. To protect data from unauthorized access

b. To monitor system activity

c. To detect malware

d. To control network traffic

4. What is the best way to ensure data security?

a. Data encryption

b. System backups

c. Access control

d. Regular system updates

5. What security measures should be taken to protect a system from external threats?

a. Firewall protection

b. Intrusion detection systems

c. Antivirus software

d. Physical security measures

Answers to Multiple Choice Questions

1. (a) 2. (a) 3. (a) 4. (a) 5. (b)

REFERENCES

1. Abeygunawardane, S. K., Jirutitijaroen, P., & Xu, H., (2013). Adaptive maintenance policies for aging devices using a Markov decision process. *IEEE Transactions on Power Systems, 28*(3), 3194–3203.
2. Aissani, N., Beldjilali, B., & Trentesaux, D., (2009). Dynamic scheduling of maintenance tasks in the petroleum industry: A reinforcement approach. *Engineering Applications of Artificial Intelligence, 22*(7), 1089–1103.
3. Al-Hawari, F., & Barham, H., (2021). A machine learning based help desk system for IT service management. *Journal of King Saud University-Computer and Information Sciences, 33*(6), 702–718.
4. Almorsy, M., & Grundy, J., (2014). SecDSVL: A domain-specific visual language to support enterprise security modelling. In: *2014 23rd Australian Software Engineering Conference* (pp. 152–161). IEEE.

5. Altinkemer, K., Chaturvedi, A., & Gulati, R., (1994). Information systems outsourcing: Issues and evidence. *International Journal of Information Management, 14*(4), 252–268.
6. Armstrong, J., (1992). Knowledge-based systems for users: Enhancing the productivity of help desks. *Information Systems Management, 9*(1), 28–37.
7. Barrett, R., Kandogan, E., Maglio, P. P., Haber, E. M., Takayama, L. A., & Prabaker, M., (2004). Field studies of computer system administrators: Analysis of system management tools and practices. In: *Proceedings of the 2004 ACM conference on Computer Supported Cooperative Work* (pp. 388–395).
8. Ben-Daya, M., Duffuaa, S. O., Raouf, A., Knezevic, J., & Ait-Kadi, D., (2009). *Handbook of Maintenance Management and Engineering* (Vol. 7). London: Springer London.
9. Brajnik, G., Mizzaro, S., & Tasso, C., (1996). Evaluating user interfaces to information retrieval systems: A case study on user support. In: *Proceedings of the 19th Annual International ACM SIGIR Conference on Research and Development in Information Retrieval* (pp. 128–136).
10. Curtis, B., Sheppard, S. B., Milliman, P., Borst, M. A., & Love, T., (1979). Measuring the psychological complexity of software maintenance tasks with the Halstead and McCabe metrics. *IEEE Transactions on Software Engineering*, (2), 96–104.
11. Deeter-Schmelz, D. R., & Ramsey, R. P., (2003). An investigation of team information processing in service teams: Exploring the link between teams and customers. *Journal of the Academy of Marketing Science, 31*(4), 409–424.
12. Dunlap, G., (1984). The influence of task variation and maintenance tasks on the learning and effect of autistic children. *Journal of Experimental Child Psychology, 37*(1), 41–64.
13. Eggemeier, F. T., Wilson, G. F., Kramer, A. F., & Damos, D. L., (2020). Workload assessment in multi-task environments. In: *Multiple-Task Performance* (pp. 207–216). CRC Press.
14. Fioravanti, F., & Nesi, P., (2001). Estimation and prediction metrics for adaptive maintenance effort of object-oriented systems. *IEEE Transactions on Software Engineering, 27*(12), 1062–1084.
15. González, L. M., Giachetti, R. E., & Ramirez, G., (2005). Knowledge management-centric help desk: Specification and performance evaluation. *Decision Support Systems, 40*(2), 389–405.
16. Green, G. I., (1989). Perceived importance of systems analysts' job skills, roles, and non-salary incentives. *MIS Quarterly,* 115–133.
17. Gupta, S., Bostrom, R. P., & Huber, M., (2010). End-user training methods: What we know, need to know. *ACM SIGMIS Database: The Database for Advances in Information Systems, 41*(4), 9–39.
18. Gutierrez, R. G., Linhart, J. M., & Pitblado, J. S., (2003). From the help desk: Local polynomial regression and Stata plugins. *The Stata Journal, 3*(4), 412–419.
19. Halverson, C. A., Erickson, T., & Ackerman, M. S., (2004). Behind the help desk:

Evolution of a knowledge management system in a large organization. In: *Proceedings of the 2004 ACM Conference on Computer Supported Cooperative Work* (pp. 304–313).

20. Heckman, R., & Guskey, A., (1998). Sources of customer satisfaction and dissatisfaction with information technology help desks. *Journal of Market-Focused Management, 3*(1), 59–89.
21. Kajko-Mattsson, M., (2005). A survey of documentation practice within corrective maintenance. *Empirical Software Engineering, 10*(1), 31–55.
22. Kaplan, B., (1997). Addressing organizational issues into the evaluation of medical systems. *Journal of the American Medical Informatics Association, 4*(2), 94–101.
23. Ko, A. J., Myers, B. A., Coblenz, M. J., & Aung, H. H., (2006). An exploratory study of how developers seek, relate, and collect relevant information during software maintenance tasks. *IEEE Transactions on Software Engineering, 32*(12), 971–987.
24. Kriegsman, M., & Barletta, R., (1993). Building a CASE-based help desk application. *IEEE Expert, 8*(6), 18–26.
25. Krishna, S., Sahay, S., & Walsham, G., (2004). Managing cross-cultural issues in global software outsourcing. *Communications of the ACM, 47*(4), 62–66.
26. Lægreid, P., Roness, P. G., & Rubecksen, K., (2006). Performance management in practice: The Norwegian way. *Financial Accountability & Management, 22*(3), 251–270.
27. Lahtinen, E., Ala-Mutka, K., & Järvinen, H. M., (2005). A study of the difficulties of novice programmers. *ACM SIGCSE Bulletin, 37*(3), 14–18.
28. Le, N. T., & Hoang, D. B., (2016). Can maturity models support cyber security? In: *2016 IEEE 35th International Performance Computing and Communications Conference (IPCCC)* (pp. 1–7). IEEE.
29. Lorenzi, N. M., & Riley, R. T., (2003). Organizational issues= change. *International Journal of Medical Informatics, 69*(2, 3), 197–203.
30. Paradis, L., & Han, Q., (2007). A survey of fault management in wireless sensor networks. *Journal of Network and Systems Management, 15*(2), 171–190.
31. Poi, B. P., (2002). From the help desk: Demand system estimation. *The Stata Journal, 2*(4), 403–410.
32. Rose, C. L., Murphy, L. B., Byard, L., & Nikzad, K., (2002). The role of the big five personality factors in vigilance performance and workload. *European Journal of Personality, 16*(3), 185–200.
33. Sako, M., (2005). *Outsourcing and Offshoring: Key Trends and Issues.* Available at SSRN 1463480.
34. Schenk, K. D., Vitalari, N. P., & Davis, K. S., (1998). Differences between novice and expert systems analysts: What do we know and what do we do? *Journal of Management Information Systems, 15*(1), 9–50.
35. Sheut, C., & Krajewski, L. J., (1994). A decision model for corrective maintenance management. *The International Journal of Production Research, 32*(6), 1365–1382.

36. Stenström, C., Norrbin, P., Parida, A., & Kumar, U., (2016). Preventive and corrective maintenance–cost comparison and cost–benefit analysis. *Structure and Infrastructure Engineering, 12*(5), 603–617.
37. Toriizuka, T., (2001). Application of performance shaping factor (PSF) for work improvement in industrial plant maintenance tasks. *International Journal of Industrial Ergonomics, 28*(3, 4), 225–236.
38. Unckless, R. L., & Lazzaro, B. P., (2016). The potential for adaptive maintenance of diversity in insect antimicrobial peptides. *Philosophical Transactions of the Royal Society B: Biological Sciences, 371*(1695), 20150291.
39. Viana, C. M., Freire, D., Abrantes, P., Rocha, J., & Pereira, P., (2022). Agricultural land systems importance for supporting food security and sustainable development goals: A systematic review. *Science of The Total Environment, 806*, 150718.
40. Wang, Y., Deng, C., Wu, J., Wang, Y., & Xiong, Y., (2014). A corrective maintenance scheme for engineering equipment. *Engineering Failure Analysis, 36*, 269–283.
41. Weinzimmer, L. G., Nystrom, P. C., & Freeman, S. J., (1998). Measuring organizational growth: Issues, consequences and guidelines. *Journal of Management, 24*(2), 235–262.
42. Yu, M., Mokhtar, H., & Merabti, M., (2007). Fault management in wireless sensor networks. *IEEE Wireless Communications, 14*(6), 13–19.

INDEX

D

FSC
www.fsc.org
MIX
Papier | Fördert gute Waldnutzung
FSC® C083411

Kolibri 360 GmbH
Ferdinand-Jühlke-Straße 7
99095 Erfurt, Deutschland
produktsicherheit@kolibri360.de